FEB 2009

☆ ☆ ☆ ☆ ☆ ☆ ☆ ☆ ☆ ☆ ☆ ☆ ☆ ☆

The Birth of the New

NFL

☆ ☆ ☆ ☆ ☆ ☆ ☆ ☆ ☆ ☆ ☆ ☆ ☆ ☆

To the late Will McDonough of the *Boston Globe*,
the sportswriter's sportswriter and a South Boston original

☆ ☆ ☆ ☆ ☆ ☆ ☆ ☆ ☆ ☆ ☆ ☆ ☆

The Birth of the New

NFL

HOW THE 1966 NFL/AFL MERGER TRANSFORMED PRO FOOTBALL

☆ ☆ ☆ ☆ ☆ ☆ ☆ ☆ ☆ ☆ ☆ ☆ ☆

Larry Felser

with a Foreword by Ernie Accorsi

THE LYONS PRESS
Guilford, Connecticut

An imprint of The Globe Pequot Press

The Lyons Press is an imprint of The Globe Pequot Press.

Text design by Sheryl P. Kober

Library of Congress Cataloging-in-Publication Data

Felser, Larry.
  The birth of the new NFL : how the 1966 NFL/AFL merger transformed
pro football / Larry Felser with a foreword by Ernie Accorsi.
     p. cm.
  ISBN 978-1-59921-151-0
  1. Football–United States–History. 2. National Football League–History. 3.
American Football League–History. I. Title.
  GV954.F45 2008
  796.332–dc22

                         2008024728

Printed in the United States of America
10 9 8 7 6 5 4 3 2 1

Contents

Foreword

This was in late autumn of 1959. Ed Ionni, my best friend, and I were driving to a high school football game. We grew up in Hershey, Pennsylvania, and like most kids in the 1950s, we were sports fanatics. We couldn't just watch games, we had to root. We had a lot of things in common, two of them being that we loved the Baltimore Colts and hated the Philadelphia Eagles.

The latter is significant because from the time we were nine years old until our late twenties, the Eagles held their training camp in Hershey. Every day we would watch their practice and loathe them more. Maybe it was the noise they produced in our town or maybe just the rebel in us. After all, we were also Catholic kids who didn't root for Notre Dame. The Colts opened up the Eagles' preseason schedule each summer, and in 1954 they came to town and beat the Eagles, 10–0. That did it; we were Colt fans.

On this particular drive, we were talking about a brief item in that day's *Harrisburg Patriot News* reporting that a new league was being formed, the American Football League, and named the cities. Of course we had to choose teams. "I'm going to root for the Boston Patriots," said Ed. "Okay," I said. "My team is the Buffalo Bills."

So it started, and before it was over I worked for Carroll Rosenbloom, Pete Rozelle, Art Modell, and Wellington Mara, four major players in the merger of the National and American Football Leagues. I was also a participant in the AFL's greatest glories, became friends with some of its founders and greatest heroes, and was a witness to their part in the merger.

I have often wondered if the two leagues hadn't merged, would teams have gone out of business? Would they have merged eventually with some owners losing their clubs? Maybe the success of pro football was inevitable, but surely things wouldn't be exactly as they are today. Events would just have been different.

The Birth of the New NFL is the story of what did happen, the bitter rivalry, the quick financial bonanza for the college stars over whom the leagues fought, the financial ruin that lurked when the fight for those players got out of hand, the inevitability of a merger—even though it was resisted by some of the principals—and finally the uneasy peace and shocking suddenness of the realization, reached after the third and fourth Super Bowls, that the quality of play in the AFL had reached parity with that of the older league.

At first I didn't think much of the AFL; even as a teenager I was filled with NFL superiority. I remember in 1960 returning home from a Thanksgiving morning classic between two Harrisburg schools, John Harris and William Penn, in the Hershey Stadium. I was awaiting the annual NFL Thanksgiving Day game on TV, the Detroit Lions versus the Green Bay Packers, and wiling away the time watching the Bills play the New York Titans in the AFL game. To me it was a laughable interlude. That was the impression of fans in most NFL cities.

The AFL founders were determined sportsmen. For years they had wanted to get into the NFL and failed, but now they refused to be discouraged. Thirty-eight years after the AFL was formed, Lamar Hunt of Dallas—who with Bud Adams of Houston came up with the concept of a new league—told me how it all began: "I tried to buy the Chicago Cardinals from Charles Bidwill's widow on the condition I could move the franchise to Dallas. They wouldn't sell based on that condition. Then I heard that Bob Howsam tried to buy the Cardinals on the condition he could move them to Denver. Then Bud Adams who would move the franchise to Houston. Finally I thought, 'If none of us can get in the NFL, why don't we start our own league?'"

And did they ever.

Yet even after the New York Jets and Kansas City Chiefs had won Super Bowls III and IV, I'm sure that in most NFL circles there was still a lack of respect for the AFL on the playing field. From a business point of view, I'm sure they thought the merger was necessary, but as a football product I'm also sure they didn't have great respect.

I joined the Colts in the spring of 1970, less than fifteen months after Super Bowl III. The Baltimore organization was still in a state of shock. The fallout, for both the Colts and the NFL, of that devastating defeat at the hands of Joe Namath and the Jets resulted in a disappointing season for Baltimore ending in the departure of fabled head coach, Don Shula, for Miami of the AFL. When I got there, most of the people who coached, played, and worked for the Colts were still in disbelief, in denial.

Before the merger could be completed, three NFL franchises had to agree, at the insistence of the AFL, to join them to form the new American Football Conference in the newly aligned NFL. Two old-line teams, Pittsburgh and Cleveland, agreed to switch, and the third, a surprise, was Baltimore. I never could fathom Rosenbloom moving, but he did. The reward was $3 million a team, small by today's revenue standards. One of Rosenbloom's conditions was that the Colts be placed in the same division with the Jets, a rivalry that was born from Rosenbloom's pain from Super Bowl III.

I remember our first game against the Jets in Shea Stadium in October of 1970. I sat in he first row of the press box with general manager Don Klosterman, Rosenbloom, and Rosenbloom's son, Steve. I can still feel the electricity and tension and especially the mood of Carroll. The Colts jumped to a 22–0 lead, but then Joe Namath starting throwing on every play. The Jets tied the game at 22–22.

Namath threw sixty-two passes that day, but the Colts intercepted six of them, including Bob Grant's on the final play of the game. I can still hear the groans and sounds coming from Rosenbloom. I remember thinking, "We have to play this team again in two weeks and twice a year from here on? How is he going to endure these games?"

I was as entrenched an old National Football League guy as there ever existed. I loved its legacy of great teams and great games. It took me a long time to give in to the AFL and its own history. But that said, I have always envied the men of the AFL, its owners with their pioneer spirit. The writers and announcers who covered their teams with objectivity were almost as important as the owners, coaches, and players in the league's success, people like Larry Felser, Van Miller, and Stan Baron in Buffalo; Will McDonough and George Sullivan in Boston; Dave Anderson and Paul Zimmerman in New York; Dick Connor in Denver; Jerry Magee in San Diego; Scotty Stirling in Oakland; Bill Richardson in Kansas City; and Wells Twombley and Jack Gallagher in Houston.

Through it all there was one indispensable man, Lamar Hunt. We have very good men among the new breed of NFL owners, fine men. Woodrow Wilson was a very good president, but he was not Thomas Jefferson. Founders are founders.

—*Ernie Accorsi, former general manager of the Baltimore Colts,*
Cleveland Browns, and New York Giants

Introduction

In the autumn of 1957 I was in the army, stationed at Fort Sheridan, Illinois, a cozy little installation on Lake Michigan cheek by jowl with the swanky Lake Forest suburb to the north, and I was a short commuter train trip from Chicago. It was the peacetime army and I was attached to a signal corps support unit. We were supposed to be supporting the main signal corps unit, which had very little to do on its own and really didn't need our support. Ft. Sheridan was there mainly to comfortably house the generals of the fifth army, headquartered in downtown Chicago, and provide a golf course for them on which to play.

There was a great deal to keep an young enlisted man amused in Chicago, and the "City of Big Shoulders" had a big heart when it came to entertaining the men and women in uniform. While I was at Ft. Sheridan, I frequently took the train into Chicago; ate a $1.09 steak at Tad's on State Street; attended a concert by the Chicago Symphony; took in a White Sox baseball game in Comiskey Park; check out any fights scheduled in the Chicago Arena; and on Sunday, when they were at home in Comiskey, watch the NFL Cardinals play.

Actually the only point of interest about the Cardinals was their noteworthy running back, Ollie Matson, giving one of his "Ollie-against-the-world" performances. Even though my civilian job was writing sports for a big-city newspaper, the *Buffalo Courier Express*, I had never seen a regular-season NFL game in person before I was, with the intercession of the United Service Organization (USO), a guest of the Cards.

The Cardinals were in the second season of their 24-year playoff drought. They won the NFL championship in 1947, defeating Philadelphia, lost it back to the Eagles in 1948, and went the next six decades without getting close to the title. At the same time the

Cards were constructing their reputation for futility, the cross-town Bears were quite good. They had Rick Casares and Willie Galimore running the ball, Ed Brown at quarterback, and the usual rough and tough defense. I discovered quickly that even the USO couldn't produce complimentary Bears tickets for soldiers. Owner George Halas, "Papa Bear," who virtually invented pro football, had been a navy officer in World War I, but he cut no slack even for sailors. There were no freebies for the swabbies from the Great Lakes Naval Station down the road near Waukegan, IL. If you wanted to see the Chicago Bears, you paid—if tickets were available.

As the 1957 season went on and it became evident the Bears were not headed for another NFL championship game (but were still more interesting than the Cardinals), two of my barracks buddies and I made our plan to climb the ivied wall at Wrigley, the part nearest the grandstand, and sneak into a game. We got as far as gripping the top of the wall with our fingers, but then along came the security guards who rapped us across the knuckles and sent us to a movie instead.

In Chicago everyone wanted to see the Bears and virtually no one wanted to watch the Cardinals. Strangely, outside of Chicago there were a lot of cities that wanted to host the Cardinals as the home team in their stadiums. It seemed inevitable that the Cards would have to move eventually, since they were being ignored in Chicago and Halas wanted to see them depart so the Bears would have the public's complete attention. One after another the lead figures from a number of cities—Lamar Hunt of Dallas, Bud Adams of Houston, Bob Howsom of Denver, brewery executives from St. Louis and many others—contacted Walter Wolfner, who ran the Cardinals' franchise for his wife, Violet Wolfner (widow of Charlie Bidwill, who purchased the Cards in 1932). Several bids were made to buy the franchise, but when the Wolfners heard that moving the team was part of the deal, the negotiations ended. Mrs. Wolfner's attachment to Chicago was too strong, even though her husband's tenure as owner of the team was filled with heartache, including only one winning season between 1932 and 1945.

It turned out that the football suitors' unrequited lust for the Cardinals was the keystone for the founding of a rival league, the American Football League, and began the subsequent war for players as well as public attention. When the war was over and an uneasy, often-distrustful peace was forged in what amounted to a shotgun marriage, the financial and entertainment bonanza that is the NFL today was underway.

By the time the 1958 NFL season began I was no longer rushing to the USO for tickets or trying to devise a plan to get past Bears' security. I had been mustered out of the army and was being paid by the *Buffalo Courier-Express* to cover an NFL regular-season game. It seems the Cardinals had been pushed out of Comiskey for their early-season schedule. The White Sox, managed by Al Lopez and starring players such as Minnie Minoso, Luis Aparicio, Ted Kluszewski, and Early Wynn, were pennant contenders, and Sox management wanted to prepare the park for a stretch run and a possible World Series, which eventually came to fruition. In that era the most popular spectator sports were boxing, college football, horse racing, and, above all, major league baseball. Pro football ranked somewhere between hockey and college basketball.

Wolfner, a football orphan seeking a temporary home, was contacted by Pat McGroder, a wealthy liquor distributor in Buffalo who had sold his business and was named the city's parks and recreation director. McGroder had orders from Mayor Frank Sedita to see what he could do to secure a pro football team for Buffalo. That's how the Cardinals happened to open the 1958 season against the New York Giants in Buffalo's War Memorial Stadium, a Depression-era relic constructed by the Works Project Administration. The Giants had lost the last five of their exhibition games, but were loaded with stars such as Frank Gifford, Kyle Rote, and Charley Conerly on offense and a smothering defense led by future

Hall of Famers Andy Robustelli, Emlen Tunnell, and Sam Huff. New York won 37–7.

My assignment after that game was to interview the two owners, Wolfner of the Cardinals and Wellington Mara of the Giants, about their reaction to the crowd and the way Buffalo greeted the return of pro football after losing its own franchise in the All-America Conference after the 1949 season. Wolfner was disappointed in the turnout and showed no enthusiasm for transferring the Cardinals anyplace other than back home in Chicago. Mara's reaction was different. "The crowd was larger than we would have drawn in Chicago," he said. That was an accurate statement, not a guess by the Giants' owner. Only one home game in Comiskey Park that season drew more than the game in Buffalo. In fact, the next season, the Cardinals played two home games in Minneapolis, and only one, also against the Giants, boasted an attendance that surpassed the crowd in Buffalo. It made no difference. The Cards intended to stay put.

However, three factors changed their plan to remain in Buffalo. The first was the 1958 NFL championship game, the first overtime NFL game ever, won by Johnny Unitas's Baltimore Colts over the Giants on Alan Ameche's one-yard touchdown. CBS, the televising network, almost missed the winning touchdown when a spectator jostled a cable loose and the nation's TV screens went dark at the most dramatic moment. The picture was recovered just in time for Ameche's heroics.

In the wake of the exciting game, both the television industry and the viewing public came to similar conclusions: Pro football at its highest level was great theater, not just something to fill the screens between baseball seasons, and the networks were keenly interested. Around office water coolers and blue-collar lunch breaks American workers talked about how great it would be for their cities to have pro football teams.

The second factor in the NFL rethinking its resistance to change was that eight months after the Colts' dramatic victory, Lamar Hunt announced in Dallas that a new league had been formed and would begin play the following year, 1960. The third factor was that Ollie Matson, the only valid reason Chicagoans would want to see the Cardinals play, had been traded to the Los Angeles Rams for nine players, five of them starters. Despite the reshuffling, the remodeled Cardinals still lost ten of their twelve games. The Cards, at long last, were headed elsewhere.

By the time the AFL began their first season, the staid NFL, so content with doing business as usual, had been forced into radical change. On January 28 the league announced it was adding a team in Dallas for the 1960 season and a team in Minneapolis–St. Paul for 1961. On March 13 a permanent transfer of the Cardinals from Chicago to St. Louis was approved by the league's owners. Cities such as Dallas, Houston, and Buffalo were no longer interested. They were part of the new AFL, here to stay. Part of the Cardinals' deal to move to St. Louis was a significant reverse bounty reported to be as high as $500,000, paid to the Cardinals by Halas, whom Mike Ditka once described as "throwing nickels around as if they were man-hole covers." But this move was a case of money well spent by Halas, clearing Chicago, the city of competition.

Until those events, expansion had been out of the question. A twelve-team league was just fine with George Preston Marshall, the autocratic owner of the Washington Redskins. Marshall was virtually a one-man veto. He had the lowest payroll in the NFL and a segregated roster. He later became the final holdout as the NFL de-segregated. If Marshall were alive today I suspect he might still be ranting about the financial joys of an all-white twelve-team league.

Instead Lamar Hunt and Bud Adams, two Texans who barely knew each other, were joined by the mutual frustration of failing to buy the Cardinals and move them to their respective city. Finding partners was relatively simple. The entrance fee was a bargain, $100,000 per franchise with a modest $25,000 down. Think about it this way: Forty-eight years later a half interest in the Miami Dolphins would be sold for more than a half-billion dollars.

Some saw the AFL as a business opportunity. Others saw it as an end to their frustrations. Detroit insurance executive Ralph Wilson and his father owned a small piece of the Lions and came to the conclusion that they would never be able to buy a bigger slice. Wilson decided to buy an AFL franchise, which he could place in Miami, near his winter home on the Indian River. The catch was negotiating around the Orange Bowl's college football schedule. Dubious about letting the pros share their arena, the directors of the Orange Bowl demurred.

Again Wilson was frustrated, just as he had been in Detroit. Then he received a phone call from his old skipper on a Navy sub chaser during World War II. The ex-skipper's name was George Schaaf and he talked Wilson into inspecting his hometown, Buffalo, New York, where he was greeted by Pat McGroder and the editor of the *Buffalo Evening News*, Paul Neville. Neville, a dynamic graduate of the University of Notre Dame, guaranteed Wilson that if he placed his franchise in Buffalo, his paper would publish a story about the team every day the paper ran. That's how the Buffalo Bills came into being.

The NFL, which had ignored all petitioners for expansion teams, could not ignore the new league, even if it pretended to do so in public. Before the AFL kicked off its first football, the league met in Minneapolis to award its eighth franchise to that city, but the would-be owners were wooed into the NFL with the promise of a franchise that would begin play in another year. The AFL had to content itself with a franchise in Oakland, California, to be called the Raiders. That was the unwitting foundation for what later would evolve into "the Raider nation" with its bizarre followers.

The NFL had modernized against its own longtime wishes and the football war was on.

I covered the first AFL game of any sort, an exhibition game between the Buffalo Bills and the Boston Patriots in July 30, 1960. It was sponsored by the Junior Chamber of Commerce and the *Buffalo Evening News*, celebrated by a parade down Main Street, and took place in War Memorial Stadium. The parade was more entertaining than the game, and the Patriots' uniforms had not arrived from the manufacturer in time for kickoff—they were dressed in faded red jerseys and scruffy tan pants, giving the debut a definite sandlot look. The guys in the sandlot outfits won easily, 28–7, in front of a modest crowd estimated at 16,000.

The Patriots' uniforms weren't the only things to bear a "used" look. The AFL was full of hand-me-down quarterbacks in the league's first two seasons. For the most part, the Canadian Football League bore the closest resemblance to the NFL. The small NFL rosters worked in the CFL's favor by making solid talent available, and in the fifties the Canadians often outworked the NFL scouts to find small-college gems in the U.S. Each of the CFL teams had a good quarterback and plenty of other talented players to maintain a competitive balance. The Hamilton Tiger-Cats, coached by Jumbo Jim Trimble, once the head coach of the NFL Philadelphia Eagles, were the most solid organization. The Ti-Cats had outbid San Francisco to sign Maryland quarterback Bernie Faloney, the 49ers' No. 1 draft choice, plus John Barrow, a Cleveland Browns' high choice, who was considered the top offensive line prospect in his draft year. Joe Kapp, the Vancouver quarterback, and Sam Etcheverry of Montreal would come down to run NFL teams a few years later. Russ Jackson, a Canadian homebred quarterback, made the Ottawa Roughriders a contender.

The Bills, in a bid to lure some Hamilton fans to make the 45 minute-drive down the Queen Elizabeth Highway to Buffalo for Sunday games, foolishly agreed to play an exhibition game against the Ti-Cats in Hamilton's Ivor Wynn Stadium in the summer of 1961. It was an embarrassment for the AFL. Faloney picked apart the Bills' defense and so did Hamilton's second and third-string quarterbacks in a one-sided victory for the Tiger-Cats. The AFL was not yet ready for prime time, much less the high-caliber Canadian opposition.

If the AFL was to grow into a viable rival for the NFL, it would have to continue to win a lot of battles for the best American college players. That is exactly what happened. By 1963, the fourth season of the AFL's existence, its better teams were stocked with elite talent and had reasonable arguments that they could contend with the NFL's best. They were growing up together, and by 1963 the Chargers, then based in San Diego, along with Kansas City, Buffalo, Boston, and Houston had reached a point of parity with the NFL.

When the merger was enforced in 1966 and the NFL reluctantly agreed to play a championship game against the AFL titlist, I was proud to have written the Kansas City scouting report in the Super Bowl I program, now a collectors item, but I had more fun writing in the Super Bowl XI program. The format of that piece was patterned after a popular segment on CBS's *60 Minutes*, called "Point Counter-Point" starring conservative Jack Kilpatrick debating liberal Shana Alexander. It became so popular it was regularly lampooned on *Saturday Night Live* with Dan Aykroyd and Jane Curtin. Aykroyd's line, "Jane, you stupid slut!" became a national punch line.

My opponent in the pages of the Super Bowl program was Tex Maule, the longtime AFL antagonist. I argued that if the Super Bowl had come into being earlier, 1963, San Diego's offensively spearheaded Chargers would have defeated the Chicago Bears' NFL champions, who depended largely upon a strong defense coordinated by George Allen. A photo spread over the width of the article had Tex and me, with our sleeves rolled up and striking boxer's poses, duking it out over one last NFL-AFL argument.

In reality an uneasy harmony had begun to take hold among the merged owners. The merger was a business necessity. Distaste for one another bordered, in some cases, on hate. It really didn't start to subside until Kansas City soundly defeated Minnesota in Super Bowl IV, the younger league's second consecutive triumph on the field.

It took more than a victory to heal old wounds. What it took mostly was the diplomacy and statesmanship of Pete Rozelle, for my money the most talented sports executive of all time. Rozelle had been one of his league's most deeply-rooted adherents during the war, but like a wise king assuming the leadership of once-bitter foes, Rozelle governed evenly and effectively, keeping order with a mailed fist concealed in a velvet glove.

I was elected president of the Professional Football Writers Association four years into the completed merger. I am proud to have brought about three important changes in coverage of the sport by the media. One was the installation of televisions in strategic places all over NFL press boxes so that journalists covering the games could see the close-ups and replays as clearly as the fans (and readers) at home could. Another change was smoothing the way for female members of the media so that they would have access to stories in the locker rooms and other areas where their male counterparts were admitted. The third was a closer working relationship with the Players' Association so that its side of stories, especially in bitter disputes, would receive fair representation to the public.

I couldn't have been successful in any of these matters without the cooperation and encouragement of Rozelle, one of the most reasonable men and enjoyable dinner companions I ever had the pleasure of encountering.

CHAPTER 1

The Preliminaries

Major changes in the conduct of professional football take form slowly, like the development of a championship team. Events that seem unconnected a year or two before often come together as if they were drawn up on the original blueprint for the final project.

That's how it was with the football revolution of 1966. It began when Ralph Wilson went to the Winter Olympics in Innsbruck, Austria in 1964. It's probably inaccurate to say that Wilson went "to" the Olympics since he wasn't interested in seeing the Goitschel sisters of France win gold medals in slalom and giant slalom; nor was he particularly keen on witnessing the Russian ice hockey team begin an Olympic dynasty that would last through 1976. Wilson, owner of the Buffalo Bills and a member of the league's three-man Television Committee, traveled to Austria because the Olympics were being televised by NBC, the same network that was in negotiations with the AFL over a new television contract.

The other TV committee members were Sonny Werblin, who had recently become a co-owner of the New York Jets, and Billy Sullivan, managing partner of the Boston Patriots. Sullivan, named the lead negotiator, had gone to Innsbruck to be with the NBC executives who were dividing their time between supervising the telecasts of the Games and their next project, the AFL contract.

A few days after the Games' opening ceremonies, Werblin and Wilson received transatlantic phone calls from an exuberant Sullivan: "I have great news! I've just about reached agreement with the network, which will pay us $600,000 a team in each of the next five years." Werblin didn't even pause. "We can get more," he told Sullivan. "Don't accept their offer. Keep negotiating."

1

Sullivan kept arguing with his fellow owner. "Remember Sonny," he reasoned, "we received just $100,000 and change per team in our original contract with ABC. NBC's offer of $600,000 is a huge increase. I think we should take it. I'm uncomfortable with further negotiating."

Werblin, sure that if the AFL took the NBC offer it would be leaving significant money on the table, persisted. He was new to the league, having purchased the Jets along with four colleagues in the team's bankruptcy sale the year before. Werblin may have been a rookie in football terms, but no one in the entertainment industry had more experience or more success in negotiating contracts with television networks.

Sonny was the foremost individual agent in the stable of MCA, which was the foremost entertainment business agency at the time. Werblin's personal clients included Frank Sinatra and Johnny Carson, arguably the two most compelling figures in show business. A year before, when Werblin and his partners purchased the New York Titans from financially beleaguered Harry Wismer and turned them into the Jets, Werblin's clients dominated 80 percent of the prime-time programming on NBC. He negotiated their contracts. His successes with Sinatra, Carson, and other marquee clients helped create the show business adage that "pneumonia is a cold managed by MCA."

His own negotiating experience convinced Werblin that Sullivan needed his back stiffened in the negotiations with the NBC executives in Austria, but he would be unable to do the stiffening personally. Important MCA business dictated that he stay in the U.S. He phoned Wilson at his Detroit business office. "Ralph, I can't leave the country," he said. "You have to go and you have to leave as soon as possible. This could mean the survival of the AFL." Wilson flew to Austria that night.

When multimillionaire sportsmen travel to the Olympics, the arrangements are usually made by their aides months in advance.

Mansions or chalets are rented, cars and drivers are leased, chefs and housekeepers are hired. It wasn't that way for Wilson's trip.

"Innsbruck isn't a very big city now," said Wilson forty years later. "In 1964 it was very small. I couldn't find a room in a hotel, an inn, a B&B, or anything else. I ended up sleeping in the same bed with a friend of mine, Gene Ward, a sports columnist for the New York *Daily News* who was over there to cover the Games. His room was about the size of a closet."

Comfort wasn't Wilson's concern. The best possible television contract for the AFL was. His presence along with his resolve and that of Werblin changed the tenor of the negotiations. The AFL signed for $900,000 per team for each of the five years that the contract covered.

"This contract makes us secure," said Joe Foss, the AFL commissioner. "It will allow some of our teams which haven't been able to compete for high draft choices to do it now. Our partnership with NBC is the best thing that could happen to us." The rich TV contract helped, but Foss's vision of every AFL team able once and for all to compete with the NFL over the best players coming out of college was misguided. As much as the financial infusion was welcomed, management skills and recognition of talent were still essential elements in all major league team sports.

The AFL's New York franchise was no longer a target for ridicule. The name switch, from Titans to Jets, along with the attractive new green-and-white uniforms and the move from the dilapidated Polo Grounds to newly built Shea Stadium, were necessary cosmetic changes. More important than new style was new substance.

The critical change was the new owners' aggressiveness in pursuing talent—not just player talent but also talent throughout the front office and especially in coaching. They hired Weeb Ewbank, who had built the Baltimore Colts into NFL champions using a five-year plan. He promised the owners he could do the same for the Jets, and they took him at his word.

Werblin's four partners in the purchase of the team were also his partners in the ownership of Monmouth Race Track, which was near their New Jersey homes. They were Leon Hess, chairman of the giant Hess Oil Co.; Phil Iselin, a garment manufacturer; Don Lillis, chairman of Bear Stearns, one of the most prominent brokerages on Wall Street, and Townsend Martin. The term "sportsman" was going out of style at the time, but it was an authentic fit for Hess, Iselin, Lillis, Martin, and Werblin.

The people who were hired for the franchise's new management team found out what *sportsmen* really meant. The owners and their heirs were so loyal to Jets' people that most of them stayed with the team for decades. One of the first new people hired by Werblin, the original managing partner of the Jets, was a young assistant public relations director named Frank Ramos. Ramos was soon promoted to the head PR job and stayed with the team until its entry into the new millennium when the heirs of the original five owners sold the Jets to Woody Johnson.

Werblin, the master showman, understood that in order to win a football fight for the allegiance of the New York fans, his team must have a star of the highest magnitude. The Giants were revered in New York, but those who revered them most were older, affluent, more socially conservative spectators. Werblin correctly assessed the market and decided his share would lie with the young, most of whom were shut out from personally attending Giants' games because sellouts had become routine in Yankee Stadium, where the established team played. Since the NFL wouldn't play games against the AFL, foreclosing on the possibility of a gridiron battle for fans between the Giants and Jets, the new team would battle the old in the newspaper kiosks of New York's five boroughs as well as the radio stations and television channels of the Greater New York area.

Werblin also assessed the Giants and saw what steadfast Giant supporters had refused to see, that the established team's stars—glamorous halfback Frank Gifford; fullback Alex Webster; quarterback Y. A. Tittle; and defensive end Andy Robustelli—had gotten old. By the end of the 1965 season all of them were gone.

This was the 1960s, the time when college students were locking the dean in his office, when antiwar draft protestors were taking to the streets and telling President Lyndon Baines Johnson, "Hell, no! We won't go!" when young radicals were advising their peers, "Don't trust anyone over thirty-five."

What the Jets needed to upstage the Giants, decided Werblin, wasn't a hero, but an antihero. That's when Sonny zeroed in on Joe Namath, the Alabama quarterback. Namath was a drugstore cowboy from Beaver Falls in western Pennsylvania, the breeding ground for a litany of great football players. He had long hair, walked with a slouch, had a wise-guy attitude, and the furtive look of someone who might be about to hold up the local 7-11. On the football field he already had a sense of greatness.

The legendary Bear Bryant came up to Beaver Falls from the University of Alabama to recruit him for the Crimson Tide. Years later, on the eve of Super Bowl III, another great coach, Vince Lombardi, as fierce an NFL loyalist as there was, told *Washington Star* columnist Moe Siegel, "don't be too sure about our side winning," he cautioned. "This kid has the quickest release of any passer I've seen."

Werblin lusted for Namath, but he didn't have the AFL draft rights to get him. The Houston Oilers did. The St. Louis Cardinals had drafted Namath in the NFL. The University of Alabama Crimson Tide had one more game to play, the Orange Bowl against the favored University of Texas Longhorns, and it appeared that the Tide might have to do it without Namath, who had suffered a serious knee injury. Nothing—not knee injury, not long hair, and certainly not price—would deter Werblin and the Jets. Coach Ewbank traded a first-round draft choice and the rights to Jerry Rhome, who had broken a number of collegiate records at Tulsa, for the rights to Namath.

The Orange Bowl became an unforgettable game. Namath not only played hurt, but he was also magnificent. The Longhorns won, but all anyone could talk about the next day was Namath and his whip of an arm. When the Jets signed Namath for $427,000, an unheard-of sum for a pro football player, the Giants, upstaged, were moved off the back page of the New York tabloids.

The Jets took more than Namath away from that memorable Orange Bowl game. They signed Texas star receiver, George Sauer Jr., and the Longhorns tight end, Pete Lammons. Sauer and Lammons would join Don Maynard to give Namath the heart of his passing game. The four of them would collaborate with running back Snell to produce an offense that would carry the Jets to fame.

Werblin even gave Namath an immediate new identity. Beaver Falls Joe and Tuscaloosa Joe became Broadway Joe before stepping foot on the Great White Way. Right after the signing, there was Namath on the cover of *Sports Illustrated*, celebrating his new identity amid the famous marquees of Broadway. The Titans? They had already been consigned to the Lost and Found Department of New York sports history. In his first home game as a Jet, Namath drew a crowd of more than 58,000. The team hadn't drawn that many people for all seven home games in its final season playing in the old Polo Grounds as the now-defunct Titans.

Werblin's assessment of the Jets-Giants rivalry was accurate. At the end of the 1964 season, the second year of the Jets and their new management, the Giants had crash-dived from an 11–3 conference champion to a 2–10–2 last-place team. It would be five years before they would have another winning record. By that time the Jets had won a Super Bowl and were dividing the football fans of the New York area. And Broadway Joe was the biggest name in football.

The AFL was not the only one making television news. Five days before the NBC bombshell, CBS and the NFL had agreed to a contract awarding the rights to telecast regular-season games in 1964 and 1965 for $1.4 million a year. Three months later CBS acquired the rights to the NFL championship games of the same seasons for $1.8 million a game. The football war had opened a second front: television.

TV and football had been approaching each other gingerly, like cautious boxers, since the "Uncle Miltie" and *Kukla, Fran, and Ollie* days of the young industry. In 1950, the Los Angeles Rams, under forward-looking owner Dan Reeves, became the first NFL team to allow all of its games, home and away, to be televised. A year later the "home" portion of the Rams' schedule was rescinded from the agreement. It was the first-known blackout.

In the early days of television, pro football had been televised on an experimental basis by some local stations. The old Dumont Network became the first to understand that there was a future in telecasting football. Dumont paid $75,000 to show the 1951 title game between the Rams—who had moved from Cleveland to Los Angeles as NFL champions in 1946—and the Cleveland Browns. The Rams won, 24–17. Five years later NBC became the first of the big networks to show an interest, paying $100,000 to the NFL to televise its championship game.

In 1956 CBS became the first network to broadcast some games to selected markets across the country. At the end of the season the New York Giants scored a surprisingly easy 47–7 win over the strong Chicago Bears on a snowy December 30 in Yankee Stadium. CBS and the NFL were about to be locked in what was as close to a corporate-love embrace as imaginable.

The Giants had been a winning team for three years, ever since Jim Lee Howell took over as head coach. They weren't just skilled, they were glamorous as well, led by Frank Gifford, a great all-around back with matinee-idol looks. During the season many of the Giants players lived in the Grand Concourse Hotel near Yankee Stadium, just a short taxi drive away from Manhattan. As an attraction the Giants didn't rival the Yankees, who were at their all-time baseball dominance then, but New York was charmed by the winning Giants as they had never been previously.

Nobody was more charmed than the CBS executives. Mike Manuche's Restaurant, just down from CBS's headquarters on Fifty-second Street and nicknamed Black Rock by industry insiders, became the unofficial watering hole for the execs. It was common to see some of them lunching with guests such as Gifford, Charley Conerly, Kyle Rote, and Sam Huff. Tom Landry and Vince Lombardi would stop in now and then. The word *coordinator* hadn't yet been used in pro football, but that's what Lombardi was on offense and Landry on defense. Gifford once joked that "Jim Lee rakes and smoothes the field for practice, then Lombardi and Landry do the coaching." Years later, even after Lombardi had become a football god in Green Bay, he still used Manuche's as his Manhattan headquarters.

The bond between the NFL and CBS was superglued when Tex Schramm, general manager of the Rams, was hired to become assistant director of sports at the network. Promoted to succeed Schramm, at the urging of Tex, was Pete Rozelle, his handpicked director of public relations. Replacing Rozelle was Tex Maule, a Dallas sportswriter who would later become the presiding football writer and NFL advocate at *Sports Illustrated*. It was Maule who wrote that the Baltimore Colts' overtime victory against the Giants in 1958, was "the greatest game ever played."

If the Giants' victory over the Bears in 1956 had won over New York City, the excitement of the Colts-Giants overtime game and its sudden-death ending two years later captured the attention of the American sporting public via television. When the Harris poll of 1964 revealed that pro football had vaulted over baseball to become the favorite of the nation's sports lovers, it couldn't have been done without TV. Television and pro football were made for each other.

When the American Football League was formed in October of 1959, it wasn't the first time the NFL had been challenged in the modern era. In 1946 the All-America Football Conference was formed. There were plenty of players for a new league. Stars like Otto Graham, Elroy Hirsch, Marion Motley, Ace Parker, and Bill Dudley were coming back from the armed forces. There was such a backlog of the top players in the top major football powers such as Michigan and Texas that each graduating class provided new stars for the pro rosters. Notre Dame's George Ratterman was never a No. 1 quarterback in college because he played behind Heisman Trophy–winner Johnny Lujack, but as a rookie starter in 1947 he made the Buffalo Bills a contender in the AAFC. Ratterman's career continued with the New York Yankees and Cleveland Browns for another seven years when the Bills folded after the 1949 season.

The AAFC had a great champion in the Browns. It had two franchises on the West Coast, in San Francisco and Los Angeles, one in Chicago, and two more in the New York area. All were prime television markets. The new league's problem? TV as mass entertainment was little more than a marketing concept.

By 1949, the AAFC was operating as a one-conference, rickety conglomeration of a few good teams, one great one, and the others in danger of bankruptcy. The NFL swallowed up all but three franchises, Cleveland, San Francisco, and Baltimore. The Baltimore franchise was gone in a year, reconstituted in Dallas. It was reconstituted once again in Baltimore in 1953 by a group headed by Carroll Rosenbloom, a former University of Pennsylvania football player with a broken nose and a lot of money. If there had been a television contract for the All-America Football Conference, who knows how that challenge might have ended?

So when the fledgling American Football League was formed in October of 1959, the owners knew that it would be an exercise in

futility if they couldn't obtain a viable TV deal. The Music Corpora-
tion of America, the giant talent agency, was hired as the AFL's negotiating representative charged with obtaining a favorable contract
with ABC. The network wasn't sure what it was being asked to buy.
The MCA agent assigned to the new client was a handsome young
man from the West Coast named Jay Michaels. He was the antithesis
of the public's idea of a hard-driving, hard-sell agent. Michaels was
quietly forceful, a person with all the essential facts at hand and the
ability to use them to make his point. Much later he would become
best known as the father of sportscaster Al Michaels, ABC's star
play-by-play sportscaster.

When ABC signed its memorandum of acceptance to televise
AFL games starting in 1960, it was delivered to Jay Michaels. When
the AFL held the twentieth anniversary of "The Foolish Club," which
the owners called themselves, it was recalled that there were no
football people available in 1960 to make out the first schedule for
the new league. "The schedule was made out by Jay Michaels and
me," said Roone Arledge, who was the assistant director of sports at
the network then, but later became the most powerful man in sports
and probably in the whole of television as president of ABC News.

CHAPTER 2

Harry and Pete

T hat's what brought about the merger between the leagues more than anything," was Ralph Wilson's recollection. "Television and Pete Gogolak. And don't forget Harry Wismer."

Wismer was the first owner of the AFL's New York franchise, the Titans. Gogolak was the first soccer-style kicker in pro football history.

Artistically, the Titans' first regular-season game was a success. They beat the Buffalo Bills, 27–3. It wasn't even close. Financially it was a disaster. The official attendance was announced by Wismer as 10,200. It was the first of many occasions that the skeptics said, "Harry counts eyes and ears as well as noses." Titans linebacker Larry Grantham, who would stay to enjoy far better days as a Jet, later remarked: "instead of introducing us before the game, we might as well have walked up into the stands and introduced ourselves to the fans. There weren't many of them there for just about any game, nothing close to 10,000."

The small attendance, which seldom improved, failed to chill Wismer's enthusiasm. He already had the reputation of being one of the nation's most buoyantly enthusiastic citizens. He was a famous sportscaster, particularly notable for his work as a play-by-play broadcaster for college games involving Notre Dame, Michigan State, and other top schools. He had been a good athlete in his youth. He knew sports, but his accuracy sometimes failed to equal his enthusiasm. He once described a ball carrier running downfield as "reaching the 40, he's at the 45, the 50, the 55 . . ."

Wismer also had the habit of identifying mythical fans in attendance at the game he was broadcasting. "And there is the secretary of state sitting on the 50-yard line," he might say, while the secretary of state was actually in Europe negotiating a trade agreement. Those were details, and Wismer wasn't bothered by minor details.

Wismer loved to disarm people. He'd meet someone, and the first thing he would say was "Congratulations!" Quickly he would walk on, leaving the person mystified as to what he had done in order to be congratulated. Wismer reasoned that "everybody has done something for which they deserve congratulations, so why not?"

He also enjoyed startling people. He would enter a room and say something like, "So they shot Castro, eh?" to no one in particular. There would be an immediate buzz around the room, which is what he wanted.

Wismer collected important people. When he worked in Detroit, where he was very popular, he became friends with Harry Bennett, the original Henry Ford's right-hand man. It was Bennett's security force—union organizers called them thugs—that left Walter Ruether, president of the United Auto Workers (UAW), and his brother Victor beaten and bloodied outside Ford's River Rouge plant after the UAW set up a picket line one day in the 1930s. Wismer may not have approved of Bennett's methods, but he liked his connections. Through Bennett he met the old man, Henry Ford himself. A portly man, Wismer would often have an early lunch with Bennett and then a later lunch with Ford. He ended up marrying Betty Bryant, known as the favorite niece of Henry Ford.

Wismer was worth about $2 million in 1960, which is how he managed to buy a football franchise. The AFL initiation fee was $100,000. Wismer already owned about a quarter of the Washington Redskins. He had to sell that share when he entered the AFL (as owner of the Titans).

The Titans weren't that bad a football team. They had some good players like Larry Grantham and wide receiver Don Maynard, a speedy Giant reject who developed into a Hall of Famer. In their first two seasons, the Titans finished with 7–7 records. The players didn't fare as well at their local banks, however, as many of their paychecks bounced. It became the practice of visiting AFL teams to assign a couple of their front-office executives to forget about watching the game and monitor the box office instead so that they could take home the guaranteed cut of the gate they had coming.

Still, Harry retained his optimism. "The whole difference in this league is the sale of television, and your old buddy here sold it," he'd say. "The American Football League is the league of the future."

"He did sell it," said Wilson, four decades later. "He was the man who came up with the idea of all teams in the league sharing television revenue. The NFL says Pete Rozelle started it, but it was really Wismer's idea. Harry was all right. The only thing wrong with him is that he ran out of money."

At about the same time Wismer's fortunes began to fall, the fortunes of Peter Kornel Gogolak began to rise. Gogolak had immigrated to the United States from Hungary with his family at the time of the Hungarian uprising against Soviet domination in 1956. The Gogolaks settled in Ogdensburg, New York, where Pete and his kid brother, Charlie, enrolled at Ogdensburg Free Academy. They played the favorite sport of their childhood, soccer. A good student, Pete started college life at the nearest Ivy League school, Cornell University in Ithaca, New York.

A coach on the Big Red staff saw Gogolak kicking a soccer ball and invited him to try out for the football team. Placekicking would never be the same. By the time Gogolak reached his senior season, NFL scouts were no longer making Ivy League campuses a "must" stop on their campus tours. Ted Thoren, Cornell's baseball coach, tipped off Harvey Johnson, the Bills' chief scout, to Gogolak. Johnson had been a kicker himself in his playing days with the old New York Yankees of the All-America Football Conference. After auditioning Gogolak on the Cornell campus, Johnson called Lou Saban, the Bills' coach. "I've never seen anything like him," Johnson reported. "We've got to draft this guy."

Saban wasn't as excited as Johnson. The Bills selected Gogolak, but not until the twelfth round of the twenty-six-round 1964 draft. He wasn't selected at all in the NFL draft. Pro football was still skeptical about nontraditional kicking. Nevertheless, there was a great amount of national publicity when Buffalo signed him shortly after the draft. It was a one-year contract with an option year. In the first days of training camp, Gogolak did not do much to erode the skepticism. A story in the *Buffalo Evening News* staggered him. It said that if he didn't improve soon enough to impress Saban, he could be cut.

His hands shaking with indignation, Gogolak brought the newspaper story to Eddie Abramoski, the team trainer and the only confidant the kicker had in camp. "What is this bullyshit?" demanded Gogolak, still not fully conversant with American slang. "That story is accurate, Pete," Abramoski told him. "If you don't get your kicking into gear, you may not be long for this camp."

His teammates were not enthralled with Pete anyway. It was Saban's practice to excuse his kickers a few minutes early after the morning workout. It was Pete's habit to leave the field and shower quickly, then walk back out on the field to watch the rest of the team sweat and grunt under the hot July sun. It wasn't taunting. Gogolak just wasn't in tune with pro football protocol.

The Buffalo veterans had a custom of hazing the rookies, culminated by a horror of a haircut usually administered by linebacker/punter Paul Maguire, later a nationally known broadcaster for NBC and ESPN. When Gogolak heard about the custom, he complained plaintively to Saban. The coach knew that under the Soviet occupation it was the practice to give short haircuts to Hungarian youths as a matter of discipline. It was a well-remembered and despised memory from Gogolak's past. Saban cut short the hazing. The coach's award of amnesty did not help Gogolak in his relations with his teammates.

Getting it into gear was the best remedy for Gogolak's uncomfortable situation. So he got it into gear quickly. The Bills' first preseason game was against the Jets in Tampa. Gogolak kicked a 57-yard field goal, the longest on record for any pro. The story made newspapers coast-to-coast. From then on, pro scouts would take a fresh look at soccer-style kickers. In 1966 the Washington Redskins made Charlie Gogolak of Princeton, Pete's younger brother, their first-round selection, the first time a kicker had been drafted that high.

The excitement was understandable. Placekicking had been an imprecise science. When the Colts beat the Giants in the famous overtime championship game of 1958, Baltimore passed on attempting a short field goal and kept running the ball until the game was ended with a 1-yard touchdown plunge by Alan Ameche. After the game there were all sorts of questions asked and eyebrows raised because the touchdown had beaten the point spread; a field goal would have produced a "push," a tie in gambling parlance, and bettors don't collect on ties. Years later Johnny Unitas, exasperated at the accusing questions, explained: "We were afraid to try for a field goal. [Steve] Myhra missed a short one earlier, and he was having a lousy year."

Myhra was a backup guard who doubled as the kicker, fairly customary in the days when roster sizes were fewer than forty men. He attempted only ten field goals during the regular season and made just four. The Colts' long-distance kicker, Bert Rechichar, was mainly a defensive back. He tried four field goals during the regular season and made just one. The gold standard for pre-Gogolak kickers was Lou "The Toe" Groza of Cleveland, also a star tackle who is in the Hall of Fame. Despite Groza's nickname, in the twenty-one years in which he kicked, his percentage of successful attempts was under 50 percent for ten of those seasons. In 2003, the fortieth season of soccer-style booters, of all the kickers who performed regularly for their teams, the lowest success rate was 60 percent.

When Gogolak joined the Bills in 1964, they were unlike most of the other AFL teams, which were derided by the NFL and its backers as "playing basketball on cleats." The Bills' method under the conservative Saban was to play strong defense, control the ball with power running, emphasize field position, and when it was time to strike, rely on play-action passes.

Buffalo's defensive line, with All-AFL Tom Sestak and Jim Dunaway at tackles and Ron McDole and Tom Day at ends, allowed just four rushing touchdowns that season. All three starting linebackers had been tight ends in college. Strong-side linebacker John Tracey had been an All-America for Bear Bryant at Texas A&M. Mike Stratton, the best weak-side blitzer in the AFL, was from Tennessee, middle linebacker Harry Jacobs from Bradley. They started fifty-three consecutive games as a unit. Free safety George Saimes, an All-America fullback at Michigan State, was the surest open-field tackler in the league.

The running game was built around Cookie Gilchrist, the best player in the Canadian Football League, when Buffalo signed him as a free agent in 1962, beating the Los Angeles Rams in the race to get him under contract. Cookie stood 6 feet 2 inches, weighed 252 pounds, had a 32-inch waist, and possessed amazing speed to go along with devastating power. Gilchrist, who went straight from high school in western Pennsylvania to the Canadian pros, won the AFL's most valuable player award in his first year in the league.

The Bills had two strong-armed quarterbacks, starter Jack Kemp and young backup Daryle Lamonica, who later would earn fame as the Raiders' "Mad Bomber." Lamonica was an unpolished gem with enormous self-confidence. As a rookie pressed into action in one game he misfired on his first eight passes. Saban, enraged, summoned him to his side. "Don't worry, Coach," said Lamonica, "I'm a .500 passer. I'll complete my next eight."

The explosive part of the offense came from wide receivers Elbert Dubenion and Glenn Bass, two of the fastest men in football.

16

Kemp still owns two of the four longest-pass completions in Bills history, 94 yards to Bass and 89 to Dubenion. Lamonica still has the longest completion in a playoff game, to Dubenion for 93 yards.

As strong as Buffalo was in 1964, it needed frosting for its cake. The Bills had to battle Boston, the defending champions of the AFL's Eastern Conference, who possessed a vital player in Gino Cappelletti, not only the most dangerous sure-handed receiver for quarterback Babe Parilli, but also one of football's most efficient straight-ahead kickers. Cappelletti kicked twenty-six field goals in thirty-nine attempts that year. He also caught seven touchdown passes. He was voted the AFL's most valuable player.

Gogolak was the Buffalo frosting. His soaring kickoffs forced the opposition into the inferior field position, which is exactly where Saban wanted them. The fans might have been disappointed because, in his regular season games, Gogolak never came close to the 57-yard field goal he had kicked in the Tampa exhibition, but his accuracy matched that of Cappelletti. He made good on nineteen of twenty-seven attempts.

The 1964 championship game was played on an unseasonably mild December 26 in Buffalo's threadbare War Memorial Stadium, a Great Depression product of WPA construction. The stadium had been refurbished, in a manner of speaking, so the AFL Bills had a place to play. When New York columnist Jimmy Cannon saw it, he wrote, "It's like putting rouge on a corpse." But the place never looked better to Bills fans as Gogolak kicked off to the San Diego Chargers.

Tobin Rote, an ex-NFL quarterback who had been lured to the Canadian Football League and eventually back across the border by the Chargers, threw a 26-yard touchdown pass to tight end Dave Kocourek to open the scoring on their first possession of the game. They wouldn't score again. Gogolak's kickoffs, Maguire's punting, and the Bills' smothering defense saw to that.

Later in the first quarter, Rote looped a short pass to Keith Lincoln, one of the best backs in the AFL who had been the outstanding player in the San Diego Chargers' one-sided victory over the Patriots in the AFL title game the year before. Arriving at Lincoln just as the ball did was the blitzing Stratton. The hit, still referred to as "the tackle heard round the world" by reporters who covered the game, broke Lincoln's ribs and San Diego's momentum. Buffalo played it conservatively for the rest of the game with their running game producing steady yards and devouring time as Gilchrist thundered over tacklers for 122 yards. Gogolak kicked a couple of gimme field goals in the 20–7 victory, but more weren't needed.

There wasn't much time for celebration. A few weeks after winning the championship, Saban dealt Gilchrist to the Denver Broncos in a punitive trade. The coach had had his fill of Cookie, dating back to a November game against the Patriots, with whom the Bills had dueled for the Eastern championship all season long. Buffalo's game plan centered around Kemp's passing, a tactic with which Gilchrist strongly disagreed. In the midst of the game, Cookie walked off the field and told his backup, Willie Ross, to replace him. It caused an uproar on the bench and in the huddle.

The Patriots won, 38–26, putting them back in the race for the championship. Saban suspended Gilchrist that night. On Monday, Kemp called the players together and told them there would be a team meeting later that night at the Hotel Sheraton in downtown Buffalo. The quarterback also arranged for Saban and Cookie to make appearances. At the meeting, Gilchrist made an apology to the team, and Saban later reinstated him. The coach's actions were reluctant.

It was melodrama enough for an HBO movie if HBO had been in business at the time. The Bills won the division by beating the Patriots in Fenway Park in the last game of the season. On the Bills' first play from scrimmage, Cookie carried the ball around the left end, then, rather than avoid cornerback Chuck Shonta, ran straight at him and hit him with a hammerlike forearm, knocking him unconscious. As Gilchrist walked past Boston's defensive huddle, he scornfully asked, "Which one of you motherfuckers is next?" The rest of the contest seemed to be a formality. The Bills won, 24–14, and six days later Cookie played his final game as a Bill in the championship victory against San Diego.

Walking off the field in the midst of a game was more than enough for both Saban and Wilson, since Cookie had already been the center of a Page 1 incident earlier in the season. Gilchrist, street-smart and, believe it or not, normally affable, always said of himself: "I don't drink, I don't smoke, I don't do drugs, and I never went to bed with a woman who didn't want to go to bed with me."

It was all true, but he could be stubbornly difficult. That's what happened on East Ferry Street in Buffalo one afternoon during the season when he doubleparked while visiting a restaurant. When he came out, a policeman was writing a ticket. One thing led to another, doubleparking escalated to resisting arrest, and it took seven cops to get him into a cell.

A few weeks later the charges were dropped, and after the Bills beat the Patriots for the Eastern Division championship, two Boston policemen posed with their arms around Cookie in the Fenway Park dressing room. Saban and Wilson were not amused. Days later Gilchrist was traded for Billy Joe, a big back whose talent couldn't match Cookie's.

Joe had developed a history of bunion trouble, and he was never the ball carrier he might have been otherwise. He would become notable as the longtime head coach at Florida A&M years later. Even at his best, Joe couldn't approach Gilchrist's production. The trade was far from value-for-value. The Bills without Gilchrist were a much different offense. They passed more and took more risks, but they still won their first four games. They were impressive victories, as they rolled over the Patriots in the opener and then beat Cookie and the Broncos, Joe Namath and the Jets, and Al Davis's Raiders.

But there was more unwelcome change to come. By mid-October, the Buffalo offense was altered beyond recognition. Both speed receivers, Dubenion and Bass, suffered knee injuries that would keep them out for the remainder of the season.

Saban made a desperate trade with the Raiders for a pass catcher with some speed who might keep the Bills from being squeezed into an offense that couldn't function to produce plays beyond 20 yards.

Knowing the Bills were desperate, Davis demanded Tom Keating, a promising defensive tackle, for Bo Roberson, a Raiders backup who once was a world-class long jumper at Cornell University. Roberson never came close to replacing the Buffalo starters, and Gogolak became far more important to the Bills.

Buffalo's chances of successfully defending its championship came down to a four-game road trip in November and early December. It started in Boston where Gogolak kicked three field goals and the Bills won, 23–7. The next two games were on the West Coast, in Oakland and San Diego. Early in the season the Bills had beaten the Raiders, 17–12, in Buffalo, but the Chargers pummeled them, 24–3, the following week.

Since his days at Cornell, Gogolak had practiced kicking with an imaginary clock ticking in his head. He whispered to himself a mantra from his own script: "Ten seconds to play, the game is on the line . . . ," then he would kick. For the first time as a pro football player, his field goals made the difference in actual games, defeating Oakland and tying the Chargers on this road trip. Buffalo would go on to end the trip unbeaten and eventually win the Eastern Division again.

When the Bills arrived in San Diego to prepare for a week at the Marine Corps Base in advance of the title game, they were greeted by a large cartoon on Page 1 of the *San Diego Tribune*'s sports section. It depicted a figure of the Chargers' huge defensive tackle, Ernie Ladd, hovering over a tiny, freckle-faced, obviously frightened Kemp. The Chargers had been established as 14-point favorites.

It was a coaching triumph for Saban and his chief defensive aide, Joe Collier. Saban decided to go with a double tight-end attack, young Paul Costa on one side and veteran Ernie Warlick, who had earlier lost his starting job to Costa, on the other. Kemp, voted the AFL's most valuable player for his direction of a wounded offense, completed just nine passes, one of them to Warlick for a touchdown. The game was in the hands of the Buffalo defense—and Gogolak. The defense, a concoction by Collier in which 300-pound Ron McDole often dropped off the line of scrimmage in pass coverage, strangled the Chargers. Lance Alworth, the fastest receiver in football at the time, broke away for what had the appearance of a touchdown run that would put San Diego back in contention, but Bills cornerback Booker Edgerson caught him from behind, to the astonishment of the Chargers as well as his own teammates.

Edgerson's big play choked off the Chargers' last breath. Gogolak kicked three field goals in the second half. The Bills had their second consecutive league championship and the first shutout in AFL title game history. So much for "basketball on cleats." Gogolak's name was in the headlines, and the headlines would get much bigger. He was about to create one of the biggest stories in football history.

CHAPTER 3

The Neighbors

oward the end of the 1965 season it was becoming clear to some owners in both leagues that the big money contracts they signed with CBS and NBC were not enough to keep them competitive in the player war. The cost of signing college stars drafted in the high rounds was getting far beyond the realm of good business. It was approaching the point where a number of franchises in both the NFL and AFL were selecting players for cosmetic purposes, a big splash in the headlines but questionable productivity on the field.

"Teams were getting to the point where they wouldn't ask 'Can he help us?'" said Gil Brandt, the NFL's Dallas Cowboys' personnel chief, "but instead, 'Can we sign him?'"

"After we signed our original contract with ABC TV in 1960, the NFL knew we [our league] were here to stay because we had the money to compete for players," said Ralph Wilson, the Buffalo Bills' owner. "For the first few years of the AFL there was no talk among us about a merger. The owners knew the new league was going to be a money loser. We all got into it because we loved football.

"We sat down and calculated what it would take financially to keep us going for three years—how much we would charge for tickets, how many fans we would need to attract, the size of the player payrolls," Wilson continued. "We had it figured out pretty closely. No one talked about a merger for the first few years of the league."

Even without major television money, most of the AFL teams aside from the Denver Broncos and the New York Titans did fairly well in assembling college talent in the beginning. They shocked the NFL in their first year of operation when they signed half the players the NFL had selected in the first round of its draft, including the No.

1 pick in the entire draft, Louisiana State running back Billy Cannon, the Heisman Trophy winner.

It took a federal judge to decide that the Houston Oilers held a valid contract with Cannon. He had already signed with the NFL's Los Angeles Rams, ostensibly under the goalposts minutes after the 1960 Sugar Bowl ended. In reality the contract had been signed weeks before and postdated. The judge ruled that the contract with Los Angeles was not binding, that the Rams' general manager—Pete Rozelle, who was into his sixth month as the new commissioner of the NFL by the time of the trial—had taken advantage of a "rustic," Cannon. Cannon was awarded to the Oilers, owned by the AFL's cofounder, Bud Adams. The signing cemented ABC's decision to become the AFL's telecaster. Having the Heisman Trophy winner as an attraction was a selling point for prospective sponsors.

The Dallas Texans, owned by the AFL's other cofounder, Lamar Hunt, signed two of the NFL's first-round picks, Johnny Robinson, Cannon's running mate at LSU, and another running back, Jack Spikes of Texas Christian. In the NFL draft, Robinson had been picked by the Detroit Lions and Spikes by Pittsburgh Steelers. The Steelers had previously traded away all but two of their first six selections, and the Texans signed both of them, the other being North Texas State running back Abner Haynes, who became the AFL's first homebred star.

Buffalo signed Penn State quarterback Richie Lucas, the Washington Redskins' top draftee, and the Boston Patriots signed Northwestern running back Ron Burton, the Philadelphia Eagles' first choice.

The AFL's Los Angeles Chargers, owned by hotel scion Barron Hilton, scored a coup by snatching Southern California offensive tackle Ron Mix from the Baltimore Colts.

Not signing Mix was a huge loss to Baltimore. In his nine seasons as a Charger, he was penalized just twice for holding, an amazing statistic since many offensive lineman have been penalized twice in a quarter. Mix was also speedy and quick on his feet. His pulling and blocking became a key to the Chargers' successful running game, allowing coach Sid Gillman to employ running backs Paul Lowe and Keith Lincoln on quick tosses.

Wayne Valley, the Oakland Raiders' managing partner, once asked his coach, Al Davis, why the Raiders didn't use more quick tosses like the Chargers. "Because we don't have tackles like Ron Mix and Ernie Wright," Davis answered.

Of all the NFL owners who lost important draft choices in that first year of competition with the AFL, Carroll Rosenbloom of the Colts was the most embarrassed. Upton Bell, son of the late NFL commissioner, was a scout for the Colts at the time. "After the AFL held its first draft in the fall of 1959, the Colts did not rush out to sign the guys we drafted," Bell said. "We were the NFL champions. We weren't going to fall all over ourselves for a bunch of rookies."

So the Colts were wiped out in the draft. Four of their first five selections signed with the new league. The Colts' second-round pick, defensive end Don Floyd of Texas Christian, played eight years with the Houston Oilers. Third-round selection Marvin Terrell, a guard from Mississippi, played four seasons with the Dallas Texans–Kansas City Chiefs. The loss of those players cost Baltimore the edge that it had on their Western Conference rival, the Green Bay Packers, the next year. "Weeb Ewbank, the coach, blamed Don Kellett, the general manager," said Bell. "Kellett blamed Weeb. From then on it was war."

Rosenbloom would never suffer such an embarrassment to the AFL again. Later in his career, Mix, by that time an established leader in San Diego's Jewish community, said, "I heard that Carroll found out I was Jewish. The next time I saw him he told me, 'If I had known that I would have signed you.'"

Rosenbloom was a man unaccustomed to and ferociously unwilling to have anyone stand between him and something he really wanted. In 1975 when he owned the Los Angeles Rams, the team signed a journeyman free agent, wide receiver Ron Jessie, from the Detroit Lions. Jessie maintained that he had played out the option in his contract. In theory, that made him a free agent. In practice, it was rare that an opposing team would sign a free agent. To skirt the antitrust implications of what amounted to holding a player in bondage, the NFL devised the Rozelle Rule. The rule mandated that when a team signed a player who was ostensibly a free agent, Commissioner Pete Rozelle would decide on compensation for the team that lost the player. In the case of a valuable starter, the compensation was a first-round draft choice. In Jessie's case, the Lions' owner, Bill Ford, argued that Detroit deserved more than a top draft choice, and Rozelle agreed. He ruled that Cullen Bryant, a promising power back for the Rams, be awarded to Detroit.

The Rams protested the ruling, and Bryant was returned to them. Rosenbloom would demonstrate how unforgiving he could be toward anyone who opposed him, and at the next owners meeting, he strode into the room, headed directly to Ford—one of America's industrial royalty—and told him, "Billy, I've got a dog who shits bigger turds than you do," loudly enough so that everyone in the meeting could hear.

Rosenbloom would never again lose draft choices on the scale of 1960, but he was a realistic businessman. He knew the price for talent had risen to alarming heights and the market would be unlikely to drop while there was still competition. By the autumn of 1965, the football war was taking its financial toll, and the idea of peace was becoming not such a bad idea. "I don't know how the talk of a merger started, except that it wasn't initiated by us," the Bills' Ralph Wilson said. "We heard that they might be interested in a merger. It was sort of in the rumor stage when we had an AFL owners meeting in Houston."

Barron Hilton, who moved the Chargers from Los Angeles to San Diego in 1961, was serving as president of his league in 1965. "I'm going to name a committee to talk to a representative of the NFL about merging our two leagues," Hilton announced. "We'll see what comes of it." Hilton named a committee of two, Wilson and Sonny Werblin, as managing partners of the New York Jets.

"Sonny, who had become one of my best friends, was against a merger because he was operating in New York against the Giants," Wilson recalled. "Wayne Valley, the Raiders' owner, was also against it because Oakland was right across the bay from the San Francisco 49ers. They knew there would be demands over invasion of territory." The AFL commissioner, Joe Foss, was not informed of any merger talk or even the formation of the committee. For Foss's future, it was an omen.

The first merger talks became a matter of neighbors talking to one another. Rosenbloom and Wilson were a pair of South Florida snowbirds. The Colts' owner had a winter home in Golden Beach, and Wilson had one farther south on the Atlantic shore, nearer Miami. The snowbirds were not birds of a feather, however, as Rosenbloom and Wilson were of different natures. Rosenbloom was an aggressive, almost forbidding entrepreneur. Anyone negotiating a business deal with him knew immediately that it would not be an easy or comfortable time. To Rosenbloom, life was a contact sport.

There was a distasteful cloud that hung over Rosenbloom's reputation after the famous overtime game won by his Colts for the 1958 championship. Baltimore had gone into the game as a three-point favorite, but as the Colts got nearer the goal line on their final, 80-yard drive, it became clear that they would not attempt a field goal. Alan Ameche ran the ball into the New York Giants' end zone from 1 yard out for the touchdown that not only won the game but also beat the spread.

There was a great fuss made over the Colts' decision not to kick once they were in point-blank field-goal range. Most of the fuss was made by people who think fishing is fixed—in this case, bettors who had taken the points. They noted that Baltimore's kicker, Steve Myhra, had kicked a 20-yard field goal with seven seconds left in regulation time to produce the first overtime in football history. Defenders of the Baltimore strategy pointed out that the Colts were farther than a yard away when Myrha was sent on the field to tie the score. It was also pointed out that Myrha, despite his clutch field goal in the fourth quarter, had a poor season kicking and there was not great faith in him.

The suspicions hounded Rosenbloom the rest of his life. The NFL conducted a quiet investigation and found no evidence that the Colts' owner had bet on the game. Rosenbloom was known to gamble, especially on horse racing, but so did a lot of other NFL owners. Wilson once owned a Kentucky Derby hopeful and many other thoroughbreds. Two of the NFL's early owners, Tim Mara of the Giants and Art Rooney of the Pittsburgh Steelers, earned their living as bookmakers. In fact, Rooney was a skilled bettor who had some legendary days at the racetrack. In 1936, in the midst of the Depression, he swept the card at old Empire City Downs near New York, winning his bet on every race.

"I never bet on football," Rooney told Pittsburgh author Jim O'Brien. "And I didn't buy the Steelers with the money I won at Empire City. That came later."

Later came at the venerable track at Saratoga Springs, New York. That day Rooney was accompanied by Bill Corum, a famous New York sportswriter. Rooney won five consecutive races, rolling all his winnings from one bet to the next. Corum estimated Rooney's winnings at between $250,000 and $300,000, which would be about $10 million in new millennium dollars. After the races Rooney celebrated by treating Corum to a milkshake.

Ralph Wilson's family business was insurance and car hauling, trucking automobiles from the manufacturer to various dealers, and it was a very lucrative business for Wilson. It was also very different from Rosenbloom's business experience. Wilson is a man of old-fashioned manners, approachable and pleasant. The word "classy" is often used to describe him. He has been a pro football fan from his youth. "My father and I used to go to the University of Detroit Stadium to see the Lions play," he likes to reminisce. "I remember watching the Chicago Bears of the '30s, with their great end, Bill Hewitt, playing without a helmet. I always wanted to own a team. My father and I bought a small share of the Lions, as much as we were allowed to buy, in the 1950s. We sold it when I bought the AFL franchise."

For a while, a part of the Lions—and maybe the NFL—stayed with Wilson. The Bills' first head coach was Buster Ramsey, who had been the Lions' defensive coach under Buddy Parker and George Wilson. For their first two seasons, the Bills' uniforms were Hawaiian-blue jerseys with silver pants and helmets, making them clones of Detroit's NFL team.

Despite the uniforms and the coach's background, Wilson set about giving the Bills their own identity. He was among the most aggressive AFL owners in signing players. In the AFL's second draft in 1961, the Bills acquired four-fifths of an entire quality offensive line, tackles Ken Rice of Auburn and Stew Barber of Penn State, guard Billy Shaw of Georgia Tech, and center Al Bemiller of Syracuse, the national collegiate champions. Shaw, Bemiller, and Barber would form the nucleus of the line that helped Buffalo win consecutive AFL championships in 1964 and 1965. In the 1963 draft they would outsign two strong NFL franchises, Chicago and Minnesota, for their first-round selections, Michigan State center Dave Behrman and Mississippi defensive tackle Jim Dunaway, respectively.

By 1964, however, Wilson, like some other AFL owners, was setting a financial ceiling as to the amount of money he would pay out to rookies. He felt that if the race of bonus dollars continued, it would produce ruin for the Bills. That's why he joined his wintertime neighbor, Rosenbloom, to seek a solution that would keep all of football afloat.

Rosenbloom doing anything neighborly was out of character. Pete Rozelle spent twenty-nine years as commissioner of the NFL. Courtly and patient, he made few enemies during his long tenure;

Carroll Rosenbloom was one of them. His fellow owners would tell tales of how Carroll would keep up vindictive, insulting harangues toward Rozelle at league meetings and how the commissioner would sit silently and endure it. When Rosenbloom would pause toward the end of a long tirade, Rozelle would simply say, "Let's go to lunch."

As an NFL owner, Rosenbloom was accustomed to success. He had a knack for hiring good coaches. The Colts' first experience as winners came under Weeb Ewbank (who was hired in 1954 and remained with the team until 1962). Ewbank was a roly-poly, avuncular aide to Paul Brown in Cleveland. Ewbank, whose given name was Wilbur, had been a quarterback at Miami University of Ohio, just as Brown had been. But while Brown earned fame as head coach at Ohio State, Weeb's experience as a head coach came at Washington University of St. Louis, a school better noted as an institution of learning than for college football.

Ewbank learned plenty from Brown, including the importance of being candid when necessary. "It will take five years to build a top team," he said when Rosenbloom interviewed him. The owner liked Ewbank's straight talk and hired him. Success required the full five seasons, but it came wrapped as a two-time champion at the end of the 1950s. Some luck was involved. An 84-cent phone call in 1955 brought to the Colts Johnny Unitas, who had been cut by the woebegone Pittsburgh Steelers. He would become one of the greatest quarterbacks of all time.

By 1963, Rosenbloom had fired Ewbank and hired another unknown, the Detroit Lions' defensive coach, Don Shula, who at thirty-three became the youngest head coach in pro football. Shula was a major success, but he would also preside over Rosenbloom's greatest disappointment—the shocking upset loss to the Jets in Super Bowl III.

After that landmark Super Bowl, Shula coached one more season in Baltimore, then exited for Miami, whose owner, Joe Robbie, had sought permission to speak to Shula about taking their coaching job when Rosenbloom was out of reach on a trip overseas. In his absence, his son Steve granted permission. When Carroll returned, he was furious at Steve. He wanted major compensation from Miami. Eventually he was granted compensation by Rozelle, but not to the extent he wanted.

In 1971, Shula was coaching the Dolphins, and one of his former aides, Don McCafferty, was coaching the Colts. At midseason the Colts were drooping a bit, partly due to their aging quarterbacks, Unitas and Earl Morrall. As Baltimore was losing the game, Rosenbloom left his seat in the owners' area and ordered his public relations director, Ernie Accorsi, to get on the press-box loudspeaker and inform the media that on draft day the year before, Rosenbloom himself had ordered Shula to draft Dennis Shaw, the San Diego State quarterback eventually drafted by Buffalo in the second round. Shaw became the Bills' quarterback by default and was a surprise winner of the Rookie of the Year award.

Accorsi knew two things: 1. At the time of the 1970 draft, Rosenbloom didn't know Dennis Shaw from George Bernard Shaw; 2. The owner would cool down and forget about it, especially since the Colts came back to win the game. Accorsi ignored Rosenbloom's command. Later that season, when the Colts did lose a game and Morrall played poorly, a story appeared in a Baltimore newspaper citing Shula's "failure to draft Dennis Shaw as ordered by the owner." Rosenbloom had leaked the little gem of misinformation himself.

Shaw was a Roman candle of a quarterback, a player who ended up having just one good year. Ewbank, then coaching the New York Jets, was asked for his assessment of Shaw after his big rookie year. Weeb paused, then answered, "I think his two receivers, Marlin Briscoe and Haven Moses, made a lot of great catches."

Rosenbloom was on his best behavior, however, when dealing with Wilson in the matter of a possible merger. The Bills' owner represented something Rosenbloom wanted, an opponent's financial cooperation without which he and his NFL partners could be seriously damaged. "I was very much in favor of a merger," Wilson admitted. "I knew that we could last a while, but eventually the NFL was going to put us out of business. They had more people in bigger markets and more TV money. I went ahead and met ten or twelve times with Carroll, then I talked hard and fast with Sonny Werblin and Wayne Valley, who was also a close friend of mine.

"Carroll set the parameters," Wilson continued. "He said there was so much animosity between the leagues—and I agreed—that we couldn't have a complete merger right away. We would have to keep the leagues separate for about four years. We wouldn't play any regular-season games, but we'd play exhibition games. We would have one commissioner, and that would be Pete Rozelle. What the AFL started the NFL copied, so we would pool our TV money; all teams would get the same cut.

"We had more meetings between the two of us, and what we talked about struck a favorable chord with me. It got to the point where Carroll set up a lunch at the Sea View Hotel in Miami. We were joined by Rozelle and Tex Schramm, the Cowboys' general manager," Wilson said.

Schramm had immense power and prestige among the NFL owners. As Rozelle's patron he served as an important counselor to the entire league. Rosenbloom's parameters were set out with Wilson presenting the AFL's ideas. Finally came Rozelle's reply. "It sounds all right to us," he said. "So we'll go ahead with this." Then he paused once more before continuing: "But it will cost you fellows $50 million to join us."

That statement virtually brought Wilson out of his seat. "Fifty million! We won't pay that!" he said, angrily. "Not only me, but the rest of our owners won't agree to pay it." Wilson's fellow AFL owners decided that Rosenbloom and a few of his colleagues might want the merger, but Rozelle didn't and neither did the majority of NFL owners. The $50 million demand was a roadblock they knew the AFL wouldn't even try to negotiate.

CHAPTER 4

The Ace

It's an old-fashioned description, and in this era of political correctness, it's taken as a pejorative. Old-fashioned or pejorative, it describes Joe Foss from his young manhood to his death: a man's man. That is a large part of the reason why the AFL chose him as its first commissioner.

Commissioners of major league sports are chosen because their skills fit the need of the times. Bill France became the head of NASCAR because the sport had outgrown its original personality as southern entertainment with a national audience only on each Memorial Day in Indianapolis. Kenesaw Mountain Landis, a federal judge, was hired as commissioner of Major League Baseball in the wake of the 1919 Chicago "Black Sox" scandal when the sport needed a law-and-order image. Bud Selig was named commissioner of baseball in the 1990s because the owners didn't want a people's commissioner, as Fay Vincent, Selig's predecessor, had been. They wanted an "owner's commissioner," and Selig was it.

In the NFL, it took twenty-three ballots to elect thirty-three-year-old Pete Rozelle commissioner on January 26, 1960, after Bert Bell had died of a heart attack at Philadelphia's Franklin Field in the last two minutes of a Pittsburgh Steelers–Philadelphia Eagles game the previous October. The NFL wanted the right man to lead them against their most serious challenge in a decade, the formation of the American Football League. Rozelle was the right man.

The AFL owners, on the other hand, wanted someone to introduce their league to America. Foss was their guy.

As World War II broke out, the term *ace* was reserved for a fighter pilot who had shot down five enemy airplanes during combat. During

World War I, Eddie Rickenbacker had earned enormous fame as the USA's antidote to the Red Baron, Germany's scourge of the skies. Rickenbacker shot down twenty-six enemy planes over Europe.

Joe Foss flew F-4 Wildcat fighters against Japanese Zeroes and enemy bombers over the Solomon Islands in the South Pacific as world war reached a dangerous crescendo in the autumn of 1942. In just over a month, Foss had shot down twenty-three Japanese planes. By the time he was rotated back to the U.S. and awarded the Congressional Medal of Honor, the nation's highest military award, he had equaled Rickenbacker's kill count.

When Foss returned to the U.S., it didn't take long for America to discover that, with or without the Medal of Honor, Foss was a magnetic personality. Men jockeyed to be in his company. He could comfortably mix with the wealthiest and most famous of them, using the earthy vernacular of his rural South Dakota upbringing even though he was college educated. He drank his whiskey straight, gave cigar smoking a polished look, and told great stories of the outdoors, hunting tales that would expand into big-game hunting stories, just as his horizons and his bank account expanded after the war ended.

He left the Marine Corps after World War II, but he became the head of the South Dakota Air National Guard with the rank of general. His profile having been kept high, Foss entered Republican politics and was elected governor of his native state. His political career ended when he was defeated in a race for a seat in the U.S. House of Representatives. The victor was another war hero, Democrat George McGovern, who would go on to become a U.S. Senator and the party's losing candidate to President Richard Nixon in the 1972 presidential campaign.

Sixteen years after he shot down his last enemy plane, Foss was still in demand at a variety of dinners, conventions, golf outings, business meetings, and veterans reunions across the country. He was still well known and recognizable, which made him an excellent fit for the AFL. The days were over that football men like Elmer Layden and "Sleepy Jim" Crowley, two of the old Four Horsemen of Notre Dame, were popular choices to serve as league CEOs. It was the age of television and along with it the sophisticated business-men who bought commercial time on football telecasts. Foss talked their language, even though he might address them as "you ginks."

After the league was formed, AFL operations were conducted out of Lamar Hunt's Dallas offices. While Bert Bell was commis-sioner of the NFL, its offices were in Bala Cynwyd, Pennsylvania, a suburb of Philadelphia, because Bell was a Philadelphian. When Rozelle succeeded Bell, NFL operations were moved to 1 Rockefeller Plaza in Manhattan, close to the television networks, the Associated Press, and other communications giants.

The AFL's location made little difference to Foss, as he was usu-ally on the road anyway. His assistant commissioner with the title of league president was Milt Woodard, an ex-Chicago newspaper-man and executive of the golf tour. Woodard operated in the back-ground, but his work was vital to the success of the new league. His finest moment came in the wake of President John F. Kennedy's assassination. Foss was out of the country and could not be located. Woodard, in Foss's name, ordered the AFL games to be postponed out of respect for the president. "Milt kept trying to locate Joe, but time was running out," said Jack Horrigan, the AFL's public relations director. Woodard knew he couldn't wait any longer. "Playing foot-ball now is not the right thing to do," he said. Then he made the decision to postpone play. Meanwhile, over at NFL headquarters, Rozelle was about to make what he later admitted "was the biggest mistake of my career." He ordered the weekend's slate of games to be played as usual.

The media's knowledge of Woodard's decisive role in that deci-sion contributed to an image of Foss as a figurehead commissioner. It was partially true, but there was at least one important occasion when he rescued the league from disaster, which came at an owners meeting in Monmouth, New Jersey, in late June of 1965. The meetings were conducted at Monmouth Race Track, owned by the Jets' five new owners.

They wanted to make the convening a gala event, especially since the Atlanta Falcons would be welcomed as the AFL's ninth franchise, the first expansion city in the league's history. The NFL figuratively blew up the meeting, just as it had blown up the AFL's formative meeting in Minneapolis in 1960 when it snatched the host city from the new league. The coup was made more embarrassing when the NFL awarded its Minneapolis franchise to the same owners who had petitioned for an AFL franchise.

The Minneapolis fiasco was eventually repaired when the AFL awarded a franchise to Oakland. Outright disaster at the Monmouth meeting was avoided when Foss suggested that a group headed by attorney Joe Robbie of Minneapolis be awarded the franchise that had been first committed to Atlanta. It was another case of politics making strange bedfellows. During Foss's days as Republican governor of South Dakota, Robbie had been chairman of the state Democratic Party. Political affiliation did not play a role when Foss had a strong conviction about someone. Besides, he and Robbie had become friends years before.

As a prospective franchise owner, Robbie did not possess the right-size bank account for the role, however, his main legal client, entertainer Danny Thomas, a fellow Lebanese-American, did. Robbie and Thomas had been seeking an AFL franchise in Miami for months. When Ralph Wilson acquired his AFL franchise in October of 1959, he wanted to place it in Miami, near where he owned a winter home. "I couldn't get the Orange Bowl as our stadium," Wilson recalled. "Miami had a franchise in the All-America Football Conference, the Seahawks, when that league began and the team didn't do well at all. They lasted only one season and left a lot of bad memories. Besides, the University of Miami played in the Orange Bowl, and they didn't like the idea of professional football as a competitor."

Things change. Like sports fans in the rest of the nation, Miamians had a far more favorable view of pro football than they did twenty years earlier. They also had a favorable view of Danny Thomas. "Outside of show business, Danny has two big interests, getting an AFL franchise and raising money for St. Jude Hospital in Memphis," Robbie explained.

When Foss informed Robbie of the turn of events vacating the AFL franchise earmarked for Atlanta, he rushed from a St. Jude's Hospital meeting in Memphis to the Monmouth meeting. Once he got there he was stunned when informed that the cost of an AFL franchise had inflated to $6.5 million, an enormous number for the time. He called Thomas in Hollywood, but had to leave a message. Late that night, Thomas returned his call.

Robbie decided to open the conversation diplomatically. It went this way:

"Danny . . . this is Joe. We raised $17,000 for St. Jude yesterday."

"Seventeen! That's great!"

"The AFL met today."

"I know."

"Danny, they want six and a half million . . ."

" . . . Danny? Are you there, Danny?"

After a long pause, Thomas's voice returned in a lower pitch, "Tell me again, Joe. How much did we make for St. Jude?"

One of the most important allies the AFL had in pro football's return to Miami was Edwin Pope, an immensely popular columnist and sports editor of *The Miami Herald*, the dominant newspaper in South Florida. Pope had been a boy-wonder sportswriter in Atlanta before he moved to Miami. He had influence not only in the southern part of the state but all over Florida as well. "If Miami gets this franchise," Pope said, "it will become the best franchise in the league." Pope was prescient.

In 1970, five seasons after they began play, the Miami Dolphins hired Don Shula as their head coach. A year later they were in Super

Bowl VI. A year after that, they won their first of two consecutive Super Bowls. Miami was atop the pro football world.

On the other hand, Foss's luck in handling the problem of the New York Titans and their owner Harry Wismer was less sunny. Near the end of the AFL's second season, the commissioner, slow to anger against any person short of an enemy fighter pilot, had had his fill of Wismer. A few days before, Wismer had denounced him in the New York newspapers, suggesting that Foss get a new job. "He should be assistant commissioner of the NFL," Wismer sneered.

Foss was making a routine visit to the Bills-Titans game, a sparsely attended attraction in the Polo Grounds, when a group of reporters asked him about the latest in a barrage of vituperative attacks. "New York should get a new owner for the good of the league," the commissioner shot back. "He's more interested in publicity, any publicity, than in running a good operation. I have to do something about him or resign, and I don't intend to resign. He can be kicked out by a three-quarters vote of the owners. I'm pretty sure I have the votes."

Foss admitted he had never met Wismer before he took the job as commissioner in late 1959. "I'll clue you in on that one," he said grimly. "If I had met him, I would never have taken the job."

The Titans just kept getting worse. They were merely mediocre in their first two seasons, finishing 7–7 in both 1960 and 1961. Steve Sebo, their general manager, had done a good job of assembling available talent. Experienced and promising talent was fairly abundant since there were just twelve NFL teams, and their rosters were small, fewer than three dozen active players. Coaches seldom had either the time or the inclination to develop young players who didn't have the right stuff as soon as they entered the NFL. Exhibit A was Johnny Unitas, who was playing semipro football in Pittsburgh after the Steelers cut him. Pittsburgh had a trio of quarterback talent ahead of him: Bobby Layne, Jim Finks, and Ted Marchibroda.

In stocking their rosters in the beginning, all AFL teams operated in the same manner as the Titans. George Blanda, the Chicago Bears' quarterback/kicker, retired, frustrated at not getting enough playing time. As a free agent, he reconsidered his retirement and signed with Houston of the new league. He became the AFL's first Most Valuable Player. The Titans became respectable when Sebo signed Don Maynard from the Giants and Art Powell from the Eagles as the team's starting wide receivers. Maynard was a diamond in the rough that needed polishing that the Giants didn't have time to give. Powell had an impressive rookie season as a defensive back, but he proved so difficult and disruptive that he was released at the end of the season. Coach Sammy Baugh, one of the greatest passers in football history, switched him to wide receiver. Al Dorow, a vagabond quarterback with six years' experience in the NFL and Canadian Football League was signed as the man assigned to get the ball to Powell and Maynard. Powell led the AFL in touchdowns in its first season, and Dorow threw twenty-six touchdown passes.

What the Titans weren't able to do, which was essential in the credibility race against the NFL, was sign its college draftees. From the three drafts in which the New York team participated as the Titans, only two players of significance, linebacker Larry Grantham of Mississippi and center Alex Kroll of Rutgers, were signed. Lost were players such as future Hall of Fame cornerback Herb Adderly, who signed with the Packers; tight end Bernie Casey and offensive tackle Joe Scibelli, who chose the Rams; tight end John Mackey and running back Tom Matte, who signed with Baltimore; and defensive tackle Roger Brown of Detroit and running back Don Perkins, who went to the Cowboys.

Wismer didn't have the money to compete with Dan Reeves of the Rams, Carroll Rosenbloom of the Colts, Clint Murchison of the Cowboys, and their brethren with deep pockets. Eventually Foss found some men who did—Sonny Werblin, Leon Hess, Townsend Martin, and Phil Iselin. As the prospective new owners were performing their due diligence with a background of enormous publicity in New York, Wismer exited figuratively kicking and screaming. The kicks and screams were aimed at Foss.

The commissioner was sleeping comfortably in his Omaha hotel suite when a knock at his door awakened him at 5:40 a.m.

"Room service!" came the announcement.

"I didn't order room service," answered a sleepy Foss.

"Sir, we have an order that you called in last night; it says breakfast for ten, no later than 5:45."

"I'm the only one in this room," Foss protested. "No one else is coming. I have no idea who called in that order."

By the time Foss had shaken the sleep from his head, he figured it out. He was being harassed, and it wasn't difficult to finger the harasser. Apparently Wismer had some sort of mole in the AFL office or its travel bureau, and the mole provided Harry with the ingredients for mischief making. Two weeks later at an airport gate, Foss discovered that his airline reservations to Denver had been cancelled by someone using his name. This went on for months, until the sale of the team became final and the Titans morphed into the New York Jets.

Wismer wasn't finished with his mischief making. Selected sportswriters who covered the AFL began getting phone calls at 7 a.m., or even earlier. Wismer wouldn't announce himself; he'd merely deliver his message and hang up. One morning it would be, "Did you know that Shea Stadium is sinking into Flushing Meadow?" (Shea Stadium, its construction nearly completed, was to be the new home of the Jets.) A week later he'd say, "Isn't it silly for a grown man to insist that people call him Sonny?"

Eventually the mischief ended. Foss thought that Wismer might be out of his life for good, but months later he received a phone call from his nemesis, and this time it was different. Wismer informed Foss that he was getting married again, and his betrothed was the widow Zwillman from New Jersey. Her late husband was Abner

"Longie" Zwillman, a notorious leader of the Jewish arm of the mob, a confederate of the late Bugsy Siegel, the mob's pioneer overlord in Las Vegas. Bugsy had met his end in an infamous mob hit in the living room of his moll, Virginia Hill. At least Zwillman died of natural causes. It's likely that Wismer's bride-to-be had a better chance of finding happiness with Harry than she did with husband No. 1. Longie was short on fidelity, and his mistress was the 1930s "platinum blonde of the silver screen," Jean Harlow. Harlow was Marilyn Monroe when Monroe herself was a mere toddler.

When Wismer called Foss, he wasn't fishing for a wedding present. In fact, he asked Joe to be his best man for the nuptials. When Wismer took the widow for his lawfully wedded, it was Foss, letting bygones be bygones, who handed his onetime tormentor the ring. Wismer's wedding was one of the last connections Foss would have to football. The AFL owners were looking for someone less forgiving and kind as their commissioner.

CHAPTER 5

Brooklyn Al

Erasmus Hall, the legendary Brooklyn high school established in 1787, has seen generations of famous people file through its halls, from Barbra Streisand and Chicago Bulls and White Sox owner Jerry Reinsdorf to the late chess wizard Bobby Fischer and Moe Howard of the *Three Stooges*. Nevertheless, the school may never have graduated a student more distinctive than Al Davis, the most popular boy in his senior class.

By the time he reached thirty, the "most popular boy" was working in professional football as an assistant coach for the Los Angeles Chargers of the new American Football League and already becoming extremely unpopular with Charger opponents. By the time he was thirty-three, he was head coach of the Oakland Raiders, and the unpopularity had turned to loathing in both the National and American Leagues. By the time he was thirty-six, he was the second commissioner of the AFL, and loathing had collected a partner, fear, that of the NFL owners who had to contend with Davis's agenda of piracy.

Davis always had a deep interest and respect for the military. His first big college coaching job was at the Citadel, the military school in Charleston, South Carolina. During his time there, his only child, a son, was born. The Davises named him Mark, in honor of General Mark Clark, hero of the Italian campaign in World War II. In retirement Clark had become superintendent of the Citadel. By April 1966, Davis would have a command of his own.

When the AFL owners convened their 1966 spring meeting in Houston, it was public knowledge that they intended to change commissioners. Joe Foss had been their Colin Powell, a diplomatic general. They needed a George S. Patton, the swashbuckling "Blood and Guts" commander of the armored phase of the invasion as the war in Europe intensified and was won by the Allied forces. On April 7, Foss resigned. On April 8, the owners hired their Patton, Al Davis.

The day after the new commissioner was named, the Houston newspapers carried front-page photos of a fistfight at the AFL meetings between Houston Oilers owner Bud Adams and Jack Gallagher, a popular sports columnist for the *Houston Post*. Adams and Gallagher, Bud's frequent critic, had often traded barbs in a semi-friendly manner. This time, however, the banter was not friendly. The photo showed the backsides of the combatants as they tussled on the floor, with Davis between them, breaking up the fight. It was the only peacemaking in which Davis was involved during his short reign as commissioner.

His status as a football man was the main reason Davis was chosen by the owners. After his hitch at the Citadel, he moved to the University of Southern California as an assistant to Don Clark. Clark had outstanding aides on his staff, including John McKay, who would succeed him as head coach and became a giant in the college game. Davis coached the USC Trojan receivers and also served as a recruiter. It was a happy time for him, but USC was already an established power, and he was both ambitious and interested in tougher challenges.

Davis's drive may have been born of frustration as a player. He was a good athlete in high school, less so at Syracuse University where he played football and basketball on the Orange's freshman teams. He never made a traveling squad. A decade later he spoke of his bitterness about Andy Mogish, the freshman coach in both sports. "I can't hear his name without grinding my teeth," Davis admitted. Like many other coaches, his frustrations as an athlete would be translated to excellence as a teacher of the game.

When the Chargers were founded as an original franchise in the AFL, they were based in Los Angeles. Sid Gillman, who had spent five years as coach of the NFL's Los Angeles Rams, had been fired just as the new league was formed. Barron Hilton, the hotel scion and original owner of the Chargers, had been impressed by Gillman's work with the Rams, especially his sophisticated passing offense. Sensing that an entertaining offense would be a help in attracting customers to a start-up operation, Hilton hired Gillman.

The Chargers, with Jack Kemp at quarterback, won the Western Division championship in their first year, but they stayed just one season in Los Angeles. The reason might have been found in a famous response Hilton gave after the master of ceremonies offered an error-filled introduction of him as an after-dinner speaker.

"Barron has an interesting history," the emcee said in his remarks. "He was married to both Zsa Zsa Gabor and Elizabeth Taylor, he bought a baseball team and realized a $1 million profit in his first season."

When Hilton reached the microphone, he thanked the emcee for the introduction, then asked to make a few corrections: "I wasn't married to Zsa Zsa Gabor, that was my father, Conrad; I wasn't married to Elizabeth Taylor, either. That was my brother, Nicky; it wasn't a baseball team I bought, it was a football team; and I didn't make a million dollars, I lost three million."

Barron was in charge of the hotel chain's blossoming credit-card business—hence the name "the Chargers"—and Gillman ran the entire football operation. His selection of his first coaching staff was a masterpiece. First hired were two members of his former Ram staff, Jack Faulkner and Joe Madro. Then came Davis and Chuck Noll. Coaching staffs in those days were miniscule compared to the ones of the twenty-first century, and five men was the limit. It was enough, and three of them—Noll, Davis, and Gillman himself—ended up in the Hall of Fame. Faulkner breathed the first fresh air into the moribund Denver franchise as head coach and general manager. Noll coached the Pittsburgh Steelers to four Super Bowl victories. Davis created "Raider Nation," a dynasty and its raffish followers, which stayed near or at the top of pro football for more than four decades and into the new millennium.

Not only was Brooklyn Al a superb teacher of wide receivers, he was also a tutor who demanded attention to detail, disciplined route running, and a commitment to excellence. Among his gifts were uncommon intelligence and foresight. He could also talk birds out of trees, a valuable asset when recruiting the best athletes coming out of the draft into professional football.

Slick recruiting was second nature to Al from the time he worked at the Citadel. Paul Maguire, an ESPN sportscaster, told the story of when he came out of Youngstown, Ohio, as a coveted tight end and punter. "Al told me if I came to the Citadel I wouldn't have to take military and he'd get me a car," said Maguire. "When I got there, I found out that everybody takes military at the Citadel. When I asked Al about the car, he said, 'I'll introduce you to this used-car dealer I know in Charleston. He'll give you a good price.'" Maguire stayed at the school, and in his senior year he caught eleven touchdown passes. When he graduated, he signed with the Chargers to a contract proffered by a coach named Al Davis.

In 1963 it was time for Davis to graduate from the ranks of assistant coaches. The Oakland Raiders were the nuclear waste of pro football. They won only two games in 1961 and one in 1962. In three years, the only college player of consequence whom they had signed was an undersize center from the University of Miami, Jim Otto. Otto's body developed into pro size, he became the AFL's all-time center, continued to excel, and when he retired, was inducted into the Hall of Fame. Almost half a century later, he was still with the Raiders as an aide to Davis.

The early Raiders went through coaches so quickly that it was difficult to remember who was in the job at any one time. The first was Eddie Erdelatz, who had established a good reputation at Navy during the 1950s with what he called A Team Named Desire. He tried the same approach in Oakland, but there was little desire and less talent. When the Raiders beat the Bills in a game at San Francisco's Kezar Stadium, an earnest young radio reporter asked the losing coach, Buster Ramsey, "Do you think this is A Team Named Desire?" Ramsey replied, "They quit like a bunch of turds when we beat them 38–9 in Buffalo."

By the end of the 1962 season, it appeared the Raiders would either relocate, probably to New Orleans, or close down operations. Instead Wayne Valley, the managing partner, convinced his board of directors to give it another year, mainly because the team had received a $400,000 infusion of cash from Ralph Wilson, owner of the Bills, in exchange for 25 percent of the team. Wilson later said, "I knew it was against the constitution, but the league would have folded. I did it for the sake of the league."

The Raiders then got an infusion of professionalism by hiring Davis as head coach and general manager. He had been recommended by Gillman. One of the first moves Davis made was to trade for Art Powell of the New York Titans, a big, fast, enormously talented receiver who had previously worn out his welcome in one year as a Philadelphia Eagle. It took him three years in New York to become a dispensable asset. The trade with the Titans came about because Davis was unafraid to take big risks. Powell caught sixteen touchdown passes in his first year as a Raider. Davis made other risky moves, and they were what made the 1–13 Raiders of 1962 into the 10–4 Raiders in his first season as a head coach.

Forty-three years later, Davis would take a similar risk. He traded with the Minnesota Vikings for another megatalented but troublesome receiver, Randy Moss. In 2004 the team had been an un-Raiderlike 5–11. Davis's football philosophy had never wavered: Positive change requires taking major risks. Moss was a disappointment in two seasons as a Raider, but Davis's appetite for risk-taking was not lessened.

In 1966 after the AFL owners elected Davis their new commissioner, Davis flew to New York to hold a press conference signaling the significant turn in the events in pro football. The major thrust of most of the questions was "What are you going to do now that you have the job?" Davis grasped a vital reality of public relations: When you don't have much to say, don't say much. His basic answer was, "Just watch us."

He quickly broadened his staff. He already had a strong public-relations man in Jack Horrigan, the former *Buffalo Evening News* sportswriter whom he knew well and with whom he felt comfortable. Horrigan was a thick-skinned, wisecracking Irish Catholic with a reputation for great integrity and loyalty.

From the beginning of the AFL, the practice was to schedule each team for three consecutive games on their opposite coast. For instance New York, Boston, and Buffalo would all play Oakland, Los Angeles, and Denver on one long trip in order to save money. It was easier to billet a team in a less-than-top-scale hotel for two-and-a-half weeks than make three separate coast-to-coast trips in a chartered plane. The charters were always prop planes, not jets, which would have been more costly. For their entire eastern trip, it was the Chargers' custom to stay and train in either Niagara Falls, New York, or cross the bridge to Canada and set up camp in Niagara Falls, Ontario. They would travel to New York and Boston by short hops in chartered props. Horrigan would visit the Charger coaches in their temporary headquarters in the Hotel Niagara on the American side of the Falls. "Their language would peel the wallpaper," he said. "One day I saw a secretary in the hotel office quit her job because she couldn't stand the obscenities wafting down from the coaches' office as they argued." Those visits were where Horrigan and Davis bonded.

I had my own opportunity to bond with Davis in April of 1966. Beverly and I were departing on our honeymoon and staying in a Miami Beach hotel room when the phone rang. We were startled. The call was unexpected and unwanted. The Miami stay was a one-day layover while we awaited our flight to the Bahamas for the rest of our honeymoon. No one was supposed to know where we were. I answered the phone and heard the voice of Al Davis, who had found me somehow. He wanted to hire me for his staff. I thought it over for twenty-four hours in consultation with my bride then declined Davis's invitation. I was too happy in the newspaper business.

Two years later Beverly and I were on vacation in Vermont, staying at The Old Tavern and Inn in Grafton. It was a classic Vermont inn, once frequented by Rudyard Kipling and Abraham Lincoln, a "can't-get-there-from-here" destination as the expression of native Vermonters goes. There were no telephones and no televisions. We were having breakfast when the hostess appeared at our table. "Are you Mr. Felser?" she asked. "You have a phone call from a Mr. Al Davis." Davis was interested in hiring an ex-player I knew, Remi Prudhomme. Davis wanted to check one last detail, which was his custom. Prudhomme got the job. Al would have made a great FBI agent.

I digress from Horrigan and Davis. When Horrigan sat down in his New York office to write the first press release about Davis setting up headquarters, Davis began to look over his shoulder. "Can you get the words *young genius* in there somewhere?" Davis asked. Horrigan didn't even look up from his typewriter. "Get lost," he told his boss. Davis left. Not long after Horrigan was diagnosed with leukemia. While he was in a New York hospital undergoing his first treatments, Davis, a Jew, bought a votive candle in a Catholic religious supply store. Back in his office, he lit the candle as a devotion, a prayer in flame—a Catholic custom. When the office was about to close that evening, a cleaning lady informed him it was against building policy to leave a burning candle unattended. Davis took off his coat and stayed the night.

The new commissioner's idea was to hire people who had strong contacts in every phase of sports. Davis paid well and offered an adventure. Hired were Mickey Herskowitz, a Houston columnist widely respected across the southwest and beyond; Val Pinchbeck of Syracuse University, a former president of COSIDA, the organization of college sports information directors, who was to be the contact man for the colleges; and Irv Kaze, a well-known baseball public-relations man who knew just about everyone worth knowing in sports.

"I needed a football man as an assistant," Davis said about completing his staff, "so I hired Mel Hein, the Hall of Fame center who was the greatest New York Giant of them all. He would be returning to New York as an AFL man. We had coached together on the USC staff. The Giants were stunned that their all-time great had come with us. Mel had an explanation for people who asked why he did it. He said, 'The Giants never did anything for me except use my name.'"

The most pressing administrative problem Davis encountered when he began the job was smoothing the way for Joe Robbie and Danny Thomas with the new franchise in Miami. It was during his conversation with Ralph Wilson that more interesting news broke. "About six weeks after I was named commissioner," Davis said, "I was visiting Ralph Wilson in his Detroit insurance office, since Ralph was serving as president of the league. We were talking about Miami. Suddenly one of his top people, Lou Curl, walked into the office with some big news—the New York Giants had just signed Pete Gogolak. Ralph was indignant, since Gogolak was his player, very important to the Bills.

"I told him, Ralph, don't be indignant," Davis said. "The NFL just handed us the merger."

When Davis left Syracuse and his playing days behind, he became a football coach. Coaching is teaching. It's not a rare story to hear that outstanding coaches do not have a background as outstanding players. When Davis was drafted into the Army, he ended up coaching his base team whose players included commissioned officers who had played football in college. The officers listened to Davis respectfully, because they could quickly tell that he knew what he was talking about when it came to football.

CHAPTER 6

The NFL Owners in Shock

In an Appleton, Wisconsin, steak house, noted for the Green Bay Packer memorabilia on its walls, there hangs a framed letter from Wellington Mara, president of the New York Giants, to Vince Lombardi apologizing for the language he had used in a heated conversation with Lombardi, his best friend and the Packers' legendary coach. It is dated 1966.

The letter doesn't refer to the subject of the conversation, but those familiar with it explain the note in two words: Pete Gogolak. When the owners convened in New York for a May meeting in the NFL offices, Commissioner Pete Rozelle went through all the items on his agenda, and after he had dispensed with them, he made an announcement: "The New York Giants have signed Pete Gogolak, a free agent from the Buffalo Bills."

"Oh, my God, Well!" shouted Carroll Rosenbloom of Baltimore to Wellington Mara, owner of the Giants. "If you had let me know you wanted a kicker, I would have given you one!"

One after another the other owners denounced Mara's action. Lombardi, who had some advance notice, was seething nonetheless. "You've put us all in jeopardy," he told his fellow Fordham University graduate. Rozelle tried to explain away the signing by pointing out its legality, that Gogolak had signed a one-year contract including an option with Buffalo in 1964 and that the option had expired. The kicker was a free agent. Even the persuasive Rozelle wasn't able to offer a valid explanation for the financial abyss that the signing had broke open. Free agents were the forbidden fruit of the football war, and Wellington Mara had become Eve to the NFL's Adam.

The owners were in shock, but the NFL's football people, the general managers and coaches, were in a state of puzzlement. Their question was "Why did he choose Gogolak?" On the surface it might have been explained by examining the Giants' field goal record in 1965. The New Yorkers had attempted twenty-five field goals and made good on just six of them. Their record from 40 yards and beyond was a study in ineptitude, 1-for-17. Bob Timberlake, who began as the kicker, lost his job after he made good on just one field goal in fifteen attempts. Coach Allie Sherman switched to defensive end Andy Stynchula, then middle linebacker Jerry Hildebrand, and eventually to backup fullback Chuck Mercein to little avail. To put this in historical perspective, Lawrence Tynes of the 2007 Super Bowl Champion Giants kicked twenty-three field goals in twenty-seven attempts, including 8-for-8 within the 40-49 yard lines.

Still, beyond the miserable kicking, the Giants made progress in the standings, from a 2–10–2 record in 1964 to 7–7, which tied them with the Dallas Cowboys for second place in the Eastern Conference. They won two of their last three games of the season, but Mara wasn't deluded by the improvement. None of the team's seven victories came against an opponent with a winning record. In their seven losses the Giants were outscored, 239–92, an average differential of twenty-one points. They were swept by their chief competition in the East, as the Cleveland Browns beat them 38–24 and 38–21. The improving Cowboys outdueled the Giants 31–2 and 38–20. None of the Giant losses was by the margin of a field goal or even three of them.

The authentic reason Gogolak was suddenly a Giant was due to the competition in Flushing Meadows in Queens, New York. The Jets, with Namath gaining polish and the quality of his support inflating, were winning the race for publicity and public interest not only in New York but also in the important fan bases of New Jersey and Connecticut. Sonny Werblin was far ahead of Mara in the battle of the newspaper kiosks.

Gogolak never made any sort of difference that would have compensated for the anger and alienation from Mara's fellow owners. If only Mara had done his due diligence on the kicker, consulting his football people along the way, the signing might not have taken place. Also, the other owners might have pressured Rozelle into refusing to approve the contract.

For all his value to Buffalo, Gogolak was not a good fit for what the Giants needed. He never came close to the 57-yarder he kicked in his exhibition debut in Tampa. His longest as a rookie was forty-seven yards, a distance he converted once in 1965. Of the forty-seven field goals he kicked in his two years with the Bills, twenty-seven were shorter than 20 yards.

In his first season as a Giant, 1966, Gogolak kicked a pair of 47-yard field goals and was 16-for-28 overall, but the team went into a steep decline and won only one game, finishing last in the East with a 1–12–1 record. He played nine years with the Giants, during which they had just one winning season, finished no higher than second in their division, and never made the playoffs.

The most interesting question of all about the Gogolak signing was, "Why didn't Rozelle disapprove the contract on his own?" The commissioner was aware that merger talk had resumed sub-rosa, almost a year after the preliminary talks between Carroll Rosenbloom and Ralph Wilson had blown up after Rozelle informed Wilson that any possible merger agreement between the leagues revolved upon the AFL paying an indemnity of $50 million to the NFL.

The answer was that Rozelle didn't want a merger. Beneath his suave, gentlemanly appearance, Rozelle was a fighter, and he wanted to win this fight in order to finish off the competition.

CHAPTER 7

Show Them the Money

It wasn't called the "First Super Bowl," and "virtual football" was far off in cyberspace—an unknown concept in 1964—but it was the first game played between the NFL and AFL; the mythical first game, that is. It took place in the pages of *Sports Illustrated* as the product of sportswriter Tex Maule's imagination.

The AFL had been in business for five seasons, and it had signed its landmark television contract with NBC. But in the perception of many owners, general managers, and coaches in the NFL, along with their allies in the media, it was still a "Mickey Mouse League."

Both league championship games in 1964 had been unexpectedly one-sided. The Baltimore Colts possessed the NFL's No. 1 offense and defense that season and were heavy favorites to beat the Cleveland Browns. Instead, the Browns' defense throttled Johnny Unitas, Baltimore's great quarterback, while Cleveland quarterback Frank Ryan threw three touchdown passes and wide receiver Gary Collins averaged 26 yards on his five catches in a 27–0 victory. The AFL title game was similar. The Buffalo Bills were a heavy underdog, but its defense smothered the San Diego Chargers' high-scoring attack and the Bills' run-oriented, conservative offense slowly pounded the Chargers into submission.

The public may not have shared the NFL old guard's feelings that their young rival was a Mickey Mouse League, but there was no clamor for an interleague playoff to settle the matter. In the minds of most football fans outside the franchise territories of the AFL, there was nothing to settle: The NFL remained clearly superior.

Maule's "playoff" between the Bills and Browns in *Sports Illustrated* gave hints that it was strictly his idea, not the editors'. The article was placed far back in the magazine, and there were no accompanying boxes nor a "teaser" placed on the contents page. It read like an appeasement to Tex in order to give his bias toward the NFL, which was considerable, a national forum.

Since Maule became *Sports Illustrated*'s No. 1 pro football writer shortly after its founding in 1954, his work had been notable. He was a must-read for serious football fans. The *Sporting News* was still mainly a baseball weekly, and *Pro Football Weekly* was just a foundling. Anyone looking for the inside story of the big NFL games wanted to read Maule in *Sports Illustrated*. The NFL owes no small debt to the writings of Tex for its burgeoning popularity in the 1950s and 1960s.

It was no surprise that Maule took sides in the NFL-AFL war. He felt he was part of the established league. In fact he actually had been part of it at one time, succeeding Pete Rozelle as public relations director of the Rams when Rozelle was promoted to general manager of the team. The PR genes of Maule didn't disappear when he returned to journalism with *SI*. His first story on the founding of the AFL was headlined THE SHAKY NEW LEAGUE, a redundancy that apparently escaped the notice of both Tex and the editors; it seems inevitable that a new league would also be shaky, made clear by the two attempts to launch a rival league. When Maule sat down to create a faux super bowl after the 1964 season, the outcome was preordained: The Browns won, 47–7. Maule had Buffalo scoring only in garbage time near the end of the fourth quarter as backup quarterback Daryle Lamonica ran into the end zone on a bootleg.

In April 1966, Al Davis, the new commissioner of the AFL, didn't need any literary license. Wellington Mara, owner of the New York Giants, had given him a great gift to create a compelling story; it came under the heading of nonfiction. Mara signed Pete Gogolak, Buffalo's kicker, who was technically a free agent. NFL Commissioner Pete Rozelle had approved Gogolak's contract with the Giants. The AFL's new warlord was happily stunned that his enemies had given him a license to go to war. As soon as the signing became public, Davis told his staff at AFL headquarters, "The NFL will never know what hit it."

   To a certain extent, the NFL people had been deluding themselves for years. At first, when the challenging league made do with NFL retread quarterbacks on most of its teams, there was understandable scoffing among the established league's players. The Boston Patriots' quarterback was Butch Songin, who had kicked around the Canadian Football League for years. Al Dorow and Cotton Davidson took the same route to quarterback the New York Titans and Dallas Texans, respectively. Tommy O'Connell, once the Cleveland Browns' starter, came out of retirement after serving as head coach for a year at Drake University to lead Buffalo. Frank Tripucka, who had led a gypsy life in the pros, was the Denver Broncos' starter. Babe Parilli, the Oakland Raiders' starter, had been a great college quarterback for Bear Bryant at Kentucky, but he had been a disappointment in the NFL. Jack Kemp of San Diego was getting a second chance. Kemp, who played college football at little Occidental, had such a strong passing arm that three NFL teams had him developing on their taxi squads at different times. Taxi squads were made up of a handful of players who were in their developmental stages and not ready for inclusion on the small active rosters, which had recently increased from thirty-three to thirty-five players. The Houston Oilers had a jump on the seven other teams, as they signed George Blanda, who had retired from the Chicago Bears in frustration at not receiving enough playing time. Blanda had plenty left and provided a big boost, as he remained one of the game's best kickers.

   Kemp, twenty-five, was the only young starting quarterback in the league. Songin was thirty-six years old, Blanda thirty-three, Tripucka thirty-two, and Dorow and O'Connell were thirty, giving the AFL the look of a "jock Jurassic Park." It stayed that way for several years due to a quarterback drought in the college draft. In the six years that the NFL and AFL fought it out for prize rookies, there were just seven quarterbacks drafted and signed who became consistent NFL starters—Joe Namath of the Jets, Don Meredith of the Cowboys, Fran Tarkenton of the Minnesota Vikings, Norm Snead of Philadelphia, John Hadl of San Diego, Billy Kilmer of the San Francisco 49ers and Roman Gabriel of the Los Angeles Rams. The most productive years for Kilmer and Gabriel occurred after the merger.

The only difference makers among the group of seven were Namath, Meredith, Hadl, and Tarkenton—who was a surprise to everyone but himself. Tarkenton was selected in the third round of the NFL draft by the expansion Minnesota Vikings and in the fifth round by the AFL's Boston Patriots. The consensus of pro scouts was that Tarkenton was too small to excel in the pros. The prototype pro quarterback in those years was statuesque, in the sense of both physique and mobility.

Tarkenton's first coach with the Vikings was Norm "The Dutchman" Van Brocklin, who came straight from quarterbacking the Philadelphia Eagles to the 1960 NFL championship. Van Brocklin, a Hall of Famer, preferred pocket passers like himself, but as the commander of a ship with limited weapons, his only option was the scrambling Tarkenton. With the former Georgia star as his rookie quarterback, Van Brocklin watched the Vikings upset the Chicago Bears in their very first NFL game. The Dutchman learned to live with, if not love, scramblers.

Once, while riding as a passenger in a car driving down Florida's Interstate 95 north of Miami, Van Brocklin did play-by-play as he described the reckless driver ahead of them weaving in and out of heavy traffic. "He takes off to his left, cuts to his right, cuts back to his left, and then appears to prepare for a pirouette," Van Brocklin kidded. "It's Francis Tarkenton, son of a preacher man, and he's giving us a thrill a minute."

With their quarterback supply line from the colleges failing them, the AFL teams improvised wherever they could in order to stay competitive. One of the most famous improvisations came in

1962 from the Buffalo Bills. Lou Saban was in his first season as the Buffalo coach, and he was not satisfied with the quarterbacking of Warren Rabb, who had been so successful in college leading Louisiana State's "Chinese Bandits." Saban wanted better for his improving team.

In the Bills' time of need, it happened that Kemp, who had led the Chargers to the AFL's Western Division championship in 1960 and 1961, was on the injured list with to a broken capsule on the middle knuckle of his passing hand due to hitting an opponent's helmet while following through after throwing a pass. The forecast was that Kemp would be off the field for many weeks.

The AFL then had a little-known technical rule mandating that if an injured player were officially placed on his team's injured list twenty-four hours or closer to a weekend game, then that player would be exposed to a waiver claim until twenty-four hours after the game. Sid Gillman badly needed the extra roster slot for San Diego's upcoming game, so he took the risk of placing Kemp on waivers over the weekend. Gillman reasoned that the rule was so arcane and furthermore had never been used before, and that no one would be alert enough to claim Kemp. He was wrong.

The Bills did not understand the rule until they were secretly made aware of it by Jack Horrigan, the league's public relations director who previously covered the team as a *Buffalo Evening News* sportswriter. Equipped with such solid information, Saban put in the claim and the Bills had their quarterback for the next eight seasons. Ironically, if Buffalo had not claimed Kemp, the Denver Broncos would have. Jack Faulkner, the Broncos' new head coach and general manager, was the one opponent aware of the waiver rule. Faulkner had been Gillman's lieutenant with the Rams and Chargers for the previous seven years. He knew about the fine print.

Kemp's departure pointed up a flaw in San Diego's high-powered offense: Young John Hadl wasn't ready to be the starting quarterback yet, and his inexperience ended the Chargers' two-year run as Western Division champions. Gillman, the best-informed coach in the league, knew that Tobin Rote would be available for the next season. Rote had helped the Detroit Lions capture NFL title in 1957. In 1960 he jumped to the Canadian Football League, signing with the Toronto Argonauts for three years. His contract expired at the end of the Canadian season in November 1962. Gillman signed him immediately. In 1963 he led the Chargers to their first AFL championship.

Al Davis was about to leave Gillman's San Diego staff to become head coach and general manager of the Raiders. The signing of Rote by San Diego was just one more page in Davis's portfolio of life's lessons: "They follow the money."

The Giants' signing of Pete Gogolak so soon after Davis took office as AFL commissioner in 1966 may have surprised him, but it didn't find him without a plan. One of the conditions that he presented to the league owners before he agreed to take the job was that a war chest be built with contributions from the coffers of every franchise. If he was to be a wartime commissioner, he told the owners, he had to have funds to fight the war.

Davis knew that sooner or later the gentlemen's agreement between the leagues concerning the signing of one another's veterans would be abrogated. Like any good commander—General Mark Clark, his old boss at the Citadel, for instance—he had to set up options. One of Davis's options was to make a list of loyal and capable football men who could be counted on to carry out whatever plan of attack he decided upon.

One of the men he enlisted was a fellow member of Sid Gillman's organization when he began with the Chargers in 1960—Don Klosterman. Klosterman was a talent scout who played an important role in making the Chargers one of the new league's most formidable teams from the AFL's very beginning. Hank Stram, one of Gillman's major rivals, once conceded, "Sid taught everyone else in the AFL how to be professional." Klosterman was part of the Chargers' professionalism.

Klosterman had once been a star college quarterback at Loyola of Los Angeles in the 1950s, attracting attention with his success passing to Gene Brito, later a noted Washington Redskin. Klosterman himself played briefly in the NFL, then more successfully in the Canadian Football League. His football career ended when he suffered a shattering injury in a skiing accident, which resulted in a medical prognosis that he would never walk again. Klosterman beat the odds. He learned to walk with a gait that made him look like an escaped prisoner hobbling as fast as he could with his ankles in chains. No one seemed to notice the hobble after they spent a few minutes in Klosterman's company. He was a handsome, wise-cracking, irreverent man with a personality that made him seem as if he couldn't wait to start each day. As a scout he related to football players by making them laugh, marvel at his encyclopedic knowledge of what was going on in the sport, and wowing them with his familiarity of their own personal backgrounds. A signing still depended on money, but Klosterman's charm offensive often made the difference if it was close between the Chargers and an NFL team.

Three days after the NFL adjourned its meeting in which the staggering news of the Gogolak signing was announced by Commissioner Rozelle, Davis struck. Roman Gabriel, the young quarterback for the Los Angeles Rams, signed a $400,000 contract with the Raiders, Davis's old team. The $400,000 wasn't quite as much as Joe Namath had received from the Jets, but Gabriel had three years' experience, and besides, it was more than any NFL quarterback was being paid.

Gabriel had played just seven games for the Rams in 1965. He had not distinguished himself in four pro seasons. But like all good commanders, Davis had the gift of foresight. In Gabriel's case it was positive foresight. In his seven games, Gabriel had thrown for 1,321 yards, eleven touchdowns, and just five interceptions for a passing rating of 83, all personal highs for a team that won only four games. At just twenty-five years old, standing 6-feet-5 and weighing 220 pounds, Gabriel's chances of playing another ten years were very good.

For the AFL, he was a sound investment. Besides, Gabriel represented the Rams' future. The team had been stockpiling solid draft choices for several years and felt it had enough young players to make an eventual run at Western Conference domination. There would be no run without Gabriel. There were other Davis targets on the L.A. roster such as twenty-six-year-old Deacon Jones, the best pass rusher in the league, and the two young offensive tackles, Joe Scibelli and Joe Carollo.

Beyond raiding for talent, there was the intangible value of crippling the Rams and handicapping the organization. Owner Dan Reeves and what he stood for in the NFL made Los Angeles a special franchise to the league. When Reeves decided to move the Rams out of Cleveland after winning the 1945 championship, it marked the first major league franchise in any sport to open for business on the West Coast. Reeves also signed the first black players in the modern NFL.

Then there were the heritage personalities, dear to the NFL and despised by the AFL. Tex Schramm, who didn't found the Dallas Cowboys but virtually invented them, was once Reeves's general manager. Rozelle succeeded Schramm as GM. Tex Maule of *Sports Illustrated*, who succeeded Rozelle as public relations director of the Rams, was considered an NFL propagandist by Davis and the AFL.

Davis also took into consideration that successfully targeting the Rams would mean that three of the largest NFL markets would be in dilapidated conditions. The New York Giants had already become a punching bag and the proud Chicago Bears were vainly attempting to battle out of mediocrity.

The NFL owners were still vibrating from the news of Gabriel signing with the Raiders when a rumor began circulating that John Brodie, the San Francisco quarterback, was about to sign with the

Houston Oilers. Lou Spadia, the 49ers' president, was still trying to deal with the idea of Gabriel quarterbacking the AFL team across the bay, when he received a phone call from Brodie himself from the Warwick Hotel in Houston. Spadia was more strongly opposed to a merger with the AFL than any other figure in the NFL. He was nearly speechless when his veteran quarterback informed him that he signed a $750,000 contract to jump leagues.

The third shoe dropped with the news that the Oilers had signed Mike Ditka of the Chicago Bears, the best tight end in football. Davis had carefully thought out his plan of attack. The NFL's two West Coast franchises had been stripped of their starting quarterbacks. The Bears still had Gale Sayers tied up, but the AFL might cripple their passing game by taking away Ditka. The Giants were already a mess. In less than a month of raiding, the pirate commissioner had overseen the diminishing of four of the NFL's major markets.

Lou Spadia and his colleagues had a sour ball named Al Davis in their bellies.

CHAPTER 8

Texas Showdown

While Al Davis was busy digging a collapsible tunnel under the NFL, a secretive tunnel was being dug under him. The diggers were Tex Schramm, archenemy of the AFL, and Lamar Hunt, cofounder of Davis's own league.

Schramm and Hunt were clandestinely carrying out the wishes of most of the owners in their leagues. The exceptions were the four franchises in New York and the San Francisco Bay area—the Giants, Jets, Raiders, and 49ers. The majority of the NFL owners had thrown up their hands when Davis began signing veteran stars of the NFL in the wake of the Pete Gogolak signing. The majority of the AFL owners just wanted peace under the cover of one league and a balance sheet written in black ink.

Schramm and Hunt, despite their Texas roots, were not cut from the same cloth. Schramm was pin-striped sharkskin, Hunt muted gray flannel. Schramm was the cliché Texan—hearty, enormously self-confident, voracious once he set a goal for himself, and not at all reluctant to make enemies. When Hunt was selling his idea of a football league to challenge the NFL, the Texan he sought out was his total opposite in personality, the flamboyant Bud Adams, jokingly known in Houston as "the rich Texan who bought his dog a boy." After Adams and Hunt departed following their first meeting in 1959, Adams wasn't even sure what Hunt wanted. There was a popular television series at the time called *Mister Peepers*. Played by actor Wally Cox, who bore a slight resemblance to Hunt, the lead character was unnervingly shy, almost apologetic about his very presence. That was Lamar's nickname in the early AFL, Mister Peepers.

Schramm's full name was Texas Ernest Schramm. The sound of it suggests he might have been a colleague of Sam Houston and Stephen F. Austin, but in truth Schramm was born in California, and although he was reared in Texas, his background contained a liberal sprinkling of both the state of his birth and New York.

He graduated from the University of Texas at Austin with a degree in journalism and was working in the sports department of the *Austin American-Statesman* while he was an undergraduate. Texas has a long history of distinguished sportswriting. In Schramm's journalism period, the state was populated by more talented sportswriters than almost any other state in any other era. These sportswriters included Blackie Sherrod, whose East Texas sayings would find their way into the hit Broadway show *The Best Little Whorehouse in Texas*; Dan Jenkins, author of the comic football novel *Semi-Tough*; Mickey Herskowitz of Houston, who collaborated with Howard Cosell, Dan Rather, and actress Gene Tierney on their biographies; Bud Shrake, later a screenwriter and ghostwriter of *Harvey Penick's Little Red Book of Golf*; novelist Gary Cartwright; and other stars such as Dave Campbell of Waco and Jack Gallagher of Houston.

For a time, Schramm might have wished for a career like the celebrities of the sports sections, but he wasn't in the newspaper business for long when he decided the path for him was a managerial role in sports rather than writing about them. He returned to California to take a job as public relations director of the Los Angeles Rams. Not long after, Rams' owner Dan Reeves made Schramm the team's general manager. He left the Rams for New York, where he was hired as assistant director of sports for the CBS network. There he earned a reputation as an innovator. When CBS televised the Winter Olympics in Squaw Valley, California, in 1960, it was Schramm who insisted that Walter Cronkite, the network's news anchor, be the lead CBS announcer for the games.

The Olympics would be Schramm's last big television assignment. Clint Murchison, owner of the NFL's newborn expansion team in Dallas, the Cowboys, asked him to run the franchise. Schramm not only accepted the job, he devoured it. His touch was uncanny. For the Cowboys' first coach he selected Tom Landry, who ran the New York Giants' offense. Landry was a Texas purebred who had played football at the University of Texas but hadn't been a major star on the level of Longhorn greats like quarterback Bobby Layne or defensive tackle Bud McFadin, so there had been no clamor by the public for Landry as coach.

Still, Schramm had his convictions. He hired Gil Brandt as the Cowboys' chief scout. Brandt had earned his living as a baby photographer in Milwaukee, but his avocation was following college football stars and their potential for a career in the NFL. That made Brandt an amateur freelance scout who wrote reports on collegians for the entertainment of friends or for the occasional pro team, who might send him a small check for his submissions. In other words he was a *draftnik* before there was such a description.

Eventually Schramm would introduce the first cheerleaders in pro football; the "ring of fame," enshrining the Cowboys' best players ever on the walls of their stadium; and the nickname America's Team, a name despised by the Cowboys opponents but one that was relatively accurate. Years later, at a Super Bowl reception, Beano Cook, sometime ABC college football analyst and full-time Pittsburgh character, announced to Schramm that "I've named the Cowboys the second-most efficient organization of the twentieth century."

Schramm beamed. "Thank you very much, Beano," he told Cook. "But who is No. 1?"

"The Third Reich," Beano answered.

Tex was not amused.

But all of the Cowboys' glory was in the future. When the NFL owners sued for peace in the spring of 1966, just about all the Dallas team had done up till then was lose. The "Boys" on paper had promise, but not until the 1965 season did they avoid a losing season, finishing 7–7 and playing the best football in their six-year existence.

The consensus around the NFL was that Schramm's long-range plan was approaching fruition. When Schramm began negotiating with Hunt, he was not operating from a personal position of power, but he did have the confidence of the large majority of NFL owners who had had enough of the financial war.

Schramm began the negations with little respect for Hunt, whom he thought was weak. The major reason was that, in the true style of *Gunfight at the O.K. Corral*, Dallas turned out not to be big enough for both the Cowboys and Texans, the name of Dallas's AFL franchise. The Texans won the AFL championship in 1962, beating their Texas rivals, the Houston Oilers, 20–17, in the second overtime game ever played. The AFL team had a new quarterback, Len Dawson, who had thrown for twenty-nine touchdown passes in his first season in Dallas. It already had one of the league's first stars in running back Abner Haynes, who had played his college football at North Texas State. They had other homegrown stars like linebacker E. J. Holub of Texas Tech and defensive end Jerry Mays of Southern Methodist.

The year the Texans won the AFL title, the Cowboys won just four games and averaged fewer than 17 points a game, 10 points fewer per game than the Texans. The Cowboys' starting quarterback was still little Eddie LeBaron, an undersize curiosity. The prize draftee from 1960, Don Meredith of SMU, had not yet developed enough to take over the offense. Their primary ball carrier was journeyman Amos Marsh, their top receiver Frank Clarke, another journeyman.

But the Cowboys were an NFL team, and enough Dallas fans favored association rather than performance. Hunt decided that his team would be better off in Kansas City, which Schramm considered a cow town, not a Cowboys' town. Unexpectedly, Schramm's Cowboys had Dallas to themselves, for what it was worth. Even the optimistic Tex knew that it was still a Southwest Conference college town and a high school football town. That would change quickly.

Lamar Hunt had gone through life with people underestimating him. What many mistook for lack of self-confidence was actually the underrated quality of humility. At the time there was no such thing as "The Forbes 400," a list of America's wealthiest people, but the consensus opinion was that if there had been, oilman H. L. Hunt, Lamar's father, would have been No. 1. H. L. was an eccentric. Despite his vast wealth, he still brown-bagged his lunch. Lamar's brother, Nelson Bunker Hunt, once cornered the world silver market. After attending a game between Lamar's team and the Titans in New York's Polo Grounds, which adjoined Harlem, Bunker sat on the team bus awaiting its departure to LaGuardia Airport. He silently surveyed what he could see of the famous borough and its citizens through a chain-link fence, finally uttering to no one in particular, "So this is the great unwashed."

There is an old story, probably apocryphal, that an acquaintance of H. L. once said to him, "Did you know that Lamar is losing $1 million a year on his football team?" To which the elder Hunt supposedly responded, "At that rate, in 100 years he's going to be broke." Lamar himself lived modestly, much like a common person. His Dallas home telephone number was listed in the phone book. *Boston Globe* sportswriter Will McDonough regularly played tennis with Hunt at owners meetings. "I have to play with my billfold in my pocket because we always stop for Cokes afterward, and Lamar doesn't carry any money," McDonough said.

The Mister Peepers in him surfaced most often when he was communicating. When he and his first wife decided to divorce, Hunt took out an ad in the Dallas newspapers to announce it. He felt that because he was a public figure, he owed the public an explanation. He often had trouble getting to the point, particularly when the point was unpleasant. Tex Schramm wasn't the first person to look down on Lamar, nor the first to find an inner toughness in the quiet man. Lamar played football as a walk-on at Southern Methodist University despite his relatively small stature. As a member of the scout team, he occasionally lined up opposite Forrest Gregg, one of the greatest offensive linemen of all time. Gregg remembered him not for his lack of athletic talent but for his doggedness. "He was all heart," Gregg said years later.

Schramm resented Hunt from the start of the football war. Tex saw Lamar as a product of Daddy's money, ironic since the man who owned the Cowboys, Clint Murchison, had a similar profile—a wealthy father via Texas oil. The genesis of Schramm's ill feelings toward Hunt stemmed from how difficult his job was made by the presence of Lamar's Texans. It was tough enough overcoming the popularity of college and high school football in the Dallas–Fort Worth area in order to create a sizable niche for the Cowboys, but when the Texans won far more often than the NFL expansion team, they attracted a stronger public following. It didn't make any difference if the Cowboys' competition was much stronger, they both played in a region of Texas where winning, no matter against whom, was what excited the fans. When Hunt agreed to have the Texans leave the market for Kansas City, no word was said about compensation, which was a face-saving part of the agreement for Schramm. The Cowboys quietly agreed to take over the Texans' training headquarters in exchange for payments of about $100,000 a year for ten years.

But Schramm's antipathy toward his rival did not trump his desire for peace after five bitter seasons without it. Despite his personal feelings, he knew that Hunt was the perfect enemy with whom to deal—discreet, honest, a man of his word, and, most important, someone who fervently wanted the merger as much as Schramm and most of the NFL owners did. After all, what led Hunt to cofound the AFL was his desire to obtain an NFL franchise. So Tex initiated phone contact with his adversary and Hunt agreed to meet him at Love Field, then Dallas's main airport. The meeting, both agreed, would be secret. They talked where they couldn't be observed, in Schramm's car.

The man from whom both Schramm and Hunt wanted most anxiously to keep their meetings secret was Al Davis, whose tactics during his short command were, in a sports sense, similar to the World War II tactics of General Patton. But with financial peace within reach Davis was kept in the dark, even by his allies. Finally, with the merger all but agreed to by most of the owners, word leaked to the AFL commissioner. This time the military comparison was to another general, Douglas MacArthur, commander of the U.S. troops who halted the enemy advance in the Korean War in 1950. But when MacArthur later wanted to bomb China, North Korea's patron, he was fired by President Harry Truman.

Once word of the approaching merger seemed all but confirmed, a friend called Davis to ask what was happening. "They don't know how to fight," Davis said bitterly, referring to the AFL owners. "We could have won this thing. We could have wrapped up the whole NFL." He referred to his plan for signing NFL players, even those under contract for another year or two, to "future" contracts which would put them in AFL uniforms as soon as their pacts with their original team expired. Clearly it would have crippled the established league but may have destroyed the financial fabric of the sport in the process. In one last, defiant move, Davis brushed aside Hunt's order not to finalize any more contracts with NFL players by having Don Klosterman sign John Brodie to a contract that dwarfed Joe Namath's. Brodie signed for three years at $250,000 a year.

The merger never would have taken place if Davis hadn't used pirate tactics. The two NFL franchises most opposed to a merger were the ones most threatened by competition from their AFL rivals—the San Francisco 49ers by the Raiders across the Bay in Oakland; and the New York Giants by the New York Jets just a borough away.

The financial war would have gotten far bloodier. "I knew of about one hundred NFL players who wanted to sign with us," said Bud Adams, the Houston owner. A short time after Davis returned to Oakland to run the Raiders, he ran into the Los Angeles Rams' great pass rusher, Deacon Jones, at a charity event. "Hey, why didn't you sign me?" Jones asked. Why wouldn't NFL stars have wanted to jump to the new league? After the news broke of Namath's big rookie contract, Cleveland quarterback Frank Ryan said publicly, "If he's worth $400,000, then I'm worth a million!" Browns' owner Art Modell had no inclination to pay Ryan $1 million or anything near it.

What accelerated the Schramm-Hunt negotiations was the AFL's willingness to meet the NFL asking price of an $18 million indemnity, which came to $2 million per team over the course of ten years, a pittance compared to what the accrued interest on $2 million in escrow would have brought over two decades. It was also far lower than the $50 million Pete Rozelle informed Buffalo's Ralph Wilson that the NFL wanted when they met in Florida during the truncated merger talks in 1965. The $18 million, the NFL owners later decided, would be split between the Giants and the 49ers, with New York getting $10 million and San Francisco $8 million.

It turned out that Davis wasn't the only principal behind whose back the merger talks bore fruit. Pete Rozelle, whose decision to approve Pete Gogolak's contract with the Giants, allowing Davis to charge into action, had alienated many NFL owners, not the least of whom was his old antagonist, Carroll Rosenbloom. Rozelle, whose entire reputation seemed to be built upon reason and compromise, wanted neither reason nor compromise with the AFL. He was a hardliner; he wanted to destroy the enemy. "Tell Rozelle," Rosenbloom instructed Schramm when he learned of the commissioner's balking at a merger, "that we're going to do this with him or without him."

CHAPTER 9

Cease Fire

All but four of the owners in the two leagues desperately wanted the merger. For them it was a case of "Stop us before we overspend again!" Nevertheless, as much as the moguls wished to end their financial bleeding, there were messes to sweep up, egos to soothe.

In their haste to close the merger deal, Schramm and Hunt left some things unclear. The biggest misunderstanding was Schramm's belief that two of the AFL franchises, the New York Jets and the Oakland Raiders, had agreed to move out of their competitive markets. He said he understood that the Jets would be moving to Memphis and the Raiders to Portland, Oregon. Wrong. When the conditions of the merger were first revealed to their fellow owners by Schramm and Hunt, one of the most controversial clauses in the deal was that the AFL would pay an indemnity, about $18 million, to the NFL. The Jets' managing partner, Sonny Werblin, was furious. "They should be paying us!" cried Werblin, who knew a great deal about hardball negotiating. The idea that the Jets, with Joe Namath and a mushrooming young fan base, would move to Memphis was ludicrous.

It was equally ludicrous that the Raiders would consider moving north to Portland. Wayne Valley, their majority owner, despised the owners of the San Francisco 49ers, the Morabito brothers, Vic and Tony, whom he called "those fucking dagos across the bay." Besides, Valley had anticipated the return of Al Davis to run his team in the wake of the merger.

Talk of franchises moving anywhere was dicey stuff to those in both leagues. A year before the merger talks began, the NFL was forming plans to expand by 1967. One of their target cities, along with New Orleans and Seattle, was Houston. That would have been an outright invasion of AFL territory and a shot across the bow of Oilers owner Bud Adams, who, along with Hunt, was cofounder of the AFL.

NFL Commissioner Pete Rozelle made an exploratory visit to Houston in August of 1965. He attended a Houston Astros baseball game in the new Astrodome, the first major domed stadium in the nation. Adams had resisted moving his Oilers to the new stadium because of the expensive lease demands. "If the Astrodome is the ninth wonder of the World, then the terms of the lease are the tenth," complained Adams. Rozelle made it clear to Judge Roy Hofheinz, the majordomo of the Astrodome, that he did not wish to be introduced nor any fanfare made of his presence even though Hofheinz was clearly wooing the NFL. But the public address announcer introduced him anyway, as Rozelle's likeness appeared on the giant screen. The crowd booed. When the PA announcer asked that all who wanted a football team in the Astrodome stand up, not many stood.

The Houston sports public made it plain that it was an AFL town.

The AFL itself went poaching the same year. Its target was Philadelphia, where the Eagles had recently finished their fourth consecutive losing season. At the time the AFL was formed, however, the NFL headquarters were located in a Philadelphia suburb and the suburb was also the home of Bert Bell, the NFL commissioner. Reason prevailed and the AFL honed in on Atlanta, only to have it snatched from its grasp at the last moment by the NFL. The young league's compromise choice was Miami, at the time of the merger still an unproven pro football town.

Expansion, however, was a subplot. The most important element for the majority of owners in both leagues was a merger, which would cut their costs and bring about far more financial improvement than collecting expansion fees. Consequently two of the pillars of the merger agreement were that all existing franchises would make up the new, merged league and that no franchises would be transferred to new locations. There had also been consideration of keeping the AFL's identity in a separate conference, playing separate schedules with separate league presidents and one overall commissioner, Rozelle. Briefly, it was suggested that the AFL president should be Al Davis. Whoever suggested that possibility obviously was not acquainted with Davis, who would chafe at being No. 2 to anyone, especially Rozelle. The idea of keeping the AFL and NFL in football segregation did not fly since the future expansion plans would have created a sixteen-team NFL and a ten-team AFL, giving the established league preference in the draft, the waiver system, and other important segments of the way pro football was conducted.

Hence the additional pillars included a single league schedule starting in 1970 and a common draft beginning in January of 1967. Existing contracts for hotels, chartered aircraft, and especially for television commitments did not allow for a single, interlocking schedule for four years, 1970. Missing many of the details of the merger settled would not keep the leagues from playing a championship game the following January of 1966.

The major points of the merger were as follows:

- A game for the championship of pro football each year, beginning in January 1967
- Interleague preseason games starting in the summer of 1967
- A single league schedule starting in 1970
- All existing franchises retained
- No franchises transferred from present locations
- A single league commissioner, Pete Rozelle
- Two new franchises no later than 1968
- A common draft, beginning in January 1967

From a historical perspective, it wasn't up to the standards of Martin Luther's 95 Theses, a document which was nailed to a church door in Worms, Germany, in 1517, but from a business perspective, what it meant to the pro football owners was a sacred part of their balance sheets: cost certainty. They felt that, with a common draft, they no longer were compelled to sign Namath-size contracts with unproven rookies. As for the treasury-rattling contracts that Davis's agents signed with John Brodie, Mike Ditka, and Roman Gabriel, peace between the leagues meant that free agency returned to being a theory, not a model established by Pete Gogolak.

The college stars who were preparing for the 1966 season understood their new status immediately. The forecast was that Michigan State was likely to be the best college team in the nation, and Coach Duffy Daugherty had four seniors who were likely to go extremely high in the first common draft. They were defensive end Bubba Smith, wide receiver Gene Washington, running back Clinton Jones, and linebacker George Webster.

In the previous draft, their former teammate, defensive tackle Harold Lucas, had been selected in the second round by the St. Louis Cardinals. The Cards lost their first-round pick, Oklahoma linebacker Carl McAdams, to the Jets, so they overpaid Lucas by giving him a $300,000 contract. Back in East Lansing, Michigan, Smith, Washington, Jones, and Webster figured Lucas's contract would be a barometer of how much they might expect in 1967.

"He had nothing," Washington said of Lucas. "And then it seemed he had all the money in the world. Now I guess it will be take-it-or-leave-it again."

Chicago attorney Arthur Morse, who served as the agent for a number of top players including Illinois running back Jim Grabowski, Green Bay's first pick, saw it another way. "If the two leagues were selling electric appliances instead of football," said Morse, "in my opinion such an attempt on their part to destroy the avenues of commerce and competition would be actionable." Morse thought

73

the merger was a violation of the federal antitrust laws. Pro football must have thought Morse had a point. The attorney had made his remarks to the *Miami Herald* on June 9. On August 4, Commissioner Rozelle suggested that if Congress didn't give the leagues congressional approval of their agreement, the finalization of the merger by 1970 might not happen.

The reaction of veteran players from the AFL and NFL was different. Jack Kemp, president of the young American Football Players Association was prescient. "I think a merger is for the common good of the owners and the players," Kemp said. "I think you'll see profits rise quite a bit and players' salaries rise along with the profits. I wouldn't be surprised if the minimum salary figure soon doubles, from $6,000 to $12,000."

Kemp had been a political activist from his college days at Occidental in Southern California. A conservative Republican, he spent off-seasons working for Herb Klein, editor of the *San Diego Union*, and Klein's successor, Gerald Warren. Both Klein and Warren had served as press secretaries to Vice President Richard Nixon. Later in his football career, Kemp spent his winters working for the governor of California, Ronald Reagan.

His role as the president of the players union was not out of character. Back then Kemp described himself as "a bleeding-heart conservative," a play on the political cliché *bleeding-heart liberal*. It wasn't just talk. Kemp was famous among his peers for taking up the cause of even the most marginal AFL players. Once when the league owners were meeting in San Diego, he got out of a sickbed and waited hours while plainly ill to plead the case of Tommy Minter, a backup defensive back for the Chargers who had been released by the team without what Kemp considered full payment for which the collective bargaining agreement called.

In 1970, with the merger completed, Kemp retired as a player to enter politics as a candidate for U.S. Congress from western New York. "He threw his hat into the ring," kidded Jack Horrigan, by then a vice president of the Bills, "and it was intercepted." His heavily Democratic district elected him by a healthy margin. Four decades later Kemp was proud that his prediction about the merger had proven true. "It was an example of the benefits of a free-market economy," he said.

Most players agreed with Kemp, for a variety of reasons. Len Dawson, the Kansas City quarterback, said, "For the fans and all connected with the game, this is the best possible thing that could happen."

Dawson's teammate, defensive end Aaron Brown, who had just finished his rookie season, bubbled with anticipation. "Holy smoke! That's the best news I've heard in years. Now we'll find out who can play. And all any of us want is the opportunity to test our ability with the best." Nine months later, Brown and the Chiefs would get the opportunity they sought.

Emanuel Celler, Democratic congressman from Brooklyn who was chairman of the powerful U.S. House Judiciary Committee, held his enthusiasm in check. "Go ahead, and play your game," he told Pete Rozelle in regard to the first championship clash between the NFL and AFL. Without the approval of the Judiciary Committee, there would be no merger, and Celler made no promises about the proposed merger beyond that one game.

But for the owners of NFL and AFL franchises, it was the difference between writing their balance sheets in red ink and blue ink. Events would soon transform their bottom lines from lakes to oceans. The owners were now certain of their labor costs, by far the most important item in their overhead.

CHAPTER 10

A New Challenge

Three months after the terms of the merger were announced, the players and coaches from the two leagues began concentrating on just a single term—a championship game between the NFL and AFL would be played at the end of the 1966 season. The challenge was a thrill for them and it was immediate. The old league championships were now semifinal playoff games. The ultimate game was for the world championship of professional football.

Street & Smith's football annual and its growing list of imitators normally started planning for their July newsstand sales in May. The first item of business was to figure out what teams in the NFL would most likely end up defending the honor of the long-established National Football League and from where the most likely challenger from the AFL would emerge.

Since the Green Bay Packers were the NFL's defending champions, it was reasonable that they would wear the favorite's designation. The Cleveland Browns were the runners-up in 1965, but their greatest star, running back Jimmy Brown, had abruptly retired from pro football between seasons in order to pursue a career in the movies. The Baltimore Colts, still quarterbacked by the great Johnny Unitas, were always a contender. The dark horse would be the Dallas Cowboys, who had a mere 7–7 record the previous season but bore watching because they closed so strongly with three consecutive victories.

In the American Football League, the Buffalo Bills won championships in 1964 and 1965, but after the 1965 season their coach, Lou Saban, abruptly resigned and took the head-coaching job at the University of Maryland. His successor was Joe Collier, a young defensive assistant with no head-coaching experience. There was another important subtraction in Buffalo. The New York Giants had signed the Bills' soccer-style kicker Pete Gogolak, the move that had triggered the merger in the first place.

The Boston Patriots, who battled Buffalo to the end of the schedule for the AFL's Eastern Division championship in both 1964 and 1965, were still an imposing team. In the West, the San Diego Chargers had won the championship in four of the AFL's five seasons under the leadership of Coach Sid Gillman. The Oakland Raiders, built by Al Davis who was about to rejoin the team after settling his contract as AFL commissioner, were considered dangerous.

Steadily improving and infused by more impressive talent each year were the Kansas City Chiefs, owned by AFL cofounder Lamar Hunt. The Chiefs had added Southern California's Heisman Trophy winner, Mike Garrett, for whose rights, surprisingly, they won a bidding war with his hometown Los Angeles Rams of the NFL.

The Dallas Cowboys broke out of the 1966 starting gate with four consecutive victories, giving them an overall winning streak of seven games over two seasons. The Cowboys hadn't achieved a winning record since their founding in 1960, but no one considered the streak a fluke. For one thing, the three closing victories in 1965 included road games in Philadelphia and New York. The Cowboys had lost their first five road games that season, so the upbeat closing was taken as a sign of their maturity.

The four victories that opened the 1966 season were an outbreak of offensive power. They beat the Giants, 52–7; Minnesota, 28–17; Atlanta, 47–14; and Philadelphia, 56–7. This was their fifth season with Don Meredith as the starting quarterback, and the Cowboys had demonstrated in 1965 that they finally had the skills to protect him, cutting his sacks by twenty, from fifty-eight to thirty-eight. In 1966 Dallas would not lose consecutive games. Finally, there was cohesion in the offensive line, with most of the starters carrying over from year to year. There was an important stabilization at right tackle, because in 1965 the Cowboys signed Oklahoma star Ralph Neely, but so did the Houston Oilers of the AFL. Neely opted for the Cowboys and started as a rookie in 1965, but Bud Adams, the Houston Oilers' owner, intended to fight the Dallas contract in court. The matter was resolved in November of 1966 after the Oilers won the court case, followed by a deal whereby the case was settled with the Cowboys giving Houston their first and second selections along with two fifth-round picks in the first common draft in exchange for permission to keep Neely.

Most of the explosion in the Dallas offense was provided by Bob Hayes, the great Olympic sprinter. Hayes gave Meredith opportunities to unleash his strong arm, and he caught sixty-four passes for a 19.3-yard average. Thirteen of his receptions were for touchdowns. There were also some important infusions of fresh talent in the offense. Dan Reeves, a quarterback at the University of South Carolina who was signed as a college free agent, had learned his new position, running back, mostly from the bench in 1965, but by the next season, coach Tom Landry had worked him into the offense with major payoffs. Reeves teamed with Don Perkins to produce just under 1,500 yards on the ground and also served as Meredith's No. 2 target, catching forty-seven passes, eight of which went for touchdowns for an overall total of sixteen scores, best on the team. The Cowboys were becoming noted for signing skilled athletes from other sports. Hayes was the most visible, but starting cornerback Cornell Green from Utah State and wide receiver Pete Gent from Michigan State were basketball players. Gent was an underrated producer in 1966, averaging 17.6 yards on his twenty-seven catches. He later became a novelist; his most-famous book, *North Dallas Forty*, based on his experiences as a Cowboy.

The defense, with young stars such as tackle Bob Lilly, safety Mel Renfro, and linebackers Chuck Howley and Lee Roy Jordan in the lineup, allowed 14 or fewer points in six of Dallas's ten victories.

The Cleveland Browns had changed but not for the better. When it was time to prepare for the 1966 season, Jim Brown was in England, a member of the cast of the movie, *The Dirty Dozen*, along with Lee Marvin, Charles Bronson, Telly Savalas, and other big-name actors.

The only recourse Cleveland had was to turn to Leroy Kelly, Brown's backup. Kelly was a little-known college player at Morgan State whom the Browns drafted in the eighth round in 1964. He carried the ball from scrimmage a mere forty-five times in two years, but he established himself as one of the premier kick- and punt-return specialists in pro football. Kelly averaged over 19 yards on punt returns as a rookie and over 15 yards in his second year, returning three punts for touchdowns in those two seasons. He averaged over or near 25 yards as a kickoff returner. At six feet tall and over 200 pounds, he was sturdy enough to be a full-time back, even demonstrating the type of body control that enabled Brown to avoid absorbing serious hits during his career.

As a starter in 1966, Kelly was a startling surprise. In his final season, 1965, Brown gained 1,544 yards, scored seventeen touchdowns, and averaged 5.3 yards each time he carried the ball. In his debut season, Kelly gained 1,141 yards, scored fifteen touchdowns, and averaged 5.5 yards. Kelly didn't get as much work as Brown— eighty fewer carries—and he shared the workload with Ernie Green, Brown's running mate who played the same role alongside Kelly, and Green averaged 5.2 yards per carry.

The Browns as a team averaged 5.2 yards a carry, outrushing their opponents by 20 yards a game. They scored 403 points, which averaged to nearly 29 points per game. Frank Ryan, the veteran quarterback, increased his passing yardage by almost 1,200 yards, his touchdown pass total from eighteen to twenty-nine, and his passer rating by 13 points. The constant for the Browns' outstanding offensive play was their line, one of the most underappreciated offensive lines in pro football history. Dick Schafrath was the left tackle, John

Wooten the left guard, John Morrow the center, Gene Hickerson the right guard, and Monte Clark the right tackle. Coach Blanton Collier used his No. 1 draft choice, Milt Morin of the University of Massachusetts, as the starting tight end. Most of the interior line had been together since the late 1950s.

What took the Browns out of contention for the approaching Super Bowl in January were two losses late in the season, one to the Cowboys in Dallas on Thanksgiving Day and the other to the Eagles in Philadelphia on December 12. The Browns' soft spots were a defense that had undergone five changes since the previous season and the decline of the great kicker, Lou Groza, who was successful on just nine of twenty-three field goal attempts.

Baltimore opened its 1966 season against Green Bay in the manner in which it usually fared against Vince Lombardi–coached teams: The Packers won, 24–3, in Milwaukee, the sixth time in eight games that they had defeated the Colts. But Johnny Unitas, still the best quarterback in football, rallied his team, and the opening loss was followed by seven Baltimore victories in the next eight games.

By November things had changed dramatically. Unitas suffered a shoulder injury. Hindered by a mediocre running game, the Colts went into an offensive slump. The career of Lenny Moore, the great halfback, was dwindling down, and the attack produced just seven rushing touchdowns, the lowest number in Don Shula's four years as head coach. They scored an average of just 13 points a game as they lost three of their next four games, the last of which was another loss to the Packers at home, causing them to finish three games behind Green Bay in the Western Conference.

Meanwhile, the Packers had exploded to begin the season, beating the Browns in Cleveland and then two more formidable opponents, the Los Angeles Rams and Detroit Lions, both in Green Bay. This was to be the spectacular season of Packer defense and Bart Starr. The defense allowed 16 points or fewer in ten of fourteen games, with half a dozen foes held to single digits. Green Bay intercepted twenty-eight passes and sacked opposing quarterbacks forty-seven times. Enemies were discouraged quickly since the Pack outscored them 62–13 in the first quarter. If there were any thoughts of regrouping at halftime, they were quickly dispelled as the Packers held a season-long advantage, 61–23, in the third quarter.

Since November of 1959, when the Pack began a four-game winning streak, which ended Vince Lombardi's first year as head coach and resulted in the team's first winning season in twelve years, the coach's light had outshone that of everyone else in the organization. Lombardi's only competition, if you could call it that, came from the Golden Boy, Paul Hornung, who had won the Heisman Trophy while playing with a rare losing team at Notre Dame. Hornung was a vanishing species in football, the triple threat. He was a smart and dogged runner, if not a swift one. A college quarterback, he could pass as well as serve as a reliable receiver. He was an NFL leader in scoring, as he also served as Green Bay's kicker. Hornung was a personable, witty star with a reputation as a playboy. He had enough stature, even with Lombardi, that he could get away with quite a lot.

As an after-dinner speaker, Hornung often kidded his coach by claiming that when Vince climbed into bed with his wife, Marie, one frigid Green Bay night, Marie cried out, "God! Your feet are cold!" To which the coach was supposed to have replied, "Marie, when we're in bed, you may call me Vince."

Ordinarily Lombardi was not enthused about sharing the spotlight with anyone. In the midst of the Packers' spectacular defensive streak, the team's public relations director, Chuck Lane, wrote a press release praising what he termed "Phil Bengtson's defense." Since Lombardi was also the general manager, it was Lane's custom to forward the press release to the boss for approval. Instead of approving the press release, Lombardi angrily stormed down the hall into Lane's office. He made it emphatically clear to Lane that it wasn't Bengtson's defense, that it was his, Lombardi's, and that Bengtson was the assistant carrying out the head coach's commands.

Lombardi enjoyed Hornung, but that did not alter his businesslike approach to reevaluating him at age thirty. Hornung's numbers had slipped in the previous two seasons. Don Chandler had been brought in as the field-goal kicker after Hornung had been successful on just twelve of thirty-eight attempts in 1964. Once celebrated as a big-game player, the only notable play Hornung had contributed in his last few years was a 13-yard touchdown run which was vital to the Western Conference championship sudden-death playoff victory over the Colts. That wasn't enough to cloud Lombardi's judgment. Lombardi drafted Donnie Anderson and Jim Grabowski to replace Hornung and the superb fullback Jim Taylor. After the 1966 season, Hornung would become a New Orleans Saint via the expansion allotment. That led to the public emergence of Bart Starr as a star of the highest magnitude. He had been one of the best quarterbacks in football for several years, a fact sometimes overlooked by the fans and even the media since Hornung and especially Lombardi overshadowed him.

Humility and small egos are not usually associated with big-time pro quarterbacks, but Starr was the exception. He never changed, which an incident in a Dallas-area hotel many years after Starr was finished with both his playing and coaching career demonstrated. The Cowboys were playing host to the Detroit Lions in a Monday night game that was celebrating the NFL's "Throwback" promotion—when teams first began wearing their "retro" uniforms as a salute to the league's past. The Cowboys had invited a few Hall of Fame quarterbacks such as Starr and Sid Luckman of the Chicago Bears as their guests for the game.

The afternoon of the game, a fan stopped Starr in the lobby and asked him to autograph a football for her son. Starr said he would be happy to oblige, but neither he nor the woman had a pen handy. So Starr asked her to stay right where she was, not to leave. He then took the elevator back to his room, found a pen on his dresser, and came right back down to sign the ball for the woman. That was the essential Bart Starr.

Lombardi's coaching philosophy seemed simple enough: aggressive defense, ball-control offense, discipline, and, above all, don't make any mistakes. All coaches preach about not making mistakes, but it's hard to follow through. Making mistakes is human, everyone does it. The idea is to keep mistakes to a bare minimum. By choosing players who lent themselves to discipline, who tolerated his constant nagging, abuse, and insults, who believed in what he preached, Lombardi achieved a team that kept mistakes to his desired bare minimum. Whether he would admit it or not, he could not have achieved it without Starr as his quarterback.

High school All-America teams are fairly common in these times, with the most prominent being those selected by *Parade* magazine and *USA Today*. In 1952 the only one of any note was that selected by an organization called The Wigwam Wise Men of America, appearing in the *Sporting News*, which was still mainly the bible of baseball. The quarterback on that team was a youngster from Montgomery, Alabama, named Bart Starr. It was the only prominent national publicity Starr would receive for the next five years. He received a scholarship from the University of Alabama and had some mild success in his first two seasons, but as a junior he suffered a back injury that virtually put an end to his college career. By his senior year in 1956, a new offense had been installed, and the coaches felt he did not fit it. In those days the NFL draft lasted thirty rounds, mostly because the owners weren't keen on having a lot of undrafted free agents at large who, at least theoretically, might pit one team against another for pricier contracts. Starr, on the basis of his early promise, was drafted in the seventeenth round, the two-hundredth player selected. In a happy irony the Packers used their second-round selection to draft Forrest Gregg of Southern Methodist and their fifth to draft Indiana's Bob Skoronski. When the Lombardi era would reach fruition, Gregg would protect Starr from his right-tackle position and Skoronski from left-tackle.

Starr had been a Packer for three years before Lombardi arrived in Green Bay. It was not love at first sight, at least from the coach's perspective. Lombardi inherited four quarterbacks when he was hired to coach Green Bay in 1959—Starr, Lamar McHan, Babe Parilli, and Joe Francis. He wasn't particularly impressed with any of them. McHan started the first nine games, but when the Packers lost five straight in the middle of the season, Starr was promoted. After losing Starr's first start, the Pack won four straight, including the last three on the road. In the final game Starr completed all twenty of his passes in a victory over the 49ers in San Francisco. The Packers averaged 25 points a game in those closing victories.

If Starr convinced Lombardi that he was the man for the job, it was a short-lived convincing. The coach again opened the quarterback assignment to McHan and Starr in training camp. Starr was given the start on Opening Day in 1960 in Chicago, but when the Pack lost to the Bears, Lombardi demoted Starr and promoted McHan once again. It was the wrong decision. Green Bay won four straight, but McHan was disturbingly erratic, compiling a dismal quarterback rating of 36.3. Despite a 19–16 victory over Pittsburgh on October 30, according to Michael O'Brien in *Vince*, his biography of Lombardi, the coach told Starr, "You're now my quarterback, and there will be no more changes."

Lombardi kept his word. Green Bay lost three of Starr's next four starts, but he remained in the job. The Packers won their last three games and the Western Conference championship. In the NFL championship game against the Eagles in Philadelphia's Franklin Field, Starr put the Packers ahead, 13–10, in the fourth quarter. The Eagles rallied to win the title, but it was the last postseason game Lombardi and Starr would lose.

CHAPTER 11

The AFL Contenders

One of the most confident teams in the AFL, the Buffalo Bills, two-time defending champions in the league, had lost a major portion of that confidence a few days after they upset San Diego, 23–0, for the 1965 championship. Lou Saban shocked the organization and the city by resigning as the Bills' coach to take the head-coaching job at the University of Maryland. Saban cited "the pressure of professional football. It's strictly business. There is nothing outside of it."

Stunned and uncertain about what he should do, owner Ralph Wilson gave the job to Joe Collier, Saban's brilliant defensive aide who had concocted sophisticated game plans to throttle high-scoring San Diego in both title games, allowing the Chargers just 7 points in the two games. In the 1965 championship game he used a variation on the Oklahoma defense popularized by Bud Wilkinson at the University of Oklahoma. The key was frequently dropping huge defensive end Ron McDole into coverage to confuse San Diego's young quarterback, John Hadl. McDole, christened "the Dancing Bear" years later by Washington quarterback Sonny Jurgensen after he was traded to the Redskins, was amazingly nimble for his 6-foot-4, 310-pound frame.

For all his skill as a defensive strategist, Collier had never been a head coach at any level. Most of his coaching career had been as Saban's assistant, first at Western Illinois University and later with the Boston Patriots before coming to Buffalo to rejoin his mentor. Collier himself was caught by surprise at Saban's resignation, and he quickly retained the other assistant coaches under the departed coach when Wilson promoted him. It may have been more prudent to hire his own staff since the assistants had been candidates to succeed Saban, too. Collier made some other early mistakes that would haunt him. One was not making enough use of Daryle Lamonica, Jack Kemp's backup quarterback, as Saban had. Another was choosing vagabond kicker Booth Lusteg as Pete Gogolak's successor, rather than the experienced Mike Mercer. Collier's decision on the kicker was cemented by a bizarre transaction. Mercer had been claimed on waivers from the Oakland Raiders early in the season and was placed on the Bills' taxi squad. Reasoning that Lusteg had a better preseason, Collier agreed to lend Mercer to the Kansas City Chiefs with the proviso he be returned to Buffalo after the season. Amazingly the AFL office went along with the loan. Mercer, as a Chief, then led the AFL in kicking.

Lusteg made just half of his thirty-nine attempted field goals, and his misses cost Buffalo two victories. With 6 seconds to play in a 17–17 tie with San Diego, Lusteg was wide right on a 23-yard attempt, his third miss of the game. The next day Lusteg told a dubious story about walking home from War Memorial Stadium, the Bills' home field, and being attacked and beaten by a group of unhappy fans. The story did not pass the sniff test with his teammates, especially since it soon turned out that there were other matters concerning Lusteg that were not as he claimed. To begin with his name was not "Booth" as he claimed, nor was he a twenty-five-year-old former Boston College player. He had assumed the identity of his younger brother who spent just one day on the Boston College team. "Booth" was really twenty-seven-year-old Jerry and a cum laude graduate of the University of Connecticut. "Who would have taken a chance on a twenty-seven-year-old rookie?" he reasoned.

The Bills got as far as they did mostly because of their superb defense and a surprising rookie star, running back Bobby Burnett of the University of Arkansas. Burnett produced 1,185 total yards, scored eight touchdowns, and not only was named the AFL's Rookie of the Year but also his own team's most valuable player.

In their ten seasons in the AFL, the Patriots never won a league championship, but it wasn't for lack of heart, true grit, and a refusal to stay down when it appeared they would be counted out. In 1966, the football prophets were counting out the Pats after the opening game, which they lost in San Diego, 24–0. In the previous season, it was almost mid-October in 1965 before they won their first game, and they wouldn't win again until Halloween, but, surprisingly, they got back into contention and won their last three. Their reputation as a lionhearted team was well deserved.

The 1966 Patriots, however, had gotten old. Quarterback Babe Parilli was thirty-six, kicker/wide receiver Gino Cappelletti was thirty-two. Wide receiver Jim Colclough was in decline. That trio was the engine that enabled the Pats to recover from a disheartening 51–10 loss to San Diego in the league championship game of 1963. The next year their resilience allowed them to battle Buffalo to the final game of the season before the Bills defeated them for the Eastern Division title. Now they were not only a much older group, they also didn't have much speed or any particular size either. What they did have was the wonder player of the 1966 season, second-year fullback Jim Nance.

Nance had been overshadowed at Syracuse University by the Orangemen's spectacular All-America halfback, Floyd Little. It was no shame since Little overshadowed everyone who played with him or against him, including Nance's successor, Larry Csonka.

Nance, who normally weighed 235 pounds, constantly battled his weight. In his rookie season, 1965, he led the Patriots in rushing but with a mere 321 yards. He didn't even average 3 yards per carry. Coach Mike Holovak kept warning him about his poor conditioning and his eating habits, and it finally took a benching to win his attention. During the break in seasons, Nance subsisted on a diet of a boiled egg for breakfast, a diet soda for lunch, and a normal dinner. Big Jim proved that he knew how to be disciplined when it was necessary. When he was a young child, his brother was attempting to switch a pot of boiling water from the stove to the sink. "I grabbed his arm," said Nance, "and the boiling water scalded me. My left shoulder got the worst of it. I spent seventy-seven days in the hospital." His Spartan diet in 1966 was motivated by something else. "I wanted to feel hungry, hear my stomach growling when I was playing," explained Nance. He claimed he didn't eat a morsel sixteen hours before kickoff.

More than his stomach was growling when the Patriots met the Raiders in late October. He ran over them for 159 yards in the first half, finished with 208, and celebrated Boston's vault into first place in the East with a foodfest afterward.

On December 4 against Buffalo in Fenway Park, the Patriots began thinking seriously about their chances of playing the NFL champions in the first game between the leagues. The notion was born on one great play by Nance early in the game against the Bills' defense, famous for its ability to choke off almost any team's running game. Nance broke the tackle of defensive end Tom Day at the line of scrimmage, then darted into the clear by breaking away from middle linebacker Harry Jacobs. Coming up to meet him, however, was George Saimes, the all-time AFL free safety and the finest open-field tackler in the league. Nance ran over Saimes like a sixteen-wheeler disposing of road kill. The Patriots walked out of Fenway with a one-game advantage over Buffalo and what seemed like a clear path to the AFL championship game. All the Patriots had to do was win two road games against teams with losing records, the Houston Oilers and the New York Jets. The Pats hadn't lost on the road since opening day in San Diego against the Chargers.

Houston was a 38–14 cakewalk for the Patriots. New York was different, mainly because Joe Namath was in his learning period as a pro quarterback. Namath would be efficient in one game, erratic in the next. He would pass more than any quarterback in the NFL, but he was intercepted twenty-seven times, and his quarterback rating was a sickly 62.6. The Patriots came into Shea Stadium on Saturday,

December 17, to play a Jets team that had won just once in its last eight games, and not at all in the last month. The Pats could taste the Eastern Division championship and then a chance to challenge the best of the NFL. Instead, Namath incinerated them in New York's 38–28 upset victory.

The next day the Bills played in War Memorial Stadium after a three-game road trip and then a bye week. They hadn't played since losing to Boston two weeks before. They were refreshed, healed of most of their injuries, and anxious to take advantage of the mulligan with which Namath and the Jets had presented them. Their opponent was Denver, a bottom-feeder all season long and who were now shaken by the news that their coach, Ray Malavasi, would be replaced the next season. (Malavasi's successor would be Lou Saban, the same man who had walked out on the Bills a year earlier, citing the stress of coaching in pro football.) Buffalo won the game easily, 38–21, and along with it the Eastern Division championship.

There was far less excitement in the Western Division of the AFL. San Diego, coached by the brilliant Sid Gillman, father of the modern pro passing game, had won the division championship in five of the AFL's six seasons of existence. The 1966 season started off well, with the Chargers disposing of the two Eastern powers with ease. They beat the Bills, 24–7, and the Patriots, 24–0. They beat the Raiders in Oakland by 9 points and the expansion Miami Dolphins by 24 on October 2. After that they didn't win another game until December.

San Diego's two outstanding running backs, Paul Lowe and Keith Lincoln, had declined. Lowe, who produced 1,000-yard seasons in two of the previous three years, was thirty, and most of his old flash had vanished. Lincoln had not been the same player since being the recipient of the famous tackle by Buffalo linebacker Mike Stratton, a game-breaking play that turned around the 1964 championship game in the Bills' favor. Lincoln suffered a serious rib injury that put him out of the game and had lasting negative effects. Gillman, noted for mentoring promising young assistant coaches, had also suffered a steady brain drain. First Al Davis, his receivers coach, left to take over the Raiders. Davis was followed by Jack Faulkner, who became head coach and general manager of the Denver Broncos. After the 1965 season Chuck Noll left to join Don Shula's staff in Baltimore with the Colts.

There were grand hopes in Oakland for the Raiders after they closed the 1965 season by winning three of their last five games, the only losses coming from the division champions, Buffalo and San Diego. But the Raiders team was coached by Al Davis, and he was now operating out of the commissioner's office in New York. John Rauch, his most experienced assistant, inherited the head-coaching job.

Rauch's Raiders ended with the same win-loss record as the 1965 team, but instead of advancing as a contender, they were merely a pest. Other than a mid-season upset of the Chiefs in Kansas City, they failed to make an impact on what turned out to be a short-lived race.

It was the year of the Chiefs. Management was so successful in identifying talent in two of the earliest drafts, and then aggressively signing much of that talent, that it began to ferment at just the right time, when the two leagues were in the process of coming together. In 1961 and 1963, the franchise added a total of ten starters for Kansas City's historic era between 1966 and 1969. In the first round in 1961, the Chiefs (then operating as the Dallas Texans) selected and signed E. J. Holub, the tough linebacker/center from Texas Tech; in the third, Ohio State offensive tackle Jim Tyrer; in the fifth, Southern Methodist defensive lineman Jerry Mays; and in the seventh, Michigan State tight end Fred Arbanas. In the thirteenth round they picked Kansas fullback Curtis McClinton as a redshirt, a player with college eligibility remaining but who was barred from being signed to a current contract. A year later McClinton became a Texan/Chief.

In 1963, the franchise, now ensconced in Kansas City, had two first-round draft choices, including the first overall pick in the draft. The No. 1 selection was used on Grambling defensive lineman Buck Buchanan, the first time a player from a historic Negro college was given that honor. With their other first-round selection they chose Michigan State's huge guard, Ed Budde. In the seventh round, Bobby Bell, Minnesota's All-America defensive end, was taken; in the eleventh Southern Mississippi punter Jerrell Wilson; and in the twenty-fourth, Auburn offensive tackle David Hill. Buchanan and Bell would wind up in the Pro Football Hall of Fame. The names of those two, along with Holub, Tyrer, Mays, McClinton, Budde, Hill, and Wilson would be attached to the Chiefs' Wall of Fame after Arrowhead Stadium was built.

In 1965, when the Chiefs finished in third place in the West, they lacked consistency. Their longest winning streak was two games, and they did that only once. "We need playmakers, guys who can explode on an opposing defense," said Hank Stram, their frustrated coach. As if by mail order, playmaking and explosion arrived the next season in the persons of Otis Taylor and Heisman Trophy–winner Mike Garrett. Taylor was a tall, swift receiver whom the Chiefs signed when they outmaneuvered the NFL babysitters—league delegates assigned to hide out top players from the AFL so the established league could sign them. Just about everyone conceded Garrett, Southern California's great little back, to his hometown Los Angeles Rams. The Rams had used a second-round pick to draft him. Kansas City picked him in the twentieth round of the AFL draft, which seemed like a mere afterthought about a player with his skills. The disparity in the draft positions may have lulled the Rams into overconfidence. Lamar Hunt gave his scouts the word: "Sign Garrett." They did. Garrett led the Chiefs in ground gaining as a rookie, averaging 5.5 yards per carry. Taylor led them in receiving, with fifty-eight catches for 1,297 yards, an astounding average of 22.4 yards a catch. Like Garrett, Bell was expected to sign with another team, in his case the Minnesota Vikings, who played right across the Mississippi River from his school.

The acknowledged drum major for this parade of talent was quarterback Len Dawson, who at thirty-one was nearing the peak of his career. Ten seasons earlier, Dawson entered pro football as one of the most desirable quarterbacks in college football. Since they were still trying to find a suitable successor to the great Otto Graham, who had retired two years earlier, the Cleveland Browns lusted for the Purdue star, a native of Alliance, Ohio. "We had the fifth pick in the draft, and we liked Lenny more than John Brodie, who had just finished his career at Stanford," said Dick Gallagher, who was Paul Brown's personnel chief. "There was a bonus pick rule in effect at the time, which was won by Green Bay. The Packers also had the third selection. Green Bay took Paul Hornung, the Notre Dame quarterback, whom we and a lot of other teams thought would be a halfback in the pros. The Rams picked Jon Arnett, the halfback from Southern California, with the second pick and the Packers took Ron Kramer, the big tight end from Michigan with their own first-round selection. We were sure we would get Dawson because the Steelers were the next team up and they never knew what they were doing. We were shocked when they took Lenny. We had to content ourselves with a running back from Syracuse named Jim Brown."

Dawson thought he had joined the circus when Pittsburgh selected him. The Steelers hadn't enjoyed a winning season since 1949 when Harry Truman was president of the United States. The Pittsburgh coach was Walt Kiesling, in his third but nonconsecutive term with the team. The Steelers kept bringing back Kiesling during the 1930s, 1940s, and finally the 1950s, without getting a sniff of any championship. It got worse for Dawson. On August 12, Buddy Parker, who had coached the Detroit Lions to a pair of NFL championships earlier in the decade, shocked the Motor City by abruptly resigning as coach at the season-opening "Welcome Home Lions" luncheon.

Parker wasn't at large for very long. A week later, the Steelers hired him to replace Kiesling.

Parker liked veterans, and the Steelers already had young but experienced Earl Morrall on their roster. Dawson played just enough to attempt four passes as a rookie. The next season, Parker traded with his old team, the Lions, for Bobby Layne, the great star who had delivered those NFL championships for Parker and Detroit. Dawson now sat behind both Layne and Morrall. By the end of the 1959 season, Dawson's career passing line was sixteen passes attempted, one touchdown, two intercepted. The Steelers shipped him to Cleveland, the team that wanted him in the first place.

The trouble was that the Browns, having missed Dawson in the 1957 draft, settled for Penn State's Milt Plum in the second round. By the time Dawson reached Cleveland, Plum was the established quarterback, and in 1960 and 1961, he had the two best seasons of his career. In two seasons as a Brown, Dawson got to attempt just twenty-eight passes. Paul Brown was happy with neither him nor Plum. He cut Dawson and started trading. He sent Plum to Detroit in a deal that brought quarterback Jim Ninowski, and he also traded with the Rams for cerebral Frank Ryan, his kind of quarterback.

What Dawson needed was somebody to believe in him once again. The AFL was in its third season. The Dallas Texans, steadily improving, were coached by Hank Stram, Dawson's quarterback coach at Purdue. Lenny found the man who still believed in him.

Once the season began, the Chiefs, formerly the Texans, blew away their opposition.

CHAPTER 12

Manny Celler's Goal-Line Stand

By the first month of the 1966 season, the battle was galvanized for the honor of competing in the first championship game between the National and American Football Leagues. The Green Bay Packers and the Dallas Cowboys began with 4–0 records in the NFL; the Kansas City Chiefs and the San Diego Chargers had the same record in the AFL. The Buffalo Bills, the AFC's defending champion, struggled as did the Boston Patriots—who, despite being presumed contenders in the AFL, salvaged only a tie in their first four games— and the Oakland Raiders in the AFL and the Cleveland Browns and the Baltimore Colts in the NFL. The Bills were an unimpressive 2–2, and so were Cleveland and Baltimore. The biggest surprise, however, were the young New York Jets, who won three and tied one of their first four games behind Joe Namath.

What wasn't galvanized was the federal government's approval of the merger. The joining of the leagues was interstate commerce. Between the two leagues, pro football would be operated on a coast-to-coast, north-to-south basis, which meant U.S. antitrust laws must be observed. Pro football, unlike baseball, did not enjoy an antitrust exemption. The merger would create a football Goliath from a business as well as a sports perspective, but first it had to get by a figurative middle linebacker tougher than the combined strength of the Chicago Bears' Dick Butkus, the Packers' Ray Nitschke, the Detroit Lions' Joe Schmidt, and the Patriots' Nick Buoniconti.

This "middle linebacker" was a wizened, seventy-eight-year-old congressman from New York named Emanuel "Manny" Celler, and he derived his power from serving as the chairman of the Judiciary Committee of the House of Representatives. On September 8, Pete Rozelle, in his new role as commissioner of the to-be-merged leagues, went to Washington to ask for Celler's approval of special legislation to smooth the way toward the first championship game between the warring leagues and the clearing of other obstacles in the way of the merger's completion. Celler encouraged him, but he didn't approve of his plan.

"I told him I can't see any reason for them not to go ahead with their plans," Celler said after Rozelle's appearance. "There hasn't been any suit filed or questions raised." Rozelle was sure that there would be a number of tough questions to come, most of them raised by Celler. Rozelle had taken his business first to the Senate, the friendlier body of Congress, and that upper house had quickly approved the merger. The bill needed to get by the House Judiciary Committee, however, and Celler flattened it like a slow-moving little halfback. "We could go back to where we started," said a glum Rozelle. "Nowhere."

Rozelle treaded lightly around Celler. "Chairman Celler is a recognized expert on antitrust legislation," Rozelle tactfully told the media when he got back to New York. "We are pleased to have his advice to go forward." Celler's advice was better encapsulated when Rozelle returned to Washington in October and appeared before the Judiciary Committee again. "When two men ride a horse, one must ride behind," Celler said. "And I'm riding this horse."

If Rozelle had found owners of football teams such as Baltimore's Carroll Rosenbloom tough dealers, he discovered an even thornier thicket in Washington. The nation's headline writers delighted in Rozelle's problems, using sports figures of speech and cliché's such as *end around* and *goal-line stand*. The *Washington Star*'s witty columnist, Moe Siegel, outdid them the morning after Rozelle testified before Celler. Siegel wrote:

Time is growing short. The NFL is on the 2-yard line, unable to penetrate chairman Celler's man-for-man defense. To make the load heavier, the pro football people don't even have the ball yet. All they want Manny to do is help pass a law saying it is okay for the NFL and AFL to embrace legally and let no antitrust lawyer try to put this gridiron wedding asunder. But they aren't moving Manny, no matter how many high-priced blockers they hire to throw at him. Manny says he's for the affair, but like any father of the girl eager to get married, he wants to know more about the boyfriend before he gives his blessings.

Rozelle might have been in a hurry, but Celler wasn't. He had been in Congress for forty-four years. He watched unhappily as too many big corporations cut corners on too many business regulations and it wasn't to the benefit of the public. The congressman was not a fan of the U.S. Senate, either, and that august body hurriedly passed a bill back in September approving the merger without holding public hearings. It provided him great pleasure when he pigeonholed that bill in his committee, effectively killing it.

Then there was a personal grudge that he held. For his entire congressional career, Celler represented the same district in Brooklyn, Flatbush. This is where Ebbets Field, home of the late Brooklyn Dodgers baseball team, was located. A decade earlier the Dodgers' owner, Walter O'Malley, had used baseball's antitrust exemption as a vehicle to move the team to Los Angeles, opening the West Coast to Major League Baseball. Celler wasn't a fan, but his constituents were. When O'Malley's name was mentioned at the Judiciary Committee's pro football hearings, Celler's face contorted as if he were offended by an unpleasant odor.

Rozelle was discovering that politics was more difficult than a roomful of owners such as Rosenbloom, George Preston Marshall of Washington, and George Halas of the Chicago Bears. But as unfriendly as Chairman Celler was, Rozelle happily found people in Congress who were downright cordial, even obliging as long as something they dearly wanted was the price of their help. The commissioner was about to enter the spiderweb world of Louisiana politics.

Senator Russell Long was a member of one of the most famous and sometimes notorious families in Louisiana's history. His father, Huey Long, popularly known as the Kingfish, was a high school dropout who was elected governor of Louisiana three times. In 1930 he was elected to the U.S. Senate, but he enjoyed life as governor so much that he didn't show up in Washington for two years. In 1935 he announced his intention to run for president of the United States, and a month later he was assassinated in the Louisiana statehouse. At the time of the merger hearings, Congressman Hale Boggs was acting majority leader of the House of Representatives. He was the scion of a famous family. Boggs, a member of the Warren Commission, which investigated the assassination of President John F. Kennedy, was later killed in a plane crash in Alaska in 1972. His wife, Lindy, was named to fill his House seat. His son, Tommy, currently ranks among the most powerful lobbyists in Washington. His daughter, Cokey Roberts, is now a well-known NPR and ABC TV news commentator.

In 1966 what Long and Boggs wanted from Rozelle was for the NFL to give a pro football expansion franchise to New Orleans. What Rozelle would get in exchange was enormous help in getting a bill passed that would allow the merger to be completed. On October 14, Congressman Boggs and Senator Long tacked on an immunity amendment to a completely unrelated bill known as the foreign investment act. The act was needed by President Lyndon Baines Johnson as part of his postelection program after he defeated Senator Barry Goldwater in a landslide two months earlier. Boggs, who was close to Johnson and President John F. Kennedy before him, shepherded the football amendment through the House and past Celler and his committee.

Celler was angry. "There may be rejoicing in some quarters that an end run was made around me," he remarked. "But the end run was made around the public, who now have no way of knowing the whys and wherefores and the results which may flow from this merger." Celler told the *Philadelphia Bulletin* that the desire for a common draft that would end the bidding between leagues was a powerful factor in launching the merger. "They have made improvident contracts and they want and need Congress to bail them out," Celler said.

Author Michael MacCambridge, in his 2004 book *America's Game*, described the scene when Rozelle thanked Boggs in a meeting just off the floor of the House:

> *Walking up the stairs of the rotunda, when the vote looked like a sure thing, Rozelle was his usual humble self. "Congressman Boggs I don't know how I can thank you enough for this. This is a terrific thing you've done."*
>
> *Boggs had been a veteran of Louisiana politics too long to let such transparent politesse go unremarked. "What do you mean you* don't know *how to thank me? New Orleans gets an immediate franchise in the NFL."*
>
> *"I'm going to do everything I can to make that happen," Rozelle assured him.*
>
> *At that Boggs stopped and turned on his heels, heading back to the committee room, "Well, we can always call off the vote while you—"*
>
> *Rozelle took two giant strides after Boggs, turned him gently around, and said, "It's a deal, Congressman. You'll get your franchise."*
>
> *"If this doesn't work out," said the patrician Boggs, now perturbed, "you will regret this for the rest of your fucking life!"*

Eleven days after the congressional maneuver that cemented the merger, New Orleans received a franchise in professional football. Once appearing certain to become an American Football League city, New Orleans was instead welcomed into the NFL, much to the satisfaction of the city's power structure. Just three months before, New Orleans seemed destined for the AFL, and the sentiment among the city's opinion makers was decidedly sour.

In a column in the *Times-Picayune*, subtitled "Say It Ain't So," Bob Roesler, the paper's sports editor, wrote:

> *Holy smoke, it seems as if New Orleans is going to get stuck with "that" pro league. I almost ran a red light when [William Clay] Ford, president of the Detroit Lions, told me, "I understand that the American Football League has first refusal on the next city [to be added to pro football]. And George Wilson [the Miami Dolphins' first coach] told me the AFL would like to move into New Orleans."*
>
> *I turned to Ford and sighed, "Oh no. Not that." I told Ford about the scars left by the AFL walkout in January 1965. This seemed to surprise the Lions' young president, who apparently figured New Orleans citizens had forgotten how the AFL in allowing the rebels to walk out had reneged on the local promoter and Tulane Stadium.*

Roesler referred to the planned AFL All-Star game scheduled to be played in New Orleans after the 1965 season, and the "rebels" were the African-American players who refused to perform in the game. It was the first major AFL event to be played at a neutral site, an obvious reaching out to New Orleans as a potential expansion city for the young league. Dave Dixon, an energetic entrepreneur, had been on the hunt for an AFL franchise for his city since the advent of the young league, and it was at his urging that the All-Star game was coming to the southern gem that was known as "the city that care forgot."

Dixon and other city leaders had assured the AFL that there would be no racial problems for the many African-American players on the East and West rosters. They would be able to go anywhere, including the famed French Quarter, and eat in the same restaurants and patronize the same clubs as the white players did.

When the AFL All-Stars began arriving at the New Orleans Airport, it became obvious that one "care" that the city had not forgotten was racial segregation. The first trouble the African-American players encountered was getting from the airport to the city. White cab drivers would not accept them as fares. Some waited hours for cabs until they were informed by a porter that only black cabbies would drive them and a phone call had to be placed to the city for the black cabs to come out to the airport and get them.

When the black players tried to eat in French Quarter restaurants, they were denied admission even when accompanied by their white teammates. After Buffalo tight end Ernie Warlick, in the company of teammates Jack Kemp and Mike Stratton, was barred from two restaurants, he returned to his hotel. In the morning Warlick was able to order breakfast in the dining room of the hotel, "but I lost my appetite when an older woman said loud enough for me to hear, "I don't want to eat in the same room with monkeys."

That morning the African-American players began trading stories about their humiliation. A number of them immediately left New Orleans on their own, refusing to play in the game. When Milt Woodard, the top aide to Commissioner Joe Foss, heard how his players were being treated in direct contrast to the assurances the league had been given, he called Foss and they agreed to move the game out of New Orleans. Surprisingly it wasn't cancelled. Houston, a city frigidly unfriendly to the black players on AFL teams when the league began in 1960, welcomed the game on a last-minute basis.

Houston had changed in six years. New Orleans, for all its charm, was still a part of the Jim Crow South.

The AFL All-Star episode took place at a time when racial hatred was at its nadir. Less than a year earlier, Alabama state troopers had attacked peaceful demonstrators, led by Reverend Martin Luther King, as they attempted to cross a bridge in Selma. The previous August there were six days of rioting in Watts, a famous black neighborhood of Los Angeles, leaving thirty-five dead and 883 injured. *Sensitivity* was a word not yet in vogue over race relations. When the AFL's black players walked out of New Orleans, the South wasn't the only place where they were criticized for taking offense to their treatment. A *New York Times* columnist referred to their grievances as "trivial."

So it was that the NFL came to New Orleans, today a football hotbed. A perfect name was selected for the team, the Saints. They began play in 1967. They had their first winning season exactly twenty years later.

CHAPTER 13

The Semifinals

Less than three weeks after Pete Rozelle made his end run around Emanuel Celler and the House Judiciary Committee, the commissioner of the joined leagues traveled to Kansas City to watch his first American Football League game. The Kansas City Chiefs were entertaining the defending champion of the AFL's Western Division, the San Diego Chargers.

Rozelle didn't see "basketball in cleats" as described by those who loved to disparage the "other league's" offensive style. The Chiefs won, 24–14, with an impressive defensive show. Their two safeties, Johnny Robinson and Bobby Hunt, made thirty-three tackles between them. It was Kansas City's third consecutive victory, making their record 7–2. They would not lose for the rest of the season, and they swept their road schedule for the first time in franchise history, winning all seven games.

Meanwhile San Diego's fine start was dissipating. The Chargers had lost their scoring touch against the better AFL defenses. The loss to Kansas City was their third to a contender in their last five games, and they also blew a lead in the final seconds, allowing the Buffalo Bills to tie them. In the four games against contenders, the team that previously had been the symbol of offensive explosiveness averaged 16 points. Oakland was mathematically alive, but the Oakland Raiders' sorry start was a handicap that they were finding difficult to shake in attempting to keep up with the streaking Chiefs.

In the East, the New York Jets were in a swoon that would more than erase their 4–0 start to the season. The Bills were recovering from their poor start, refreshed by a 29–14 upset of the Chiefs in

Kansas City. Jack Kemp, 1965's most valuable player, had always been a Kansas City nemesis, dating back to when he played for San Diego and the Chiefs were based in Dallas. On this day he and the Bills' superb defensive line pushed the defending AFL champions back into the race.

The game did not start well for Buffalo. The Bills' starting strong safety, Tom Janik, suffered an injury and had to be replaced by backup Charlie Warner who had spent two seasons with the Chiefs. Quarterback Len Dawson picked up on the substitution immediately and called a deep pass play in which Warner was forced to cover Otis Taylor, Kansas City's game-breaker receiver. The result was a 71-yard touchdown with just 1 minute, 29 seconds expired.

It was the last time any Chief would run free that day. The Buffalo defensive line of Tom Sestak and Jim Dunaway at tackles and Ron McDole and Tom Day paired at ends overpowered Kansas City's big, talented offensive linemen. The Chiefs' running game was blunted completely, and Dawson, who completed just four of his next fourteen passes after the early touchdown pass to Taylor, was pulled in favor of backup Pete Beathard. In the second half, Kemp riddled the Chiefs' defense by completing all five of his passes, supervising a thirteen-play, 89-yard drive, finished off by his touchdown pass to Elbert Dubenion. In the last quarter he drove the Bills another 75 yards capped by his 24-yard touchdown pass to utility man Ed Rutkowski, who beat Fred Williamson. Rutkowski's moves on Williamson would be watched on film with interest by Bart Starr and the Green Bay Packers four months later.

On the November Sunday in which Pete Rozelle made his debut as an AFL spectator, the Boston Patriots had their three-game winning streak snapped at home at Fenway Park by the underdog Denver Broncos. Nothing was coming easily for the Patriots, who relied heavily on running back Jim Nance, but this gritty team still managed to stay with or right behind Buffalo. Nevertheless, just two of the Pats' six remaining games were scheduled at home.

Over in the NFL on the day Rozelle visited Kansas City, the Dallas Cowboys were visiting the Philadelphia Eagles. The Eagles beat them by a point, but it was a mere blip. The week before Dallas had scored 52 points in a rout of Pittsburgh, the third time the Cowboys had exceeded 50 points in seven games. Dallas had a stranglehold on the Eastern Conference.

Also on the day of Rozelle's diplomatic mission, the Packers had their three-game winning streak ended by Minnesota, 20–17, right in Lambeau Field. It was just their second loss of the season but they wouldn't lose for the rest of the schedule. The Pack wasn't as offensively explosive as Dallas, reaching 30 points only twice all season, but its defense was smothering. The Packers would finish with forty-seven sacks and twenty-eight interceptions, while opposing quarterbacks would have a cumulative efficiency rating of a mere 46.1.

By December it was obvious that the NFL representative in the first on-the-field clash between the leagues would be either Green Bay or Dallas. It was a different matter in the AFL. Kansas City had nailed down the Western Conference championship, but Boston and Buffalo, the two teams that played the very first AFL game, a preseason game in July of 1960, were clawing at each other once again in 1966. "I can hardly wait for that game in Boston," said Tom Sestak, the Bills' overpowering defensive tackle. He didn't have long to wait. The teams met in Fenway Park on December 4, drawing the Pats' largest home crowd in history, 39,350. It was just the second time the team had drawn a capacity crowd to Fenway, which put them, temporarily, on a level with the beloved Red Sox. The other time Fenway filled to capacity was the 1964 game against the Bills that decided the AFC-East in Buffalo's favor.

When the Patriots won the first meeting of the teams back in early October, they used run blitzes to stymie Buffalo's star rookie running back, Bobby Burnett, and his veteran backfield mate, Wray Carlton. The seasoned Boston defensive line was at the top of its game. Ends Larry Eisenhauer and Bob Dee along with tackles Houston Antwine and Jim "Earthquake" Hunt had played together for nearly the life span of the franchise, and they were the essence of cohesion. Hunt had one of the best seasons of his career, providing superb pass pressure up the middle. "I still think we're going to play Buffalo for the AFL championship in the end," said Kansas City coach Hank Stram, "but I've never seen Buffalo's offensive line handled the way Boston handled them." The Patriots couldn't muster much offense against Buffalo's strong defensive unit, but Jim Nance's 65-yard touchdown run was more than enough in a 10–3 victory. When they followed their triumph over Buffalo with an easy win over Houston, all the Patriots had to do was beat the Jets in New York and they would be a game away from playing against the champions of the NFL.

The Jets-Patriots game was played on a Saturday in Shea Stadium. Since the Bills didn't play until their Sunday season finale against Denver in Buffalo, Bills owner Ralph Wilson flew to New York to root for the Jets, his team's last hope. Some hope. The Jets had won only once since those heady days of the early season when they were still unbeaten in the first week of October, but the young New York team was a study in up-and-down development. The Boston defense that had played so well since Thanksgiving Day was cut to pieces by Joe Namath, who threw for 287 yards and three touchdowns while not giving up an interception. Babe Parilli had an explosive day for the Pats, throwing for three touchdowns and more than 300 yards, but the Jets intercepted him twice. New York's front seven controlled Nance, who was trumped by the Jets' outstanding young ball carriers, Matt Snell and Emerson Boozer. They led a running game that piled up 241 yards in their 38–28 victory.

After the game, in the New York dressing room, Ralph Wilson bent on one knee and bowed jokingly to Sonny Werblin, the Jets' managing partner. All Wilson's Bills had to do in the wake of Boston's loss was beat underdog Denver the next day in Buffalo.

"Is there anything I can send you?" Wilson asked Werblin in jest. "Champagne? I'll give them anything they want," referring to the Jets' Namath and coach Weeb Ewbank.

In the Patriots' dressing room, coach Mike Holovak couldn't believe what had happened. "We beat Buffalo twice," he muttered. "That's the toughest part of it. We beat them twice and still lose. Basically they don't deserve to win, but you've got to beat every-body if you want to win."

The next day the Bills easily defeated Denver to clinch their third consecutive Eastern Division championship. *Sports Illustrated* ran a photograph of quarterback Jack Kemp pointing to the blowup of a check for $15,000 in its next issue. Three weeks earlier, Com-missioner Pete Rozelle had announced that the first championship game between the leagues would be played in the Los Angeles Col-iseum, Sunday, January 15, and that the winner's share would be $15,000 with the losers getting half that. In winning the two previous AFL championships, the total prize money for Kemp and his veteran teammates was less than half of that.

On the Saturday the Jets ruined Boston's chances for the $15,000 pot, the Cleveland Browns defeated the St. Louis Cardinals, allowing the Dallas Cowboys to win their first championship of any sort without even playing. The Browns' victory made Dallas's game against the Giants the next day a moot point. "I don't feel as elated as I thought I would," said Tom Landry, the Dallas coach, who had watched on television. "I'm sure it hasn't sunk in yet." It sank in for most football fans. The Cowboys would be playing the Green Bay Packers for the honor of defending the NFL's reputation in Super Bowl I. That's what most newspapers were calling it: Super Bowl I. It fit much more comfortably into a headline than THE CHAMPIONSHIP GAME BETWEEN THE AMERICAN AND NATIONAL LEAGUES.

Playoffs and wild-card positions would not arrive until years later, and there was no home-field-advantage prize for the teams that compiled the best win-loss records. Consequently Dallas, who finished with ten victories, three losses, and a tie, would play host to the Packers, 12–2, in the Cotton Bowl for the NFL championship. In the AFL, the Bills, 9–4–1, would play the Chiefs, 11–2–1, in Buffalo's WPA relic War Memorial Stadium.

The Bills and Chiefs had split their season series, with Kansas City winning easily, 42–20, on September 11 in Buffalo. On October 2 the Bills retaliated, 29–14, in Kansas City. After the second game, Dave Grayson, the Chiefs' veteran safety, saluted Kemp: "You just feel those eyes of his staring at you, and all you can do is hope he doesn't throw it in your direction."

On New Year's Day, 1967, three months after their last meeting, another Kansas City safety would face Kemp far more confidently than did Grayson. Johnny Robinson, the starting free safety, had been one of the franchise's best assets since he joined in its pioneer season in 1960, first as Abner Haynes's partner in the offensive backfield, then as an even bigger hit when he was converted to defense. "Sweet Johnny" had been a starting running back at Louisiana State University, but like Jim Taylor of Green Bay he played in the shadow of the LSU Tigers' Heisman Trophy winner, Billy Cannon. Taylor, a senior, was under-classman Cannon's blocking back, but the Packers saw more potential than just blocking and drafted him in the second round. Robinson was a great all-around player, ball carrier, receiver, blocker, and defender. He was selected in the first round of the 1960 NFL draft by the Detroit Lions, but the Chiefs (then the Texans) signed him.

During the season the Bills operated as they had in their two championship campaigns: strong running to control the ball and set up the long pass; exceptionally strong defense, particularly against the run; and dependable field-goal kicking. In nine of their twelve games after September 24, the Buffalo defense held opponents to an average of 46 yards rushing. There were some worry points. In three of their biggest games, two against Boston and the first match with Kansas City, the opposition gained more than 100 yards rushing, and even though rookie Bobby Burnett and veteran Wray Carlton combined for more than 1,400 yards for the season, they were stopped in those three contests. The new field-goal kicker, Booth Lusteg, was no Pete Gogolak.

At the beginning of the AFL title game, Buffalo played as if they would become champions again by force of habit. The Chiefs struck first with a Lenny Dawson touchdown pass. Kemp sent his speediest collaborator, Elbert Dubenion, to test cornerback Fred Williamson. Williamson slipped and Golden Wheels, as the Buffalo press called Dubenion, became completely clear for a 69-yard touchdown pass, tying the game. Then it became a game of punch, counterpunch. Mike Garrett returned a punt 42 yards, but a disastrous penalty pushed the Chiefs back to the Buffalo 45. Dawson scrambled for 11 yards, but Bills linebacker John Tracey then sacked the Kansas City quarterback for a 10-yard loss. Dawson recovered with a quick touchdown pass to Otis Taylor, who beat Butch Byrd, the Bills' physical cornerback, on third-and-5.

Kemp mounted one more counterpunch in an effort to tie the game before halftime, using Burnett as his key target emerging from the backfield. Pass completions of 18 and 33 yards brought Buffalo to the Kansas City 7-yard line. When Bobby Crockett, Burnett's rookie teammate from Arkansas, beat cornerback Willie Mitchell at the goal line, it appeared the Bills were about to achieve their tie. Instead, Robinson crossed in front of Crockett, intercepted Kemp's pass and raced 72 yards downfield. Then Mike Mercer kicked a 32-yard field goal to make it 17–7 and Kansas City was in control of the game.

"I was keying on [fullback] Jack Spikes," Robinson explained of his game-changing play. "But when I saw Spikes block [linebacker] E. J. Holub, I concentrated on Kemp. He looked to the strong side, then he pumped to the weak side. I gambled when I saw Crockett cutting to the middle. I read Kemp's eyes and I got lucky." The final score was 31–7.

The National League championship was supposed to be more of a match between two brilliant coaches, onetime colleagues, and

General Manager Tex Schramm is shown holding the Vince Lombardi Trophy after
the Dallas Cowboys realized their vast potential by defeating Miami in Super Bowl VI.
Defensive coaching aide Ernie Stautner joins Schramm in the celebration.
Courtesy of the Dallas Cowboys

Having acquired Lenny Dawson as their starting quarterback, the Kansas City Chiefs finally possessed the leader to put them on par with Oakland and San Diego in the AFL's tough Western Division.
Courtesy of the Kansas City Chiefs

When a startling waiver transaction put San Diego quarterback Jack Kemp in a Buffalo uniform, the Bills became an immediate contender.
Courtesy of the Buffalo Bills archives

The decision of comedian Danny Thomas to purchase a majority interest in the expansion Miami Dolphins team in the AFL delighted his lawyer and managing partner, Joe Robbie. Here they join Dolphins' fans in the Orange Bowl. The expansion meant Miami was not only a college football town, but also a pro town.
Courtesy of the Miami Dolphins

Three years after Don Shula was hired as head coach, Commissioner Pete Rozelle hands the Lombardi Trophy to managing partner Joe Robbie and Shula after the Miami defense completely stifled Washington's offense in Super Bowl VII.
Courtesy of the Miami Dolphins

In Green Bay Vince Lombardi had loyal lieutenants in, from left to right,
Phil Bengtson, Norb Hecker, Red Cochran and Bill Austin, but there was no doubt
Lombardi (center) was the commander in chief.
Courtesy of Green Bay Packers archives

"The Foolish Club" AFL Owners, 1961. Seated left to right: K.S. "Bud" Adams Jr.,
Houston Oilers; Commissioner Joe Foss. Standing left to right: Bill Sullivan, Boston;
Cal Kunz, Denver; Ralph Wilson, Buffalo; Lamar Hunt, Dallas; Harry Wismer, New York;
Wayne Valley, Oakland; Barron Hilton, San Diego.
Courtesy of the Buffalo Bills archives

Not only did Pete Gogolak change field goal–kicking forever, but his instep was a powerful weapon in Buffalo's consecutive AFL championships in 1964 and 1965.
Courtesy of the Buffalo Bills archives

Joe Namath, the catalyst for pro football's most electrifying moment in Super Bowl III, was a special guest at the opening of the Pro Football Hall of Fame's new theater. With Namath are Don Smith of the Hall of Fame, Ray Didinger of NFL Films, and the author.
Courtesy of the Pro Football Hall of Fame

Daryle Lamonica, strong-armed quarterback acquired from the Bills in a controversial trade, was ideal for the Raiders' vertical passing game.
Courtesy of the Oakland Raiders

As the team with the worst record in the AFL or NFL, the Bills had the right to draft first in 1969, picked O.J. Simpson, and eventually signed him. Jack Horrigan, a Bills' vice president, stands with Simpson on the muddy field before a game in Buffalo's War Memorial Stadium.
Courtesy of the author

Floyd Little's vast potential bore fruit after the merger when the Broncos finally surrounded him with helpful talent.
Courtesy of Floyd Little

Without Al Davis and his canny, aggressive tactics, it's doubtful the merger between the leagues would have taken place and *The Birth of the New NFL* might never have been written. **Courtesy of the Oakland Raiders**

less a battle of quarterbacks. Bart Starr, the Green Bay quarterback, was still looked upon as one of Vince Lombardi's dependents. The identity of Dallas's Don Meredith was just emerging from the role of "amusing character" to elite quarterback. The popular scenario was forecast as a clash of Lombardi versus Tom Landry of the Cowboys, former colleagues on Jim Lee Howell's New York Giants staff of the 1950s.

Few coaches have been more distinctly different. Lombardi left the Giants for a woebegone Green Bay team that had won a mere single game the season before his arrival. He bullied, coaxed, and cajoled them into a winning record in his first season, and by the turn of the decade the Packers were more dominant than any Green Bay team since the storied franchise's leather-helmet days. By defeating Dallas, the Pack would, in Lombardi's phrase, "Go where no other NFL team had gone before"—to its third consecutive championship and the chance to defend the league's honor against the champions of the upstart AFL. Lombardi thirsted to achieve that "never-before" status and woe to the Packer who wanted it any less than he did. The week before the Cowboys' game, he nagged the Packers as they hadn't been nagged before. Anything less than total effort every day in every practice was seen as disloyalty.

Loyalty was viewed by Lombardi as the ultimate virtue, as long as it fit his ends. All his players knew the story of Jim Ringo and what happened to him when Lombardi found his loyalty wanting. Ringo was a seventh-round draft choice by the Packers in 1953. He won a starting job at center and for six years played with rare distinction on some of the worst Green Bay teams of all time. Lombardi was his fourth coach in the pros, and when he arrived, Ringo felt that he had been liberated. Under Lombardi he became the greatest cutback blocker in the history of the position, assembling his Hall of Fame credentials for five more seasons in the Lombardi regime. In 1964, after eleven years, most of them as an All-Pro, Ringo wanted a substantial raise that had been denied him in the

past, so he hired an agent. Agents, at that time, were rare crea-
tures, looked down on as intrinsically evil by big-league sports
management. Management preferred players who conducted their
own salary negotiations, much to their disadvantage. Bob Turley,
once a New York Yankee pitching ace, told of a negotiating session
between George Weiss, the Yankees' hard-nosed general manager,
and Turley's great teammate, catcher Yogi Berra. "Berra had one
of the greatest years of his career," Turley said, "but by the time
Weiss got through dealing with him, Yogi was thinking maybe he
should take a cut in pay." It was worse for most football players,
such as linemen, who didn't have the statistics baseball players
had to use in their defense.

Ringo's agent came to Green Bay to talk to Lombardi, who
excused himself from the negotiations for five minutes. Lombardi,
who disliked agents intensely, returned and told Ringo's representative that he would have to deal with the Philadelphia Eagles,
to whom he had just traded his client. Lombardi's view of agents
would change abruptly after he coauthored *Run to Daylight*, with the
noted writer W. C. Heinz. Prentice-Hall published the book, which
was illustrated by the most famous sports artist of the time, Robert Riger. Heinz and Riger each received 30 percent of the royalties
and Lombardi agreed to 40 percent. All told, the book sold more
than 200,000 copies in hardcover and paperback to become one of
the most successful sports books in publishing history. Lombardi's
take was $21,000, which did not please him. He then hired an agent
himself.

Years later, Ringo revealed that he had asked for a trade to Philadelphia so that he would be closer to his home in Easton, Pennsylvania, although his agent actually did travel to Green Bay to talk
contract with Lombardi, who often encouraged the story about his
five-minute absence and the subsequent trade. The story served his
purposes. It discouraged other players from signing with agents.
From the standpoint of loyalty, it was also hypocritical.

As the Packers approached the NFL title game against Dallas, another "disloyalty" story was circulating in Green Bay: Jim Taylor was in his last days as a Packer. The great running back was playing out the option year in his contract and would sign with the expansion New Orleans Saints, his home-state team. The Saints were in no mood for any gentleman's agreement about signing a big-time free agent since the NFL had been unkind to them in concocting the recipe for stocking their rosters. Most of the talent made available was mediocre or aged. Taylor was thirty-one, old for a running back, but at worst the Saints felt that his reputation would sell tickets for them.

Lombardi didn't see it that way. To him Taylor's decision amounted to disloyalty, not only to Green Bay but also to him personally. He didn't speak to Taylor at all during the 1966 season. When the Packers exposed Paul Hornung in the expansion draft, Lombardi was effusive in his praise of his longtime star. When asked about replacing Hornung, the coach said, "it will be difficult, but it won't be so hard to replace the other guy." He had stopped using Taylor's name. Lombardi would leave the Packers three years later to coach the Redskins, receiving part ownership in the franchise. In Green Bay the word *hypocrite* was used to describe the once-hallowed coach.

Aside from their superb coaching skills, Landry and Lombardi were unlike in most ways. People who knew Landry well could not imagine him urging his players to "hate" the opposition, or telling them "winning isn't everything, it's the only thing," as Lombardi used to do. Besides, the "winning is the only thing" motto was a line out of actor John Wayne's mouth in the 1953 movie *Trouble Along the Way*.

Since he had been in the United States Army Air Forces during World War II, Landry avoided martial descriptions of plays or game plans. Lombardi, although a good college player at Fordham, hadn't played professionally, but Landry had, which probably led him to avoid bullying his own players. A defensive back, punter, and kick returner, Landry signed with the New York Yankees of the All-America Football Conference, the NFL's rival, in 1949, even though the Giants had drafted him two years earlier while he was still playing for the University of Texas. His choice of the Yankees was influenced by another former Longhorn, tailback Spec Sanders, who had become the team's star and one of the AAFC's best players. Landry's first year with the Yankees was also his last, since the AAFC folded after the 1949 season, with just three of its teams melding into the NFL. The Yankees weren't among them, so their players went into a pool from which existing NFL teams could draft them. The 1949 Giants had allowed 298 points to opposing offenses and needed help, so they drafted three defensive backs from the Yankees—Carl Schnellenbacher, one of the most underrated defenders of his era, along with Harmon Rowe and Landry. They also drafted defensive tackle Arnie Weinmeister, who would end up in the Pro Football Hall of Fame. Giants coach Steve Owen would use the newcomers to create the nucleus of his "umbrella" defense and revive the team's fortunes. In 1950, the season the Yankee reinforcements arrived, the Giants' yield of points to the opposition shrank to 150, half the previous season's total. Late in his career, 1953–1954, Landry became a playing coach, and when he retired, the Giants made him the full-time defensive coach.

When the expansion Cowboys hired him as their first head coach, the 1960 draft had already been held, which meant he had no input into his pioneer class of rookies. The expansion veterans were, for the most part, the usual batch of retreads and has-beens. The only game Landry's team didn't lose in that first season was a tie with the Giants, his old club. Lombardi was luckier. When he was hired by Green Bay in 1959, there was a great deal of talent on the roster despite the Packers' record of one victory, one tie, and ten losses in the previous season. The players he inherited included six future Hall of Famers—Ringo, Hornung, Taylor, Forrest Gregg,

Bart Starr, and Ray Nitschke. They and half a dozen others were the core of the team that dominated the early to mid-1960s. The cupboard had not been bare, but it was Lombardi who drove that underperforming talent to greatness with his maddening demands and emotional appeals.

Landry's methods, despite his lack of talent in his first few seasons, never included emotions. "Emotions can cover up a lot of inadequacies," he said, "but in the end they always get in the way of performance. An emotional team can't stay that way consistently over a full season or even for a few games."

The 1966 NFL championship game was the fourth meeting between Lombardi and Landry's teams. The first was in Dallas's maiden season, won by the Pack, 41–7; the second, another Green Bay blowout, 45–21, in 1964. By the time they met for the third time, in 1965, the Cowboys were maturing but still lost, 13–3. When they met in the 1966 title game, both teams were rolling, Green Bay with a five-game winning streak and Dallas having won five of its last six.

The game established any future Dallas–Green Bay meeting as a potential classic, an event not to be missed. It also cemented Starr's greatness into pro football's archives. The Packers took an early 14–0 lead on a Starr touchdown pass and rookie Jim Grabowski's fumble return, but the Cowboys, playing before their home crowd, stormed back to within one point, 21–20, in the third quarter. It seemed that Starr had put Green Bay beyond reach with his third and fourth touchdown passes of the day, 16 yards to Boyd Dowler and 28 yards to Max McGee, but the Cowboys demonstrated their resilience again. First Don Meredith connected with Frank Clarke for a 68-yard touchdown, reducing Green Bay's lead to 34–27. Dallas's defense stopped the Packer offense, giving Meredith another chance, which he converted. With just 28 seconds remaining, Green Bay safety Tom Brown intercepted Meredith's pass in the end zone to send the Packers to Super Bowl I.

CHAPTER 14

The Precursor

They didn't call it the Super Bowl or even a championship game, because it wasn't. There was no national television. In 1950 television was mostly a matter of the *Texaco Star Theater* with Milton Berle; *Kukla, Fran, and Ollie*, starring a one-toothed, stuffed dragon; and a lot of professional wrestling, a megadraw if "Gorgeous George" was on the card.

Still, it was the precedent for the clash between Green Bay and Kansas City at the end of the 1966 season. This September 1950 game between the NFL champion Philadelphia Eagles and the Cleveland Browns, who had won every championship in the four-year life of the rival All-America Football Conference, 1946–49, was the precursor for things to come.

The AAFC had collapsed nine months before, mostly because it had too many weak and ailing franchises, partly because the Browns had lapped the field from the moment Paul Brown put the team together after he was mustered out of the Navy in 1946. Three of the eight teams were absorbed by the NFL—the San Francisco 49ers, the Baltimore Colts, and the Browns—in what was far more of a swallowing than a merger. Bert Bell, the commissioner of the NFL, made sure Cleveland was immediately matched against the Eagles, since the NFL was sure its best was far better than the best of the league that cost it millions of dollars and many first-rank players during their competition after the end of World War II. Cleveland was seen by the NFL coaches as strictly a "passing team," with quarterback Otto Graham throwing to his excellent ends, Dante Lavelli and Mac Speedie.

The game was a matter of rare scheduling, a Saturday night in Philadelphia's Municipal Stadium, which was not the Eagles' home under normal conditions. But baseball's Philadelphia Phillies and their Whiz Kids were making a run at the World Series for the first time since 1915, and venerable Connie Mack was in his final season managing the Philadelphia Athletics, so the Eagles' game was moved from Shibe Park. The weather was comfortably warm and the crowd huge—71,237. Before that night the largest crowd ever drawn by an Eagles' game was 38,230. The televising of a pro game nationally was fifteen months into the future, but every major city in America had at least two daily newspapers, some of the larger cities three or more, and even though pro football still lagged behind baseball, boxing, horse racing, and college football in popularity, the nation's sports sections were full of the Eagles-Browns game the week before the kickoff. Philadelphia was a heavy favorite.

The Browns and their AAFC brethren were the targets of the same sort of taunts, disparagements, and put-downs from the NFL as the AFL teams would be a football generation later. Greasy Neale, the Philadelphia coach, dismissed Cleveland as a "pass and trap" team that didn't match up to the Eagles' stellar defense, the "Suicide Seven"—the linemen and linebackers used in their 5-2 defense to hold opponents to 14 points or less in fourteen of their twenty-six games in the two previous seasons. Philly had eight shutouts in that stretch, including in the two NFL championship victories over the Los Angeles Rams and Chicago Cardinals. It was an era when coaches were not very cautious with their pregame remarks. Of the Browns, Neale said, "The high school kids are coming to play in the pros."

No NFL team, however, had experienced playing against a team prepared by Paul Brown, who had coached Ohio State to a national championship while in his early thirties, but had never coached in the NFL. As it turned out, Brown had quite a few lessons to teach the NFL. He had pioneered the practice of sending in plays to his quarterback by constantly shuttling "messenger" guards back and forth; was the first to give intelligence tests to his players, so that his roster would be full of men less prone to mistakes; pioneered the draw play with Marion Motley; was the first to emphasize classroom work; and introduced the study of film to prepare for an opponent, while reducing the importance of intrasquad scrimmages. "Scrimmaging," he said, "is what a coach does when he doesn't know what else to do." His passing game with Graham at the controls was the most sophisticated in football, using timing patterns with the great quarterback throwing to a preordained spot before the receiver had even made his break. Thirty years later some of its elements would be an important part of the West Coast offense. Bill Walsh, who popularized the West Coast passing attack with San Francisco and quarterback Joe Montana, had worked for Brown as an assistant with the Cincinnati Bengals in the late 1960s.

The Browns had also received a vital transfusion of talent from their former league, which Paul Brown put to good use. When the NFL owners rejected the application of the Buffalo Bills' owner, Jim Breuil, Breuil purchased 25 percent of the Cleveland franchise with the stipulation that he could bring three of his best players with him. They were guard Abe Gibron, defensive tackle John Kissell, and speedy halfback Rex Bumgardner. When the remaining players whose AAFC teams went out of business were placed into a draft pool, the Browns selected two helpful ones—Bills linebacker Hal Herring and Len Ford of the Los Angeles Dons, whom Paul Brown converted from offense to defensive end, launching a Hall of Fame career. When Cleveland lined up against the Eagles on that balmy September night Gibron, Kissell, Herring, Bumgardner, and Ford were in the starting lineup.

The last two seasons of the AAFC had become such a cakewalk for Cleveland that Brown found time in a number of practice sessions to work on offensive plays and special defenses against the

116

two-time NFL champions, the Eagles, in anticipation of a possible merger between the leagues. The merger never happened, but the NFL's "swallowing" of its rival did and Brown put his game plan to work as soon as he opened his training camp.

"That's what gave them a real edge," said Chuck Bednarik, Philadelphia's all-time great linebacker, in a 2004 interview with Don Bostrom of the *Allentown Morning Call*. "That's why now they scout you when you go to the bathroom. They did things we had never seen before. They shifted into different formations. They sent backs in motion. It did confuse us very much."

Brown's first idea was to set up his running game with Graham's accurate passing. He correctly decided that the Eagles would try to knock Speedie and Lavelli out of their pass routes before they even got off the line of scrimmage—Philly's usual form of double coverage. That defensive strategy was foiled immediately when Brown put Bumgardner in motion, forcing single coverage on Speedie and Lavelli. It also forced Russ Craft, the Eagles' All-Pro cornerback, into single coverage on the Browns' tall running back, Dub Jones, who wasn't yet recognized as the most dangerous pass-receiving back in football.

By the time the Eagles had adjusted to the motion, the Browns changed that device and started using a more subtle spacing of its offensive linemen, luring the Philly defensive linemen to set up wider than normal, which did two things: It isolated the Eagles' nose tackle and created holes for Cleveland's great fullback, Motley. The game had started at a fever pitch, with a number of roughing penalties called and Philadelphia guard John Magee ejected from the game in the first quarter. The NFL bunch and the AAFC upstarts didn't like each other, an atmosphere that would be repeated on a much wider stage sixteen years later in the Los Angeles Coliseum. The Browns also had four touchdowns called back because of infractions. For the rest of his life, Brown swore those infractions were undetectable on the films of the game.

The Eagles opened the scoring with a field goal, and it seemed they were taking command of the game from the start. Graham, however, was probing. When he felt the time was right, he sent Jones after Craft, and the big back gave the coverage man such a feint that it caused Craft's legs to become crossed. Jones was 10 yards beyond the coverage when he caught Graham's pass for a 59-yard touchdown. The rout was on as Graham threw two more touchdown passes, totaled an astounding 346 yards in the air, and scored a touchdown himself in a 35–10 bludgeoning. "It was like trying to cover three Don Hutsons," Craft told Bostrom in reference to Speedie, Lavelli, and Jones. "Impossible." Hutson, the great Green Bay star of the 1930s and early 1940s, was the gold standard for NFL receivers until Jerry Rice came along half a century later.

What life was left of the Eagles' defense was pounded out of them by Marion Motley. "Marion Motley was like a tank," said Bednarik, the man they called "Concrete Charley" and the last of the sixty-minute pros, players who played both offense and defense. "He was the toughest guy I've ever tried to tackle," he continued. "That was one of the worst lickings I've ever took. Usually I'd only need a day or two to shake off a loss. That one was different. I still relive some of the plays. If . . . if . . . if . . ."

Neale was far less gracious than his players. "Brown would have made a better basketball coach because all they do is put the ball in the air," said the Eagles' coach. Brown didn't reply, but when the teams met in Cleveland in the rematch later in the season, Cleveland won again, 13–7, without throwing a single pass.

Cleveland sailed through its first season in the NFL losing only twice to the Giants, whose defense, buttressed by the addition of AAFC stars Weinmeister, Schellenbacher, Rowe, and Landry, smothered Graham. The NFL championship game was a showdown with the present Cleveland team, the Browns, playing the former Cleveland team, the Rams, who left the Ohio city for Los Angeles after winning the 1945 NFL title. The Browns won in the final seconds on Lou Groza's 16-yard field goal, making him and his teammates $11,116 richer.

A strange thing happened to pro football after Cleveland won the clash of champions against Philadelphia: The nation's sports fans went back to yawning over the sport. The Browns' attendance told the disappointing story. In 1946, the team's first year in existence against unfamiliar names in the new AAFC, the team averaged crowds of more than 53,000 in Cleveland Municipal Stadium. When they won the 1950 championship in the first year of the revamped and expanded NFL, they averaged fewer than 30,000 fans. Television had not yet become pro football's partner.

CHAPTER 15

Vince's Crusade

It was January in Green Bay, not a time for beach umbrellas, but Vince Lombardi had two weeks before his Packers would face the Kansas City Chiefs in Super Bowl I, and he decided that his team was going to spend the first week at home, even if it meant forgoing a week in what might have been a more hospitable climate. He tried that in late December before the NFL championship game against the Cowboys in Dallas. The Packers had traveled to Tulsa, Oklahoma, to get in some quality practice time in civilized conditions. The weather was miserable, with freezing temperatures, an icy outdoor field, and unsatisfactory working conditions. He finally had to move the practices to an indoor facility, which he could have done in Wisconsin.

So the Packers and their coach stayed home that first week, but sleeping in his own bed did not improve Lombardi's disposition. He was confident that his team would defeat Kansas City, but the alternative was unthinkable. Honor was at stake: the honor of the Packers, the honor of the NFL, and, possibly most important, his personal honor. The constant thought of that honor despoiled put him in a cranky mood and brought out his worst side—rude, abusive, nagging, and unreasonable.

America's sporting public was more relaxed and assured. The legal bookmakers in Nevada had made Green Bay a 13-point favorite. The press was depicting the Chiefs-Packers matchup as a replay of David and Goliath. The adage that "nobody loves Goliath" wasn't true in this case. A poll featured in *Sports Illustrated* indicated that most sports fans were pulling for Goliath to cram that slingshot down David's craw.

One week before the big game, the Packers set up their West Coast headquarters in Santa Barbara, California, in sight of the Pacific Ocean, in warm comforting weather and far enough away from the bustle of Los Angeles. Yet even the famed beauty of Santa Barbara could not calm Lombardi. For him it was no midwinter break. He had too much on his mind; as he described it later, "We have not much to win and everything to lose." Pete Rozelle was closer to Lombardi than any coach in his realm. The commissioner had seen him in all manner of conditions. "I never saw Vince so anxious as he was before Super Bowl I," Rozelle said.

Lombardi may have been permanently on the edge of his seat but the football fans of America weren't. The prospect of exchanging the cold and snow of the East and Midwest for warm weather in the nation's entertainment capitol captured surprisingly few imaginations. Tickets priced at $6, $10, and $12 weren't much of an inducement. The legal betting rooms in Nevada had opened their odds at 14 points in favor of Green Bay. That number didn't move until the day before the game and then by a mere fraction, dropping to 13½ points. The fans didn't believe in the American Football League or its champions, the Chiefs. Los Angeles Coliseum, which had welcomed crowds over 100,000 in the 1950s before its size was reduced to accommodate baseball's Dodgers, would be a third empty by kickoff time. Photographs taken of the game from field level showed what seems like acres of sparsely populated sections of the stadium, something that would never occur in any Super Bowl to follow.

Press forecasts about what might happen in the game generally broke along partisan lines. The war between the leagues had been so bitter that it seemed journalistic objectivity had been suspended for the duration. The coaches and other club people were more circumspect in their statements than Greasy Neale of the Eagles and other NFL people had been when Philadelphia, the defending NFL champion, met Cleveland, the interloper champion of the defunct

121

All-America Football Conference, in the opening game of the 1950 season when the Cleveland Browns, San Francisco 49ers, and Baltimore Colts were allowed into the established league as remnants from the AAFC. Before the first Super Bowl, the press from NFL cities and national outlets were not so constrained. The same sort of put-downs that had described the Browns before their landmark victory over the Eagles had been used to describe the AFL champions before Super Bowl I—a "cheese champion from a Mickey Mouse League," as described by the *Washington Post*.

For an objective judgment from authoritative sources, the *Buffalo Evening News* interviewed six NFL coaches who previously worked in the AFL. These were their comments.

Tom Catlin, the Los Angeles Rams' defensive coach who held the same position with the Chiefs the previous season:

> *I don't expect Kansas City to win, but it's not at all possible that they might . . . they would have to play an almost perfect game . . . the Green Bay defense creates situations in which you make mistakes and you almost never play a perfect game.*
>
> *Bart Starr got caught several times in the Dallas game, but he realizes that a quarterback will be dropped three to five times a game, so he doesn't get upset. . . . We [the Rams] made them fumble 10 times in two games. We recovered eight times, but they didn't rattle.*
>
> *Kansas City has a variety of offenses, but I don't believe the Chiefs use as many formations as Dallas. . . . Green Bay, like Buffalo, does a solid job of reacting to basic formations. I thought Kansas City's idea of shifting from the 'I' worked well to slow up the time the Bills had to figure things out. It might work against Green Bay, too.*
>
> *Green Bay has an excellent pass rush, but Len Dawson is a lot like Starr. He's very deliberate, needs time and won't*

throw the ball away. . . . The moving pocket they used against Buffalo might help Dawson again.

Red Miller, offensive coach of the St. Louis Cardinals and former assistant with Buffalo and Denver:

The quarterbacks should settle the issue. . . . I don't see one team overpowering the other. . . . Green Bay plays well under pressure . . . their poise will help them a lot . . . the difference is not as great as some people are saying. . . . In my estimation one game isn't a true test. I think when we play a lot of exhibition games against the AFL teams next summer it will bear me out.

Pop Ivy, defensive coach of the Giants and former head coach of the Houston Oilers:

I think Green Bay will definitely win and by at least two touchdowns. . . . Green Bay has the best defense and more experience. . . . I realize Kansas City has a lot of variety on offense, but no one has more variety than the Dallas Cowboys.
If they played five games, I'd pick Green Bay to win four . . . the little things that happen in a pro football game could mean a three-to-four touchdown difference in the Super Bowl, too.

Chuck Noll, defensive coach of the Baltimore Colts who held the same position with the San Diego Chargers the season before:

I saw Kansas City shift out of the 'I' against Buffalo in the AFL championship game. I don't think it will bother Green Bay. I say that because we shift on every play in every game and it hasn't bothered the Packers so far.

123

If you blitz Green Bay you get to Bart Starr occasionally, but from my experience, I'd say the Packers do a pretty good job of picking up the blitz. . . . Starr needs a lot of time and he has good protection. . . . Kansas City could score on Green Bay, but I don't think the Chiefs will beat them . . . but maybe that's pride talking because we weren't able to beat them.

Bones Taylor, defensive coach of the Steelers and former head coach of the Houston Oilers and assistant with the New York Titans:

I think Kansas City has a fine chance to win. I don't see any real difference in the football in the leagues. . . . I think Kansas City has the best overall personnel. . . . They'll play it just like any other game.

The Minnesota Vikings made Bobby Bell their No. 1 draft choice a couple years ago. Just because he signed with the Chiefs does that make him any less a player? Am I a better coach because I'm in the NFL now? No sir.

Carl Taseff, defensive coach of the Detroit Lions, formerly defensive coach of the Boston Patriots:

Green Bay doesn't make big mistakes and that's important in a game like this. . . . In the NFC championship game, I think there were five penalties. Four of them were called on Dallas. That's what I mean by not making big mistakes.

The Packers have no overall weakness. They come up with the big play and their mental attitude is always the best. To me, that's 90 percent of the game. . . . Maybe the score will be lopsided, but I don't think Kansas City will be steamrolled. . . . They're a fine team.

No big mistakes . . . poise . . . they don't get rattled.

Without mentioning his name, those six coaches were talking about the coaching of Vince Lombardi. Before he even landed in California to prepare for the game, he was the game's central figure. Lombardi *was* the Packers.

As soon as the Packers reached Santa Barbara, the letters came rolling in from the owners of all the NFL franchises. It was clear to Lombardi that this wasn't just an important football game but a crusade, and he was leading it. He read some of these letters to his players, especially those from George Halas of the Chicago Bears and Wellington Mara of the New York Giants. "Papa Bear" Halas had virtually invented the National Football League. Mara was a teenager when his father, Tim, founded the Giants. Wellington Mara was such an important part of the league that inscribed on the official football of the NFL was THE DUKE, which was Mara's nickname. Lombardi wanted the Packers to keep in mind that they were defending a grand tradition.

Among football coaches, to affix the label "He's a politician" to a fellow coach means that he is voraciously ambitious and will conduct himself like a campaigning politician to reach his goal of a head job. Some of the greatest head coaches in football have been "politicians," those who as assistants endeared themselves to not only their own head coaches but to other head coaches, general managers, and especially the media. Rising in the field of coaching is difficult to do for anyone who prefers to "hide his light under a bushel." Making themselves and their good reputations known to owners and others who do the hiring is essential to getting a job interview, much less a job. There never has been a more political assistant football coach than Vince Lombardi.

I met Vince Lombardi for the first time in Palo Alto, California, on December 8, 1961, at Rickey's Hyatt House. The Packers were on their traditional, season-ending two-game trip to the West Coast to play in San Francisco and Los Angeles. As the pro football beat reporter for the *Buffalo Courier-Express*, I was in town to cover the

Buffalo Bills' two-game West Coast trip in Oakland and San Diego. It may have been the only time NFL and AFL teams stayed in the same hotel at the same time. The reason was simple: When its own football season was over, Stanford University allowed visiting pro teams to use its top-of-the-line practice facilities in preparation for their next games. Rickey's, a sprawling place that featured individual cottages, was more resort than mere hotel.

That evening, after I had driven to San Francisco to put my newspaper copy in the hands of the Western Union office down at the wharf, I returned to Rickey's to dine alone. As I was finishing, I saw Vince and Marie Lombardi sitting in a booth across the dining room. I sent a note to Lombardi with my waiter, asking if I could buy a drink for him and his wife since we had a mutual friend, Rick Marcotte from Winooski Park, Vermont. Lombardi befriended Marcotte when the Giants trained at St. Michael's College in the 1950s. Marcotte and I became friends during his internship at my newspaper.

To my surprise Lombardi himself walked over to my table, not only accepting the offer of drinks but also inviting me to join him and Marie at their table. Green Bay was on a four-game winning streak and on its way to a second consecutive Western Division championship. The coach was engaging and downright charming. He told a few warm stories of his days at West Point with Red Blaik, the Cadets' legendary coach. Then he asked where I had gone to college. Like Lombardi, I was a product of a Jesuit college, in my case Canisius College in Buffalo.

Lombardi chuckled ruefully. "Canisius was the disappointment of my career," he explained. "In 1947, their coach, Earl Brown, was hired by Auburn as its new head coach, and I wanted that Canisius job. I came to Buffalo, interviewed, and thought I had it. Instead, they hired some lawyer who had been the head coach years before." A day or so later, I wrote a small story, in newspaper parlance a sidebar to a notes column about the Lombardi-Canisius near-connection

126

and how attorney Jimmy Wilson had beaten him out for the job. At the time, Lombardi and Green Bay were a nice success story, but the Packers had lost to Philadelphia in the NFL championship game the previous year, so he wasn't the megacelebrity he was to become. Twenty days later his team humiliated the Giants, 37–0, and his days as a famed celebrity had begun.

By the time Lombardi reached Santa Barbara to prepare his team for the first Super Bowl, he was a changed man. Four league championships in six seasons had elevated him to a figure of national prominence, and Green Bay and most of Wisconsin were his fiefdom. He called almost all the shots in his daily life, including such a mundane thing as getting a haircut: after hours, doors locked, shades drawn, no conversation. As for media coverage, it was not a good career move for a local reporter to ask tough questions of the man who had breathed life into the Packer corpse eight seasons ago. Whatever treatment went beyond kid gloves usually came from Milwaukee, where the Pack still played a portion of its home games.

In 1963 I left the *Courier-Express* to join the *Buffalo Evening News*. When we arrived in California for Super Bowl week, my colleague, Steve Weller, asked if I would be doing an expanded, updated version of my Lombardi-Canisius story of five years before. I told him I wasn't planning on a reprise, so he was welcome to it. A day later I saw Weller in our hotel lobby and asked if he had spoken to Lombardi about his Canisius disappointment. "I did," Weller replied, "but Lombardi denied it ever happened, and he was hot about my asking. He said he had never been turned down for the Canisius job or any other job in his career."

Lombardi had become so much larger than life that he couldn't bring himself to admit that he once had frustrations or disappointments in his career. His denial came even though it was well known that Jim Lee Howell, his boss with the Giants, and Blaik, for whom he coached the Plebe team with Army, had often written letters of recommendation on his behalf for head-coaching jobs.

Particularly galling was his failure to get the vacant head job at West Point when Blaik retired. It went to Dale Hall, one of Blaik's former players.

There was another incident in the press briefing room in which Lombardi revealed himself as an insecure martinet on edge about a game in which his team was heavily favored. It occurred when he was being questioned about Kansas City's personnel, and his answers were full of praise and knowledge of the opposition. Then one question concerned whether he thought Buck Buchanan, the Chiefs' enormous defensive lineman was a premier player. "Of course I do," said Lombardi, snappishly. "I drafted him, didn't I?"

Up shot the arm of Tom Marshall, a small, soft-spoken sportswriter for the *Kansas City Star*, a man liked and admired by his peers for his solid reporting. "You didn't draft Buchanan in the NFL," Marshall corrected. "The New York Giants did."

Lombard exploded. "Are you trying to tell me who I drafted and who I didn't?" he loudly demanded.

Marshall stood his ground. "No. It wasn't Buchanan you drafted," said the writer, attempting to set the record straight, "you're probably confusing him with another Grambling defensive lineman you drafted, Alphonse Dotson." There was a further Lombardi explosion, while his aides, who knew Marshall was completely right but weren't about to tell their boss, shifted uneasily from foot to foot. Minutes later the press briefing ended, and Lombardi angrily stalked off the stage.

One of the Green Bay staffers must have summoned the nerve to tell Lombardi he was wrong, because the next day the coach asked Marshall to step into a side room where he apologized to him. The dressing-down had been in public, but the apology took place in private. Still, it was an apology.

Their coach might have been uptight, but the Green Bay players came to Santa Barbara relaxed and stayed that way. If a member of the media missed the official briefing with the Packers or needed something more, all that person had to do was pick up the lobby phone in the players' hotel and call his room. Minutes later Bart Starr and his roommate might be sweeping away the jockstraps from the beds, the interviewers would sit down, and there would be a conversation. Along with unsold tickets, that sort of media access would evaporate with Super Bowl I. The Los Angeles Coliseum press box accommodated all the credential print media along with NFL and AFL staff members, coaches of several other teams, politicians, and assorted celebrities. A few years later main press boxes in Super Bowl stadiums would bulge with more than 1,000 writers and broadcasters, a first auxiliary press box with 500 more members of the working press, and a second auxiliary press box with 500 more, mostly members of the international media.

The Friday night before Super Bowl I, Pete Rozelle held the first of what became an annual Commissioner's Party. Owners, front-of-fice staff, key media, and their spouses easily fit into a ballroom in a downtown Los Angeles hotel. The entertainment was Les Brown's Band of Renown, the house orchestra for Bob Hope's television show. The Commissioner's Party would evolve into gatherings of 3,000 or more, with bands of every sound playing and dancers, stilt walkers, clowns, and impersonators of Hollywood stars roaming a convention hall floor. The annual caterer seemed to be Bacchus himself.

At the first Commissioner's Party, the trappings were modest. There was an ice sculpture and a wedding cake, symbolizing the marriage of the NFL and the AFL. At the entrance to the room, young women from Rozelle's staff bore baskets of corsages and bouton-nieres. Wives of NFL owners and personnel had red rose corsages pinned on their dresses, while the men received red boutonnieres. The corsages and boutonnieres for the AFL women and men were white. The media, presumed to be unbiased, went flowerless until

Tex Maule of *Sports Illustrated*, an NFL adherent, arrived. Maule picked up a red boutonniere and unabashedly affixed it to his lapel. After dinner, Rozelle and a few other notables said a few words. Finally, an AFL wife commandeered the microphone and shouted, "Go, Chiefs!" The NFL contingent sat quietly disapproving.

CHAPTER 16

Goliath Beats David

Seven years of challenges and put-downs, of "yes, we cans" and "no, you can'ts" volleying back and forth between the warring leagues, were minutes away from a climax as the Green Bay Packers and the Kansas City Chiefs came out of their dressing room and down the tunnel of the Los Angeles Coliseum to be introduced. Words were suspended and actions were about to begin.

"Guys were puking and pissing in their pants," admitted E. J. Holub, the Kansas City linebacker. Out on the field Vince Lombardi was in no mood for distractions as the coach awaited his players at the Packer bench, but broadcaster Frank Gifford, the former Giants' star, played the longtime friendship card with Lombardi, his old offensive coach, and was granted an interview. Years later Gifford would recall, "We talked for almost five minutes, and all that time he gripped my arm and shook like a leaf."

Curiously, the Green Bay players didn't seem nervous at all. Why should they have been? Twenty-eight members of their core roster had played in at least two NFL championship games during the Lombardi era. Nine of the starters had been Packers before Lombardi arrived, and they had played in all five championship games during the Lombardi era, four of which were victories. In addition thirteen were members of the team before the AFL was founded. The Green Bay roster included six who would eventually be inducted into the Pro Football Hall of Fame: quarterback Bart Starr, running backs Paul Hornung and Jimmy Taylor, offensive tackle Forrest Gregg, linebacker Ray Nitschke, and defensive tackle Henry Jordan. Half the Kansas City starters had just three or fewer seasons' experience.

The most intense pressure on the Packers came from the NFL elders, most of whom sent messages to them before the game, urging them to successfully defend the honor of the NFL that had been in business four decades before the AFL purchased a football. The most impassionate and curious message of all came from George Halas, founder and paterfamilias of the Chicago Bears, Green Bay's most bitter rival. The Bears and the Packers had been at each other's throats since the Bears began as the Decatur Staleys, and their archenemies were the founding Indian Packing Co. Packers. Once, in the 1970s, Bob Hope, then one of the most famous entertainers in show business, was playing Chicago and received an invitation from Halas to attend Sunday's game in his private box on the roof of Wrigley Field. "When I arrived at the box suites," recalled Hope, "I was taken to a box next to the one occupied by Halas and his son, Muggs. I found out why they weren't sitting with me as soon as the game started. They began screaming all sorts of obscenities down at the officials and the opposing players and never stopped. I guess they were protecting my innocent ears, but everyone on the roof heard whatever they had to say." On Sundays when the Bears played the Packers the obscenities were louder and rawer. Now, with the Super Bowl hours away, Halas was a Packer supplicant, asking his rivals to save the league from an enormous black eye.

If the Chiefs had not shaken their nervousness after the kickoff, it didn't show on the field as they defended against Green Bay's first series of downs. Starr's first three passes resulted in completions, then a sack for a 10-yard loss by Buck Buchanan and another sack by Jerry Mays and Bobby Bell for a loss of five. Kansas City reached Green Bay's side of the field on its possession, then stalled, in part because of a damaging delay-of-game penalty. The first two series were like boxers probing each other in Round 1.

On the second Green Bay series, Starr put Lombardi's game plan into motion. The coach's signature play was the Packer sweep, a maneuver of almost delicate precision and power that pounded a long list of past opponents into submission. In this game, Lombardi decided, a surer path to success was to throw the ball. The Packers knew the Kansas City roster contained a number of skilled defensive players such as Bell, Buchanan, Mays, and safety Johnny Robinson. They also knew the defensive unit contained some flawed players, such as cornerbacks Fred Williamson and Willie Mitchell. Holub came into a different category. He was an outstanding player, but probably out of position as a pro. He had been an All-America at Texas Tech, playing both linebacker and center, but he had a series of surgeries to correct knee injuries, leading him to explain the scars on his knees by claiming, "I had a knife fight with a midget." Those past knee injuries sometimes cost him a step when he was blitzing, but the Chiefs had to play him as a linebacker out of necessity.

What Lombardi had impressed on Starr from the moment the game plan was unveiled was, "I want you to pass, and then pass some more. Don't be afraid to change the play when you see the right setup." What Starr knew to look for were the Kansas City linebackers set up inside their own tackles. Lombardi was confident that in that defensive set, the Chiefs would be unable to cover the Green Bay receivers well. On the Packers' second possession they began their 80-yard drive with a running play, and then Starr passed on four of the next five downs. The first went to tight end Marv Fleming for 11 yards; then Starr connected with running back Elijah Pitts, who was playing in place of Hornung who would not be used at all on his final day as a Packer, for 22 yards; and finally 12 yards to Carroll Dale, who beat Williamson.

That gave Green Bay a first down on the Chiefs' 37-yard line, and Max McGee was about to become the pioneer Super Bowl legend. McGee wasn't even supposed to play. Boyd Dowler, the starting wide receiver, had been the first player introduced in Super Bowl history, and he was the first injured. He separated his shoulder while attempting to block Johnny Robinson early in the game. That's when

McGee got the call. He was thirty-four years old and had announced he was retiring after the game, although he would later change his mind. He had caught just four passes during the regular season, so it became lost in his Super Bowl heroics that he had caught the winning touchdown pass against Dallas that put the Packers into Super Bowl I. When the Packers came to the line of scrimmage against the Chiefs, McGee saw the same thing Starr saw: Kansas City tipping their plans to blitz. McGee adjusted his route; Starr just barely avoided Buchanan as he threw. The ball was slightly behind McGee, and it appeared likely Mitchell could intercept, but McGee reached back, made a remarkable catch, and outran the pursuing Williamson to the end zone for a 14–7 Packer lead.

If Green Bay's 80-yard drive had not provided enough of a jolt to their confidence, the Chiefs gave up an 8-yard sack of Dawson to Lionel Aldridge and Jordan on the first play of their next series. But the Chiefs didn't rattle either, at least not yet. Dawson got up off the ground to complete three straight first-down passes—12 yards to tight end Fred Arbanas, 11 to Otis Taylor, and 27 to wide receiver Chris Burford—and the Chiefs were at Green Bay's 32-yard line. The drive stalled, but Mike Mercer's field goal sent Kansas City into the dressing room at halftime, trailing a 13-point favorite by a mere 4 points.

In the Green Bay dressing room, Lombardi was calm, assuring his players, "We'll be all right; we just have to tweak a few things." Bart Starr had seen him in a calm state in the midst of a close, nerve-fraying game before. "I saw him just as calm in a game where we trailed Detroit at halftime and he was a same way, telling us 'we're not going to change a thing,'" Starr said. Both the coach and his quarterback knew that the vulnerability of the Kansas City corners would likely yield more yardage. Williamson especially was a target. Stram had spent the weeks before the game cautioning his players not to arouse the Packers with any bravado. Williamson, an excellent athlete who had some good days as well as indifferent ones during his career, saw it differently. "We're makin' a mistake being all meek and humble," he said. "I want to worry them. I'm telling them that I'm gonna lay 'the hammer' on 'em." Williamson's "hammer" was his right forearm with which he leveled a few opposing receivers in the AFL. When Williamson began talking to the press about "layin' the hammer on 'em," it produced some light moments in the Green Bay camp the week before the game. Free safety Willie Wood began running around swinging a knotted sock at his teammates, saying, "It's the hammer!"

Over in Kansas City's room, Dawson was thinking to himself, *We could win this game.* There was food for that kind of thinking. The Chiefs had reached Packer territory on all four of their possessions so the favorites didn't appear to be invincible. Four plays into the second half, that illusion vanished.

The third quarter started well enough for Kansas City. Dawson evaded Dave Robinson and scrambled 15 yards for a first down. Two short runs and the Chiefs were 2 yards from a fifth straight trip to the Packers' side of the field. On third-and-5, Dawson set up to pass, with Arbanas the intended target. Then the Green Bay defense did something unfamiliar. For the first time in the game they executed a tactic Lombardi normally disdained: they blitzed. With linebackers Lee Roy Caffey and Dave Robinson converging on him, Dawson's pass wobbled. Arbanas was being covered by Wood. "I knew the man was blind in one eye," Wood told Dave Brady of the *Washington Post*, "so I overplayed him to his blind side."

Wood was correct. When Lamar Hunt moved Dallas's AFL franchise to Kansas City, the downtown district of the southern Missouri city was a dangerous place, with nightclubs and honky-tonks often patronized by thugs and controlled by the mob. Arbanas had been attacked on the street and blinded in the beating. When Dawson's pass made its way toward Arbanas's blind side, Wood intercepted and streaked downfield for 50 yards until Mike Garrett, a fellow USC Trojan, tackled him on the Kansas City 5-yard line.

It was time for the Packers' ground game. Hornung had missed a major portion of the season because of a pinched nerve in his neck, so Pitts had played more than at any time in his career and did well. He had come into pro football as an unknown free agent, but then so was his college, little Philander Smith in Arkansas, an unknown. There was a joke among the Wisconsin media: "Is it Elijah Pitts from Philander Smith or Philander Smith from Elijah Pitts?" A man with a sweet disposition, Pitts experienced a culture shock in Green Bay when he arrived, finding himself surrounded by big-name stars and living in a bigger city.

When Henry Jordan spoke to groups, he always got a laugh out of the crowd by describing Lombardi as a coach "who treats us all the same; like dogs." It was funny but inaccurate. Lombardi had a sound understanding of players who were out of the mainstream. When he went to coach the Washington Redskins, Larry Brown was a marginal running back who in college had been mainly a blocking back for Kansas State's tiny star, Mack Herron. Brown often blew calls in the huddle, but instead of getting angry, Lombardi asked if Brown's hearing had ever been tested. The answer was no. After he was fitted with devices to amplify voices, Brown eventually became a major star. In Pitts's case, Lombardi understood his original loneliness in Green Bay and was kind to him. "The coach made me feel at home," Pitts often said.

As a football player, Pitts always knew his way to the end zone, no matter how he was used. As Hornung's fill-in in 1966, he scored ten touchdowns, seven on the ground and three on receptions. The play after Woods's interception, Pitts followed the blocks of left tackle Bob Skoronski and left guard Fuzzy Thurston into the end zone. After Don Chandler kicked the extra point the score was 21–10, Green Bay's favor, and Super Bowl I was effectively over. The Chiefs made it to Green Bay territory just once for the rest of the game. That was in the middle of the fourth quarter when Pete

Beathard was at quarterback in place of Dawson, a sign of concession by Hank Stram. Beathard was then sacked for a 15-yard loss
by Tom Brown, and the Chiefs never crossed the 50-yard line again.
The Green Bay ground attack would bludgeon the Chiefs for the rest
of the afternoon and Pitts added his second short-yardage touchdown, the last of the game. Fred Williamson, who later became an
actor in action movies, would suffer one last indignity. Coming up to
meet a running play, Williamson was knocked out cold when Donny
Anderson's knee collided with his head, and then the Chiefs' cornerback suffered a broken arm when teammate Sherrill Headrick fell on
him. As Williamson lay on the ground, Packer guard Fuzzy Thurston
quietly hummed a few bars of "If I Had a Hammer."

The final score was 35–10. As the Packers jogged up the Coliseum tunnel, some of the Packers were jokingly shouting, "Buffalo!
Buffalo!" During one of the media sessions the previous week, someone asked Stram if he could compare the Green Bay defense to any
in the AFL. "They remind me of Buffalo," said Stram, referring to the
Bills' tough defense. The Packers had taken his answer as an insult.
The honor of the NFL had been saved.

When Lombardi finally opened the door of the Green Bay dressing room to the media, the questions were less about the game itself
than how Lombardi rated the vanquished AFL champions: "How
do they rate with NFL teams?" "Are they ready to play in the big
leagues?" He feigned a reluctance to compare teams, grinning while
he held the game ball. "It's an NFL ball," Lombardi said. "It catches a
little better and kicks a little better than the AFL ball." Finally he did
compare Kansas City, not without some quiet relish: "Dallas is a better team. Kansas City is a good team, but they don't even rate with
some of the teams in our division. There. That's what you wanted
me to say, wasn't it?"

Over in the Kansas City room, Stram was talking to a group of
reporters when Will McDonough of the *Boston Globe* walked in.

He had been at Lombardi's press conference, and he told Stram what had been said. Stram was dumbfounded. "He didn't say that, did he, Will?" Stram asked. "Vince is a friend of mine. He wouldn't say that, would he?" Stram would brood about those words for seven months, and then George Halas, not Lombardi, would pay a price.

CHAPTER 17

Unfinished Business

The Green Bay Packers, businesslike in their customs, devoted little time to celebrating their Super Bowl victory. After returning from Los Angeles, the biggest news they made was the dissipation of talk that Vince Lombardi was stepping down as their coach. With both Paul Hornung and Jim Taylor about to become New Orleans Saints, Lombardi was busy planning for the introduction of youngsters Donny Anderson and Jim Grabowski into his starting offensive backfield. There was a testimonial dinner in Green Bay for departing heroes Hornung and Taylor. Lombardi was unable to attend, but he sent a telegram expressing fond memories of Hornung, referring to his unforgettable performances as a money player, especially inside the 20-yard line. The only reference in the telegram to Taylor was oblique with no mention of his name.

The vanquished Kansas City Chiefs spent little time licking their wounds, of rationalizing "what might have been." It is in the nature of football championship games to become alarmingly lopsided. Unlike the other major team sports—baseball, basketball, and hockey—there is no multiple-game series to decide a championship. It's customary to hear the expression "there is no tomorrow" when the series dwindles down to the final game. In football, the first meeting of conference champions is also the final game. and it's always a case of "there is no tomorrow." That is why one play, such as Willie Wood's devastating interception of Len Dawson early in the second half of Super Bowl I, shattered the composure of the Chiefs. One bad play can affect a team, infecting its collective thought processes with an "all-is-lost" outlook.

This was never more evident than in the 1940 NFL title game between the Washington Redskins and Chicago Bears. The Redskins had beaten the Bears, 7–3, in a late-season game, but George Halas, the Bears' owner-coach, imported the father of the T-formation, Stanford coach Clark Shaughnessy, as a guest instructor to install his offense into the Bears' game plan. On the second play from scrimmage, the Chicago fullback, Bill Osmanski, raced around left end for 68 yards and a touchdown. The blowout was on as the Bears intercepted eight passes from a team quarterbacked by the great Sammy Baugh and astounded the pro football world, 73–0.

A game that one-sided never happened again, but in the twelve NFL championship games before Super Bowl I, the outcome in half of them were outright runaways. In 1954 the Cleveland Browns beat the Detroit Lions, 56–10, and the next season, in Otto Graham's farewell as the team's quarterback, the Browns defeated the Los Angeles Rams, 38–14. Detroit gained a measure of revenge against Cleveland in 1957, when they won 59–24. The Baltimore Colts followed their famous overtime victory against the New York Giants in 1959 with a fourth-quarter explosion that gave them a victory over the Giants, 31–16. Lombardi won his first NFL title in 1961 with a 37–0 thrashing of the Giants, his hometown team. Blowouts were not unfamiliar during the AFL's short history either. The San Diego Chargers destroyed the Boston Patriots, 51–10, in 1963, and the Buffalo Bills traveled to San Diego to shut out the Chargers, 23–0, in 1965. It was small solace to the Chiefs, but at least they had prestigious company among losers.

American sports fans were quick to turn the page on the first Super Bowl. It was the year of the Philadelphia 76ers in the National Basketball Association, as the Boston Celtics' eight-year grip on the league title was in the process of ending. For those interested in hockey, the Toronto Maple Leafs were on their way to winning their final Stanley Cup of the twentieth century. In early February the baseball training camps opened, so most sports fans put football in a mental deep freeze for six months.

On March 14, 1967, pro football was adhering to the merger agreement between the leagues by conducting a common draft. The original football draft of college players had been devised in 1935 by Bert Bell, owner of the Philadelphia Eagles, in a move to strengthen the weaker teams in the NFL. Teams were to select players in reverse position of their standings in the league when the previous season finished; in other words, last picked first. It so happened that the awarding of the Heisman Trophy, honoring the name of famed coach John Heisman, began the same year. New York's Downtown Athletic Club, for whom Heisman served as athletic director, commissioned the trophy, which would go to the year's outstanding college football player. The winner was halfback Jay Berwanger of the University of Chicago, which fielded a strong football team in those days and was a member of the Big Ten. The Eagles made Berwanger the first player ever selected in the NFL draft. Bell was unable to sign Berwanger, so he traded his rights to the Chicago Bears. NFL people learned an important lesson with Berwanger's selection: Do your homework and be prepared. It turned out that Berwanger preferred a career in business rather than professional football. He didn't sign with the Bears either and never played pro football.

As it evolved through the years, the college draft proved to be one of the few aspects of sports in which counting your chickens before they're hatched and crossing bridges before you come to them is good business. In the beginning, scouting players was largely a matter of pro coaches cultivating friendships with their college counterparts so that reliable assessments of the top seniors could be obtained on a man-to-man basis. As late as the 1960s, currying favor with college coaches was extremely important. At the annual College All-Star game in Chicago, when the NFL champions met a team of the top collegians in early August, the Dallas Cowboys rented the largest suite in the Conrad Hilton Hotel to entertain big-name college coaches. The coaches would be met at the door by buxom hostesses wearing Dallas Cowboys' T-shirts. Less avant-garde organizations would carry copies of *Street & Smith*'s annual to the draft to guide them in their selections.

The most productive drafts were usually the work of teams that put money and careful hiring into the most efficient scouting organizations, which found ways to uncover the true speed, size, and medical history of the top prospects to whom rich bonuses might be paid. Even more astute franchises delved into the background and character of prospects. The value of scouts able to project how a player might fit—or not fit—into their organization's system, or who could make a determination that a physical limitation such as short arms on a defensive linemen would handicap that player's ability to keep blockers away from him, rose as scouting became more sophisticated. Al LoCasale, who left the San Diego Chargers to run the personnel department of Paul Brown's expansion Bengals in Cincinnati, put the value of efficient scouts succinctly: "I know who can play at Michigan State; I need someone to tell me who can play at Michigan Tech."

The common draft provided an opportunity for teams to build for their future without worrying about losing their draftees to the rival league. It was an opportunity, nothing more or less, and making maximum use of that opportunity depended on the skill of the talent appraisers and those making the decisions about where draft help was needed most. For instance, the Buffalo Bills, one of the strongest AFL teams coming into the 1966 season, needed help at a number of positions in order to remain contenders, as they had withdrawn from the dollar race for top talent in 1965 and 1966. Sweeping up two or three helpful players in the premium round of the common draft, rounds one through four, was vital. The Bills' decision-makers decided they needed a wide receiver to eventually replace aging Elbert "Golden Wheels" Dubenion; an outside linebacker to groom behind John Tracey; and a couple of young guards to develop.

The Bills, as AFL runners-up in 1966, drafted in the twenty-second slot in each round. In the first round, all the wide receivers who they felt were of premium quality had been drafted, so they took Arizona State safety John Pitts with the intention of switching him to wide receiver. In round two, they selected Utah State tight end Jim LeMoine with the intention of switching him to guard. In the third round, their choice was Notre Dame defensive end Tom Rhoads, whom they ticketed for linebacker; in the fourth, it was Gary Bugenhagen, a short, strong, and blocky offensive tackle who was All-America in Syracuse's system, which used an unbalanced line. The notion was to make Bugenhagen a guard. The idea of switching one player from his college position to another in the pros is considered risky. Deciding to switch the positions of your top four draft choices is outright folly. The Bills' first common draft was a disaster. The only player who turned out to be useful to Buffalo was Pitts, and only because he was returned to his normal position of safety. The Bills paid a heavy price for such bad decision-making. In 1967, for the first time in five years, they had a losing season, and they wouldn't have another winning year until 1973.

Many teams had better luck in the original common draft. New Orleans, as an expansion team, possessed the first selection, but in a deal that seemed part of a design for twenty years of losing, the Saints traded it to the Baltimore Colts. The Colts drafted mountainous defensive end Bubba Smith, whose work at Michigan State prompted the crowds in Spartan Stadium to cry, "Kill, Bubba! Kill!" The Minnesota Vikings, with the second selection acquired in a trade with the Giants, drafted Smith's Michigan State teammate, running back Clinton Jones. The San Francisco 49ers took the Heisman Trophy winner, Florida quarterback Steve Spurrier, with the third choice. The Miami Dolphins assured their future by taking another quarterback, Purdue's Bob Griese. Griese was the first of seven future Hall of Fame members from the common draft of 1966. With their own first-round selection, the Vikings picked Notre Dame defensive lineman Alan Page and two picks later, Oakland selected Texas A&I guard Gene Upshaw. Kansas City picked linebacker Willie Lanier, and Detroit took cornerback Lem Barney in the second round. Dallas came up with a seventh-round gem in offensive tackle Rayfield Wright and Houston selected another, safety Ken Houston, in the ninth.

Green Bay, as overall champion, picked last at twenty-fifth. As the result of a trade, the Packers had an extra first-round selection, but other than Travis Williams, a star kick returner whom they picked in the middle of the draft, the Packers did little to strengthen themselves. Kansas City, as overall second-place team, selected next to last. The Chiefs had two second-round choices and they used both on linebackers, Lanier of Morgan State and Jim Lynch of Notre Dame. Both would have a huge effect on the outcome of the next Super Bowl for which Kansas City would qualify, and Lanier would become the first common draft's fifth Hall of Famer.

The fans in Denver watched the common draft with great interest since the Broncos had signed none of their previous first-round selections, losing all to the NFL. In previous drafts Denver had picked future Hall of Famers Merlin Olsen, Dick Butkus, and Bob Brown, who might have been the key to formidable defenses and offensive lines; running back Kermit Alexander, who became a star in San Francisco; defensive end Ron McDole, who was chosen on both the Washington Redskins' and Buffalo Bills' all-time teams; and fullback Jerry Hill, of neighboring Wyoming University, a stalwart on the Colts' first Super Bowl team. But all the Bronco loyalists could do was reach for the antacids, as management was underfunded and couldn't afford to sign any of their top choices.

Lou Saban was general manager as well as head coach of the Broncos during the initial common draft. At one point he seemed intent on selecting Upshaw, but the idea of obtaining a great player who could also sell tickets to a disinterested public led him to use the sixth selection in the draft on Floyd Little, Syracuse's three-time All-America halfback. When Ben Schwartzwalder, the dour Syracuse coach, recruited Little out of New Haven, Connecticut, he was uncharacteristically jubilant. Someone asked the old World War II airborne commander what made him so giddy about his recruit. "When he walks in the snow," Schwartzwalder joked, "he's so smooth he doesn't leave footprints."

After they saw Little perform in a Syracuse victory over the University of Pittsburgh late in the 1965 season, both Weeb Ewbank and Sonny Werblin, the coach and managing general partner of the New York Jets, agreed with Schwartzwalder.

"Werblin told me I was the greatest college football player he had ever seen, and if I came to the Jets he would give me the same deal he gave Joe Namath," Little said four decades later. "Then came the merger and the common draft in 1967. The Jets told me that I had to convince two teams which drafted ahead of them that I was committed to New York, which wanted me because I was from New Haven, Connecticut, and played at Syracuse, so I would help them at the gate. One of the teams was Denver and Saban was supposed to be drafting Upshaw, but then he called Val Pinchbeck to talk about me. Val was working for Al Davis in AFL headquarters, but he had been the sports information director at Syracuse when I played there, and we were good friends. Saban asked him if he could build a team around me in Denver. Val told him, 'Sure, but I'm pretty sure he's committed to New York.' Saban told him, 'If he's as upstanding a man as you say, he wouldn't want to risk being declared ineligible for those games in his senior year, would he?' So he drafted me and I ended up in Denver."

Little came to the Broncos' in the midst of a ten-year victory drought, during which there was not a season when they won more than five games. In his first six seasons as a pro, Little had a different starting quarterback each year. Somehow Saban had become enamored of Steve Tensi, San Diego's inexperienced backup quarterback. Tensi had been drafted in the fourth round by the Chargers in 1965, but Saban traded two first-round choices to obtain him, even though the young quarterback had thrown only fifty-two passes and had a flimsy 40 percent completion rate in his only season of activity.

Tensi was the starter in Little's rookie year, but Saban's dissatisfaction with quarterbacks was legendary. Tensi was replaced with the undersize Marlin Briscoe the next season, then Tensi regained the starting job in 1969. Pete Liske was the starter in 1970 and Steve Ramsey in 1971.

Except for the merger and its resulting common draft, Little would never have been a Bronco in the first place. Chances were strong that he would have either been drafted by the Jets to keep him away from the NFL, or he would have signed with an NFL team of his liking. Those options vanished with the common draft.

Little came to enjoy Denver and the American West in general, but his football career never stabilized until John Ralston succeeded Saban as the Broncos head coach and traded with the St. Louis Cardinals for quarterback Charley Johnson. A stable quarterback wasn't the only asset missing from the Denver roster during Little's years. In his nine-year career, only one Denver lineman, offensive tackle Mike Current who came to the team in the same draft as Little, ever made it to a Pro Bowl. Consequently, for the first few years of his career, some of Little's best runs barely got him to the line of scrimmage.

He led the AFL in punt returns with a 16.9-yard average as a rookie and averaged 26.9 yards on thirty-five kickoff returns, but he scored only one touchdown from scrimmage and his per-carry average was less than 3 yards. Little didn't have a breakout season until 1970, the first year in which the former AFL and old NFL teams played an intertwined season. He gained 901 yards and averaged 4.3 yards from scrimmage. The next year he became the first Bronco to break 1,000 yards, leading the entire NFL with 1,133. In 1973 the Broncos managed their first winning season in fourteen years of existence as Little scored thirteen touchdowns and ran for 979 yards. He was thirty-two years old and about to go into decline.

Years later, when the Pro Football Hall of Fame's senior committee convened to pick a candidate who might have fallen through the

146

cracks in the regular elections, one of the consultants brought in to guide the committee members was Tom Landry, by then retired as coach of the Dallas Cowboys. When Little's name was brought up in what amounted to his last-ditch chance for enshrinement, Landry was asked what he thought of him. With furrowed brow the old coach thought hard and then admitted, "I'm sorry but I don't even remember him." The Cowboys and Broncos met only once during Little's career, in 1973, with Dallas winning the game, 22–10. When Landry made his assessment, the Hall of Fame chances of a player with Hall of Fame skills, yet mired for years with a losing team, vanished.

CHAPTER 18

Thin Revenge

When August 1967 arrived, another section of the 1966 merger kicked in, the one about preseason exhibition games being played between teams from the AFL and NFL. After the Green Bay Packers' victory in Super Bowl I, the majority of fans thought they knew what to expect, but there were a great many players and coaches who weren't so sure. Green Bay was not representative of the overall strength of the NFL's play; it was several cuts above. The rest of the NFL was on its own against largely unknown foes.

On Saturday night, August 5, the Denver Broncos, one of the AFL's most notorious bottom-feeders, was matched against the Detroit Lions, a team from the Packers' own division and probably one of the teams to which Vince Lombardi was referring when he said in his post–Super Bowl press conference that teams in Green Bay's own conference were superior to vanquished Kansas City. The game was played in the University of Denver Stadium to the usual slim summer crowd of 21,228. The Broncos were in one of their frequent quarterback quandaries, so Lou Saban, the new coach, started thinly experienced second-year pro Scotty Glacken, on whom the team had invested a thrifty seventh-round draft choice when he came out of Duke.

When the captains met at midfield for the coin toss, Dave Costa, Denver's defensive captain, extended his hand to Alex Karras, the Detroit Lions' All-Pro tackle and defensive captain. Karras eyed Costa's hand as if it was something found on the floor of a dog run, refusing to shake. "If we don't win this game," Karras said with a sneer, "I'll walk home to Detroit."

The game was not a thing of beauty except to the Broncos and their loyalists.

Denver had won only four games in the previous season, and Saban announced before the meeting with Detroit, "We want to win games," meaning he would play to win. Leading 3–0 in the third quarter, Denver was confronted by a fourth down and 11 yards to go on the Detroit 44. Instead of punting, Bob Scarpitto raced down the right sideline for 28 yards and a vital first down on the Lions' 16. Six plays later, Cookie Gilchrist, whose running had allowed the Broncos to control the ball for most of the game, powered his way to a touchdown, and as Denver held on to win, 13–7, for the first victory of any sort by an AFL team over an NFL team.

Karras was ejected from the game for kicking Bronco guard Pat Matson. For the next week Colorado radio stations made sport of Alex, announcing periodically that "Alex Karras has been spotted on the outskirts of Omaha," or "Karras was reported seen in a suburb of Cedar Rapids. . . ."

Thirteen nights later the Broncos played another game against an NFL team, the Minnesota Vikings, in Denver University Stadium, this time with a crowd 10,000 larger than had watched the upset over Detroit. The Broncos had been reinforced, since Floyd Little, their acclaimed first-round draft choice, had returned from the Chicago All-Star game against the Packers to join Gilchrist in the backfield. "Alan Page, the great lineman from Notre Dame, was an All-Star teammate of mine," Little recalled years later. "The Vikings started him at end, where he had played so well in college, but Cookie just destroyed him, blocking and running. It was so one-sided that the next week the Vikings switched him to defensive tackle, where he went on to make the Pro Football Hall of Fame. Carl Eller took Page's position at end and he, too, went to the Hall of Fame." Denver won the game, 14–3, exciting the fans so much that the regular-season opener produced the largest crowd in the team's history.

On October 23 at Kansas City's Municipal Stadium, AFL hearts would beat faster than they had for Denver's twin victories over NFL teams. It was the night the Kansas City Chiefs played against an NFL team for the first time since losing Super Bowl I to the Green Bay Packers. Hank Stram, Kansas City's proud coach, had not gotten over the hurt of Vince Lombardi's stinging put-down of the AFL champions in his postgame appraisal. One of the teams Lombardi rated far above the Chiefs was the Bears. Stram warmed up his team for their encounter with Chicago by rolling over the Houston Oilers and the New York Jets in the first two exhibition games. The week before they played Chicago, they showed no mercy to their divisional rival, the Oakland Raiders, pounding them, 48–0.

Redemption was on Stram's mind weeks before the game with the Bears but the days before the kickoff, it dominated his every thought, because he had heard about what was in the soon-to-be-released highlight film of the Super Bowl. "I got the film from NFL Films. I didn't want anyone else to look at it," Stram later told Jeff Miller, author of *Going Long*, the 2003 story of the AFL years in the words of those who lived it. Recalling Lombardi's stinging appraisal, Stram explained, "I was really pissed off about it. It was terrible, demeaning. The day of the game we were at Liberty College, going to take the bus to Kansas City. I didn't say a word. I just called them in a classroom and put the film on. Nobody said a word. Smoke was coming out of their ears."

Kansas City was a better team than the one that had lost to Green Bay seven months earlier. The draft had brought two starting linebackers, Willie Lanier and Jim Lynch; kicker Jan Stenerud; and kick returner Noland "the Flea" Smith. The Chiefs released all their resentment and fury in the second quarter, scoring 32 points. They never stopped. Stram kept his regulars in the game, and they operated a game plan as if it were in the midst of the season. Lombardi's post–Super Bowl words may have been most insulting to Stram, but George Halas was among the most disdainful of the AFL. For Stram,

Halas would be perfect as Lombardi's stand-in. The final score was 66–24. The Chiefs' mascot was a white horse that was ridden around the circumference of the field every time Kansas City scored. The animal got a full workout that night. "We didn't do too well," admitted Bears' star Gale Sayers, "but we almost killed that horse." Kansas City receiver Chris Burford passed by Halas as he walked off the field after the game. "He had tears in his eyes," reported Burford.

Denver's two victories and the headline-grabbing Kansas City demolishment of the Bears made the AFL feel a lot better about itself, but those games were the only ones AFL teams would win during the brief interleague schedule. The Dallas Cowboys beat the Houston Oilers 30–17, and San Francisco won the first Battle of the Bay 13–10 over Oakland.

Kansas City wasn't the only team to acquire reinforcements. The Detroit Lions rebounded from the humiliating loss to Denver with a 19–17 victory over Buffalo, owned by Detroit resident Ralph Wilson. The Lions received thunderbolt plays from their top rookies, running backs Nick Eddy and Miller Farr. Eddy took a punt 75 yards for a touchdown, and Farr went the same distance with a screen pass to score. George Allen, the Los Angeles Rams' coach, played to win in the exhibition season, the same as Stram did. The week after the Chiefs' triumph over Chicago, they lost to the Rams in Los Angeles, 44–24. Just a week before, the Rams won the so-called battle of Southern California with a goring of the San Diego Chargers, 50–7.

The three exhibition victories turned out to be among the AFL highlights of the year, as 1967 was a season of regression for the league. Many of its experienced stars who had been with AFL teams from the beginning had reached the end of a seven-year cycle, the shelf life of most pro football players of that era, excluding offensive linemen and quarterbacks. Several of the veteran quarterbacks—George Blanda, Babe Parilli, Jack Kemp, Tobin Rote, and Tom Flores— who sat on the bench in the fourteen-team NFL then thrived because of a fresh chance in the new league. Most of the young quarterbacks such as Joe Namath of the Jets, John Hadl of San Diego, and Miami Dolphins rookie Bob Griese weren't quite ready. That left Lenny Dawson of the Chiefs and two youngsters who changed uniforms via trades. One was Pete Beathard, whom Kansas City dealt to Houston, and Daryle Lamonica, whom Oakland had acquired from Buffalo.

Lamonica had been chafing for more playing time in Buffalo, but he had received less of it after Joe Collier replaced Lou Saban as the Bills' coach in 1966. Lamonica had approached Collier for a trade between seasons, and the coach came to the conclusion that he had to deal either Lamonica or Kemp. Oakland, where Al Davis wanted to construct a vertical passing game, was Buffalo's obvious customer. Both Kemp and Lamonica had the sort of powerful passing arms around which a deep-passing attack could be built, but there was a disparity in their ages. Both were July babies, with Kemp about to turn thirty-two and Lamonica twenty-six. Both men led healthy lifestyles, so Kemp's career expectancy might have taken him another four or five seasons. One thing that Collier did not factor into making his decision was Kemp's political ambitions, a fatal misstep for the coach's own career ambitions. By 1970 Kemp was a U.S. congressman, representing a district in western New York. Lamonica was traded to the Raiders along with wide receiver Glenn Bass for Flores and All-Star wide receiver Art Powell, a man both skilled and troublesome. The Bills didn't perform due diligence on Flores. He arrived in Buffalo with a sore arm.

If the NFL opposition thought the AFL teams would scale down on what the establishment called "basketball in cleats," they were wrong, just as they were wrong about the style of football played by the Cleveland Browns when they entered the NFL in 1950. When the merger was agreed upon, the AFL owners paid off Davis for what remained on his $75,000-a-year commissioner's salary, and before that Brooklyn Al assured that his staff in Manhattan was taken care of by having them sign two-year contracts for which the newly formed NFL would be liable. Then, satisfied by a contract that gave him part ownership of the team, Davis returned to Oakland and continued to build what would quickly become one of the great sports franchises in history.

Lamonica and his powerful arm were an original building block of the new-era Raiders. Davis didn't yet have the arsenal of receivers who could fully implement his idea for a vertical passing game, but he made do by improvising. He converted Billy Cannon, who came into pro football as a promising running back, to tight end. He used Hewritt Dixon, an ex-Bronco tight end, as part running back, part receiver. Clem Daniels, whom he obtained from the Chiefs, became one of the finest receiving backs in the game. The draft brought Fred Biletnikoff, a great college receiver under a pass-oriented coach, Bill Peterson of Florida State. Biletnikoff was not a speed receiver, but he made a living on short patterns, especially hooks and comebacks. Biletnikoff wasn't wild about exposing his body, but Lamonica explained how the Raiders' system worked to compensate for the weakness of an otherwise skilled player. "Freddie wouldn't go into mid-field traffic if you put a gun to his head," Lamonica once confided, "so we don't ask him to do that. We emphasize what he does best." This strategy worked, as Biletnikoff became a member of the Hall of Fame.

During his short reign as commissioner of the AFL, Davis gave his Raiders' head coaching title to John Rauch, his chief offensive aide. When he returned to Oakland as managing partner, Davis did not resume his coaching duties, at least formally. The Raiders' game plans became a joint venture by the head coach and managing partner.

The value of the Lamonica trade was borne out immediately as the Raiders opened with three victories at home, the third of which was a two-point victory over Kansas City, the defending AFL champion. Next on their schedule was Davis's return to his home area, New York, for a night game against the Jets and Joe Namath in Shea

Stadium. Maybe the Raiders were too busy stepping back to admire their work, since the Jets beat them, 27–14, but the guys in silver and black wouldn't lose for the rest of the season.

It was a season in which the Western Division was far stronger than the East, which the Chiefs were learning to their chagrin. They lost twice each to San Diego and Oakland. The second game against the Raiders was played on Thanksgiving Day in Kansas City's Municipal Stadium, and it ended the Chiefs' hopes of playing in two consecutive Super Bowls. Lamonica carved them up, 44–22.

The surprise of the Eastern Division was Houston, who won the first two AFL championships in 1960 and 1961, but three consecutive seasons of double-digit defeats from 1964 to 1966 mandated a retooling. The most dramatic change was at quarterback, where George Blanda, winner of the AFL's first most valuable player award, was cast adrift at age thirty-nine. To replace him, the Oilers traded with Kansas City for young Pete Beathard, at one time one of the most coveted prospects in football. The Oilers' move seemed like a good idea at the time, as no one had any idea Blanda would become a football Methuselah for the Raiders. Beathard never approached replacing Blanda at quarterback. In his first two seasons combined as an Oiler he threw fewer touchdown passes and more interceptions than Blanda managed in his farewell season with the franchise.

The Houston coach was Wally Lemm, who was serving his second hitch with the team. In 1961, after the Oilers won just one of their first five games, owner Bud Adams fired Lou Rymkus, who won the AFL title the previous season. To replace him Adams promoted assistant coach Lemm. Under Lemm the Oilers won their last nine regular-season games and then defeated high-scoring San Diego, 10–3, for their second title. Lemm was voted the AFL's coach of the year and then signed a contract to coach the St. Louis Cardinals in the NFL. When Adams needed another coaching change in 1966, Lemm had been fired by the Cardinals, so Houston rehired him. The 1967 Oilers were Lemm's career jewel.

With an uncertain passing game, the Oilers ran the ball more often than at any time in the first eighteen seasons of the franchise. Hoyle Granger, a tough, thickly built Cajun, was the workhorse, gaining 1,194 yards and averaging 5.1 yards on his 236 carries. Granger also led the team in receiving with thirty-one catches for another 300 yards. He fumbled just once during his 251 combined touches of the ball. It was one of the most underrated personal accomplishments in pro football history, and Granger wasn't even named to the AFL All-Star team. What kept Houston in every game was its defense, which allowed just 14 points a game. The most points scored against the Oilers was 28, and that was in a tie game against the Jets.

One of the main reasons the Oilers were largely ignored was the success of the Jets. By Thanksgiving New York was in the proverbial catbird seat. The Jets had a record of seven victories, two defeats, and a tie. They had a bye, which, in effect, gave them off for the last two weeks over November with two straight home games awaiting them. Then they imploded. The first of the two home dates was against Denver, the worst team in the AFC-West, but any team from the West was an enigma to New York that year. They were stunned by the Broncos, 33–24. The next Sunday they were smothered by Kansas City's defense, 21–7. Namath passed for twenty-six touchdowns in 1967, but he suffered twenty-eight interceptions, many at critical times. Now the Jets, tied with Houston at identical records, seven victories, four losses, and a tie, had to finish on the road, with the first of the two away games at Oakland, the most successful team in the AFL. It was Lamonica versus Namath in the first of several major shootouts they would have over the next few seasons. Lamonica and the Raiders won, 39–28, while the Oilers were beating San Diego, 24–17, in Houston. The Oilers were on the verge of a championship and a shot at Super Bowl II, but the fans were barely interested, as fewer than 20,000 showed up to see the game. The Oilers clinched the East with an easy win in Miami the next Sunday to a minimum of fanfare. It was not an exciting year for the AFL, which seemed doomed in a Super Bowl matchup that would send either the Raiders or Oilers against some NFL team—the Cowboys, Colts, Rams, or Packers—clearly superior to whatever champion the young league would field for the final game. Football fans were a year away from seeing how the game moves in cycles.

One reason the Houston fans were unenthusiastic about the Oilers was due to the team's nondescript offense, a pale substitute for the days when Blanda made exciting connections to Charlie Hennigan and Bill Groman as they won the first two AFL titles. The Oilers had the best defense in the league in 1967, but the Raiders barely used their superb passing attack against it, instead gouging the Eastern champs for 263 yards rushing, with Hewritt Dixon racing 69 yards down the sidelines for a second-quarter touchdown. The coup de grace came with seconds left in the half when the Raiders faked a field-goal attempt and Lamonica threw a touchdown pass to tight end Dave Kocourek instead. Blanda, who kicked twenty field goals during the regular season, kicked three more in the 40–7 route.

CHAPTER 19

Triumphant Exit

Once all the excitement of the 1966 season and Super Bowl I subsided, it became clear that all the worthwhile action in the "season-after" would be in the NFL. The Dallas Cowboys, who established themselves as one of the game's most flamboyant offensive teams, seemed ready to take on the mighty Green Bay Packers. More than four months ahead of opening day Tom Landry had a speaking engagement in St. Paul, Minnesota, cheek-by-jowl to Packer territory. The normally laconic Landry was feeling downright brazen. "Within two years," said Landry, "some team will displace the Packers. They are approaching an age problem and other teams are improving." There wasn't much doubt who Landry meant by "some team."

There was also no denying Landry's contention that the Pack was getting old. Paul Hornung and Jim Taylor, the business end of the famous Packer sweep, were already members of the expansion New Orleans Saints. Quarterback Bart Starr was thirty-three, and so were defensive end Willie Davis, guard Fuzzy Thurston, and tackle Bob Skoronski. Tackle Forrest Gregg, whom Lombardi called "the greatest player I ever coached," would turn thirty-seven in October.

The first phase of realignment was the breaking down of the NFL from two conferences into four divisions, which worked in Green Bay's favor. Its two toughest rivals in the Western Conference, the Baltimore Colts and Los Angeles Rams, were both shuttled to the Coastal Division. The bottom three teams in the 1966 Western Conference—the Chicago Bears, Detroit Lions, and Minnesota Vikings—joined the Pack in the Central Division. Even with that scheduling edge, Green Bay labored heavily from the beginning even though its first two games were in Lambeau Field. The Packers were tied by

Detroit, 17–17, and barely got by the Bears, 13–10. As the season went on, it was obvious the offense was not the same as the championship attack of the previous two seasons. Starr passed for five fewer touchdowns and fourteen more interceptions than he had in 1966. Green Bay quarterbacks suffered fifteen more sacks than they had the previous season. Starr's passer rating dropped 40 points, and he threw for 467 fewer yards. Taylor led the 1966 Packers with 705 yards, and with him gone Lombardi used a committee of five running backs. In his second season as a pro, Jim Grabowski got the most carries, 120, and gained 466 yards. Among the five backs, their aggregate was a healthy 1,756 yards. One of the committeemen was Ben Wilson, a veteran journeyman whom Lombardi obtained in a trade with the Rams for a second-round draft choice. Used judiciously, he averaged 4.4 yards and his 453 yards were just 13 behind Grabowski's.

Lombardi had five picks in the first three rounds of the merged league's first common draft, but none of them had much impact. Packer luck came in the fourth round. Their selection was Arizona State running back Travis Williams, who not only led pro football in kickoff returns as a rookie but also returned four of them for touchdowns, one of the great special team feats in the history of the pro game.

The Packers were not an impressive football team in the last month of the season. They managed to get by a mediocre Chicago team by 3 points and a poor Minnesota team by 4, which wrapped up the division title. They lost the last two games to the Los Angeles Rams and Pittsburgh Steelers, one of six Eastern Conference teams that finished without a winning record. The Packers may have been gasping for air in December, but Lombardi, almost manic in his focus on winning a third consecutive NFL championship, kept driving them relentlessly, almost cruelly. It was as if the great coach were leading his most important crusade, and anyone in the Packers' employ who did not dedicate himself to the crusade was beneath contempt.

After the victory over Kansas City in the first Super Bowl, Taylor, understanding that he had just a little time left as a player, made it clear he intended to play out his option in order to return to his native Louisiana and finish his career with the expansion New Orleans Saints. Taylor's campaigning finally forced Lombardi into trading him, receiving a first-round draft choice for the onetime star. Taylor was out of football after the end of the 1967 season. Taylor gave the Packers' five consecutive 1,000-yard seasons, and Lombardi often used him as an example to the other players for his dedication and year-round attention to staying in superb physical condition. Yet when Taylor wanted to leave the Packers, Lombardi spoke warmly of the departing Hornung but airily brushed aside the departure of Taylor by saying, "we'll replace the other guy."

Meanwhile Green Bay's old rivals, the Colts and Rams, bitterly fought it out for the entire season in the Coastal Division in a duel of blossoming young coaches, Don Shula of Baltimore and George Allen of Los Angeles. Shula at thirty-three was the youngest head coach in football. Allen was in his second year as head coach of the Rams, after winning a court case against the Chicago Bears to gain the right to accept the contract offered by Los Angeles owner Dan Reeves. Both had become immediate successes as NFL head coaches. Shula's first Baltimore team won five of its last six games, then streaked to a 12–2 record in his second season. Allen's 1966 Rams won four of their last five, and in 1967 won eleven, tied two, and lost one. Football people who predicted "there will never be another Vince Lombardi" after Vince and the Packers began to win NFL championships, spoke too soon. Shula was a match for the master when it came to intensity, inner fire, full focus on winning, and unwillingness to accept less than a player's best. Allen had Lombardi's focus and inner fire, but instead of an erupting temper Allen succeeded with a con man's gift of persuasion with his players.

Defense was the key for both the Colts and Rams. Baltimore allowed just 198 points in the fourteen regular season games, Los

Angeles just 196. The Rams allowed 13 points or fewer in half their games, the Colts 10 points or fewer in half theirs. When the teams met on October 15 in Baltimore's creaky Municipal Stadium, it was a shootout that ended in a 24–24 tie. The Colts would not lose a game until the rematch in the Los Angeles Coliseum on December 17, the last regular game of the season, when the Rams stunned the superb Baltimore defense, 34–10. Even though the teams finished with the same record, Los Angeles won the championship because its point total in the two meetings was greater than that of the Colts. Baltimore had gone until the last game of the season before losing, but there were no playoffs for the Colts since the concept of wild-card teams was off in the future. All that was left for them was the meaningless playoff bowl in Miami, something Lombardi used to refer to as "a game for losers in a city for losers."

Allen brought the Rams to Milwaukee County Stadium against Green Bay for the first conference championship playoff game in NFL history. Quarterback Roman Gabriel put Los Angeles out in front early with a 29-yard touchdown pass to Bernie Casey. An Allen team had beaten a Lombardi team for the first time, 27–14, just two weeks earlier, but this was different. The previous game came at a time when the Packers had clinched their division championship. The conference playoff was part of Lombardi's crusade, which was advancing closer to its climax. Travis Williams scored on a 46-yard run from scrimmage, starting a 28-point Green Bay avalanche that was accompanied by a throttling by the Packer defense. It was a trademark Lombardi victory—faint hope for the opponent, then grim reality, a 28–7 Packer victory.

The 1967 Cleveland Browns were something of a mystery. They were good, as most Cleveland teams of that decade had been, but the question was how good? They won the Century Division easily, but they hadn't been tested much. The only time they faced one of the NFL's Big Four was the opener against Dallas, when they lost, 21–14, and most recently on November 12 when they visited

Milwaukee and were smoked, 55–7, by the Packers. The humiliating loss to Green Bay was the true indicator since their Eastern Conference championship playoff game in Dallas was another embarrassment, with the Cowboys winning 52–14.

After the game Tom Landry made another of his uncharacteristic comments when the Green Bay Packers were on his mind. "After watching the Packers on television yesterday," said Landry, "I felt that what they did carried over into this game for us. I never expected to win the game this big. It never hurts you to win big."

Dallas's blowout victory over the Browns and the Packers' smashing of the Rams set up a game that will stand forever in football lore, the Ice Bowl. Date: New Year's Eve day, 1967. Site: In the dramatic words of John Facenda, first voice of NFL Films, "The frozen tundra of Lambeau Field in Green Bay, Wisconsin." Temperature: 13 degrees below zero with a wind-chill factor of minus 46. CBS broadcaster Frank Gifford set his cup of coffee on the railing of the press box and turned to have a few words with a colleague. When he reached back to pick up the coffee, it was frozen. The heating system under the field failed to work because of the cold, but the story in Green Bay persists to this day that Lombardi ordered the system turned off. After Packer officials noticed blood on the cheeks of some of the young musicians, they cancelled the performance of the marching bands. When the game officials tried to blow their whistles, no sound was produced. The whistles were frozen. The Cowboys' bench was heated, but Packer fans kept leaning out of the stands and unplugging it. While warming up after the game, a number of fans passed out. The alcohol in their systems had thawed out. One elderly fan died from exposure to the cold.

The game itself looked as if it would be decided early, with Bart Starr rising above his subpar regular season to throw a pair of touchdown passes to Boyd Dowler, the second a 46-yard bomb. The Packers had possession of the ball again, this time deep in their own territory, when the contest abruptly tightened. Dallas's Willie

Townes sacked Starr, causing the quarterback to fumble. George Andrie scooped up the ball and ran 7 yards to the end zone for the Cowboys' first points. Just before halftime Danny Villanueva kicked a short field goal to cut Dallas's deficit to 4 points, 14–10. Four plays into the fourth quarter, the Cowboys took their first lead of the day, 17–10, on a surprise halfback option pass from Dan Reeves to Lance Rentzel. As the afternoon wore on, the numbing cold made it seem improbable that either team could score again, but with 4 minutes, 7 seconds remaining, the Packers began a drive from their own 32-yard line. The catalyst was a short pass from Starr which running back Chuck Mercein turned into a 19-yard gain to the Dallas's 11-yard line. Mercein, like Ben Wilson, was a Lombardi pickup in his effort to compensate for the loss of Taylor with a platoon of backs. Mercein was an Ivy Leaguer, a Yale man but a tough one. On the next play, the Yalie muscled his way to the Cowboys' 3-yard line. Two downs later in the huddle, Starr, who like most of his teammates was sure he was playing his last football in Green Bay for Vince Lombardi, called 35-edge, his own play. He crammed himself behind center Ken Bowman and guard Jerry Kramer into the end zone. There was a mighty struggle of the teams' linemen, then a small opening appeared through which Starr thrust his body. The extra point made the final score 21–17.

Green Bay would have assured itself of playing further in the game had it chosen to kick what amounted to a point-blank field goal. In his postgame press conference, Lombardi explained the reasoning behind his taking the risk. "I couldn't see going for the tie and making those fans in the stands sit through sudden death in this weather. That's why we gambled on scoring a touchdown." Hard-guy Vince Lombardi having compassion for the Packer fans? It may have been the final clue that his coaching career in Green Bay was coming to a close.

Lombardi may once have considered Miami "a loser's town," but its sports fans and the snowbirds anxious to migrate from the great north looked upon Super Bowl II with far more anticipation and enthusiasm than blasé Los Angeles had viewed the first Super Bowl, which was played in a Coliseum with a mere two-thirds of its seats occupied. Miami had a team of its own now, the Dolphins, and the Orange Bowl was sold out. Unfortunately, 1967 was a season in which the AFL had taken a step back in its development and, after the Ice Bowl, any game between the once-warring leagues was anticlimactic. There were to be no surprises; the game between the Packers and Raiders was the dullest of the first five Super Bowls.

The matchup of quarterbacks and coaches was not something to stir the imagination. Starr was in his twelfth professional season, the most successful quarterback in football, with five NFL championships and a Super Bowl victory in his resume. Lamonica was in his fourth season as a pro, his first as a starter, and one AFL championship to his credit. If they had much in common, it was in their unhappy experiences as college quarterbacks. With Starr it was injuries and less-than-powerful Alabama teams. In Lamonica's case, he came to Notre Dame during the Joe Kuharich era, during which a plethora of quarterbacks was recruited; too many, in fact. Lamonica had been one of the prizes of the West Coast after graduating high school from Clovis, California. In the same batch of freshmen quarterbacks was Ed Rutkowski of Kingston, Pennsylvania, one of the most desired quarterbacks in the nation. "We thought that the Golden Dome would fall off if we failed to get Eddie," said Charlie Callahan, the longtime sports information director at Notre Dame. During their careers Lamonica started some games for the Irish, Rutkowski started some, and two or three other quarterbacks started some. When he finished his college career, Lamonica was drafted in the twelfth round by Green Bay and in the twenty-fourth round of the AFL draft by Buffalo. Sensing that he would have a better chance to play in Buffalo, Lamonica signed with the Bills. Ironically, Rutkowski, by then a jack-of-all-trades player, accompanied him to Buffalo as a receiver/

return man. Just as Starr didn't begin blossoming until his fourth pro season, Lamonica didn't either.

Lombardi and Rauch, his Oakland counterpart, had far less in common. Rauch had fallen into his job when the AFL owners decided to go to war with the established league and hired Al Davis, who held the dual role of coach and general manager of the Raiders, as its hardball commissioner. Rauch, the quarterback of a good University of Georgia team in the late 1940s, spent five years with three different NFL teams in a career as a seldom-used backup and eventually began what looked like the life of a career assistant coach. Then Davis changed Rauch's career course by recommending that the Raider owners promote him to head coach. In his second year on the job, with his newly acquired quarterback Lamonica, Rauch and the Raiders compiled the best record in the eight-year history of the AFL on their way to the second Super Bowl. Still, everyone understood they were "Al Davis's Raiders," and that he was pulling just about all the important strings, including the trade for Lamonica.

As it turned out, even Vince Lombardi had needs. One of those was a much larger canvas on which to paint his next masterpiece. He had long outgrown small-city Green Bay, Wisconsin, where he was Caesar in the sticks. Being a twenty-four-hour god of football with his subjects all but genuflecting in his presence had become wearisome. He had a contract with the Packers, and he knew he had to fulfill it, even though it did not need to be as their coach. His beloved wife, Marie, was alien corn in Green Bay. She was a New Yorker with that certain sophistication that goes with it. Besides, once her husband began dominating pro football and became much larger than life in the upper Midwest, she took on a regal air. She had little in common with the women of Green Bay. Vince understood that he was now the most marketable product in sports and would have his pick of jobs with enormous perks and the highest salary in coaching. He also understood that he had a contract to fulfill with the Packers once his last coaching assignment, Super Bowl II, was completed. Something else he knew was that accommodations could be made, contract or not.

There were still the Raiders with whom he had to deal. In the Packers' first workout in Florida at the beginning of Super Bowl week, Ray Nitschke was limping, a by-product of the Ice Bowl victory over Dallas. "I have a frostbite problem with my toes," he told the press. The next day Lombardi assured the media that "only the Dallas team was hobbled by the cold." Nitschke stopped limping. Lombardi was playing one last mind game with the Pack. There were signs, however, that the rumors about Lombardi retiring as coach were true. For instance, he allowed the players to bring their wives along on the trip to Miami, something he had never done before. The Thursday before the game he had spoken to the team in unfamiliar phrases, one of which was, "I've never been so proud of you." His voice began to crack as he said it. "There were lumps in our throats," admitted Starr. The coach quickly collected himself and went on with practice, but the players knew: It wasn't a rumor. Lombardi would no longer be their coach after this game. It was the end of the Packer crusade.

On game day, there was early evidence that there would be no doubt about the outcome or the manner in which it was brought about. Nitschke blew up an Oakland sweep on the game's first play from scrimmage, and then the Raiders completed a three-and-out series, quickly punting. On their first two possessions the Packers controlled the ball for a total of twenty-seven plays, with both series ending in Don Chandler field goals and a 6–0 lead. On a short-yardage situation in the Pack's own territory, Lombardi went for the jugular. Starr faked a handoff to running back Travis Williams, Raider defensive backs Kent McCloughan and Howie Williams confused their assignments on the play, and Starr's receiver, Boyd Dowler, became scandalously open for a 62-yard touchdown. Just before halftime, Rodger Bird of the Raiders muffed a punt that was recovered by Dick Capp, an AFL castoff from the Boston Patriots. Chandler kicked his third field goal of the half, and the Packers took a 16–7 lead into their dressing room.

In few football games is a 16–7 halftime lead any assurance of eventual victory. But this was a game against the Packers who were thirty minutes away from completing their crusade with their departing coach. This Green Bay team was not nearly as strong as some of his earlier teams, but it possessed the same Lombardi-driven efficiency and refusal to beat itself. The final score was 33–14, but the yardage differential was a mere 29 yards, yet yardage totals can be like runners left on base during a baseball game. The explanation for the disparity in points was found in the turnovers. Oakland had three, including Herb Adderley's interception return for a touchdown, and all three turnovers led to Packer points. Green Bay had just one penalty. Guard Jerry Kramer explained how Lombardi could bring about team discipline with a withering comment. Once Kramer jumped offside, and the coach acidly lectured him that "the concentration span of a college student is fifteen to twenty minutes; a high school student ten to fifteen minutes; a kid in grammar school, maybe one minute. Now where the hell does that leave you?"

Eighteen days later Lombardi officially resigned as coach of the Packers, staying on as general manager. Green Bay would experience just two winning seasons in the next thirteen years; the team would not return to the Super Bowl for twenty-nine seasons. A year and four days after he resigned as coach, Lombardi resigned as general manager, leaving Green Bay forever.

CHAPTER 20

Mickey Mouse Roars

The Green Bay Packers' dominance of the first two Super Bowls gave a great many NFL players a false sense of superiority. "We were supposed to merge the AFL Players Association with the NFL Players Association by 1970 through terms of the merger," said Nick Buoniconti, the Miami Dolphins linebacker who, along with Buffalo Bills quarterback Jack Kemp and San Diego Chargers offensive tackle Ron Mix, was among the principals in starting the AFL Players Association group. "So we had sort of an informal meeting with them, and they looked down their noses at us. They insulted us, calling us 'minor leaguers' and the AFL a 'Mickey Mouse League.' I remember Ken Bowman, the Green Bay center, acting like we didn't even belong talking to them. Finally I asked him, 'Who do you think you are?'"

There was even less harmony among the merging owners. "I hated the AFL," admitted Art Modell, owner of the Cleveland Browns and about to become president of the NFL. "Even after the merger I hated them for a long time. I didn't want to do business with them." When realignment was first discussed after the merger was okayed by Congress, Modell said publicly, "The Denver Broncos will never play in Cleveland Stadium," which was a stinging put-down since the old Cleveland stadium was several light-years shy of being a sports Taj Mahal. Its grandstand poles created a sense of watching a football game sideways through Venetian blinds. The dressing rooms were shabby and miniscule, and the coaches' area was so small that the Browns finally had to rent a recreation vehicle and place it in the concourse under the stadium so the coaches of the visiting teams could hold their postgame press conferences in it. The two leagues were a mere two seasons away from an interleague schedule mandated by terms of the merger, and no genuine progress had been made toward realigning the shape of the new NFL. The Cincinnati Bengals would be the newest expansion franchise in the league, and when there was talk of keeping the AFL together along with expansion franchises New Orleans Saints and Cincinnati, Paul Brown, who was to head the management team of the latter franchise, balked. "We were promised we would be in the NFL, not the AFL," said Brown. "I wanted to come into the NFL where my old friends were." The stalling would drag on perilously close to the deadline.

The NFL players and owners were deluding themselves. They had ignored the fact that pro football operates in cycles and things change, often very quickly. The old NFL was still basking in Packer glory when in fact the Packers were already a different matter with Lombardi having moved himself to the executive suite. Phil Bengtson, Lombardi's defensive coordinator, had replaced him as head coach, an almost impossible situation, especially with a roster decaying with age. Lombardi's tyranny was a great deal of what made the Packer engine ignite, and Bengtson was not a tyrant.

The Dallas Cowboys were the most likely heir apparent to Green Bay's NFL championship in 1968, but the Baltimore Colts had great motivation—the frustration of its amazing 1967 season thwarted by a single loss to the Los Angeles Rams in the final game. The Rams would be good again and maybe Cleveland. True believers in the NFL thought its domination of the AFL could go on indefinitely.

The AFL, however, was fermenting. The Oakland Raiders, anxious to redeem themselves after their one-sided loss to Green Bay in Super Bowl II, reassembled the success of their 1967 regular season. Quarterback Daryle Lamonica was even better in his second season as a starter, and George Blanda followed his twenty-field-goal season with a twenty-one-field-goal season. Two days after the opening game, Blanda turned forty-one, but he made no concessions to age and served an important role as Lamonica's backup quarterback.

He connected with Warren Wells for the longest touchdown pass of the AFL season, 94 yards, one of Wells's twelve scoring receptions. The Raiders would score almost exactly as many points as they had in 1967 and allow an identical amount, 233. They won their first four games, in three of which they scored over 40 points.

The big difference in the seasons was that Oakland had no cakewalk in the AFL West. The Kansas City Chiefs had retooled, winning seven of their first eight games, including a 24–10 victory over the Raiders. Yet two weeks later in Oakland, the Raiders retaliated with an emphatic 38–21 victory. Those two games would cement a bitter rivalry that would last not only through the 1960s, but throughout the next five decades.

In the Eastern Division, the New York Jets had converted promise into prowess, even though the year began traumatically. In May managing partner Sonny Werblin, unhappy with the terms of the merger and sure he had won the battle of New York against the New York Giants, sold his share of the franchise to his four partners—Leon Hess, Phil Iselin, Don Lillis, and Townsend Martin. Lillis was named to succeed Werblin as managing partner but two months later he died unexpectedly, and Iselin was named to succeed him. The 1967 Jets had collapsed in December, losing three of their last four games and virtually granting the division championship to the Houston Oilers. The 1968 Jets opened with two impressive victories on the road, a 1-point victory over the Kansas City Chiefs in which they controlled the ball for close to 6 minutes at the end of the game, and then a 47–31 rollover against the Boston Patriots in what turned out to be a show-and-tell appearance by Joe Namath. Even though it was supposed to be the Patriots' home game, it was played in Birmingham, Alabama, near Tuscaloosa, where Namath had become a national sports celebrity at the University of Alabama. The Patriots were trolling for a possible new home at the time, but the attendance was just a few thousand over what the Pats had been drawing in the Boston area for Namath and the Jets.

If the Jets were disappointed in the Birmingham gate, the disappointment they would suffer in Buffalo the following week was far more devastating. Two weeks earlier Oakland administered the worst beating in Bills history, with Lamonica returning to Buffalo for the first time since he was traded. George Atkinson set a league record with 205 yards returning punts, including an 86-yard touchdown return in the first quarter. On Buffalo's next punt Atkinson returned it 54 yards to the Bills' 9-yard line, from which point fullback Pete Banaszak scored. On Oakland's next possession, Lamonica threw a 47-yard touchdown pass to Wells, giving the Raiders a 21–0 lead on just four plays from scrimmage. The final score was 48–6, and after the game Joe Collier, who had traded Lamonica, was fired.

By the time the Jets arrived in Buffalo, the Bills were on their way to ill note as the worst team in football. They started the season without their top two quarterbacks, Jack Kemp and Tom Flores, who were injured and lost for the year, then owner Ralph Wilson muddied the situation further by replacing Collier with his scouting chief, Harvey Johnson, who had sketchy coaching experience. Johnson's quarterback was rookie Dan Darragh, a thirteenth-round draft choice. In Johnson's first game, the Bills lost, 34–23, to the Cincinnati Bengals, who were in their first season as an expansion team.

Against that inviting background Namath was about to step into the blackest hole of his playing career. The Bills held a surprising 10–7 lead in the first quarter when Darragh was sacked, fumbled, and the Jets recovered at the Buffalo 10. Namath threw to fullback Curley Johnson at the goal line, but Tom Janik, Buffalo's swift and lanky safety, had shadowed Johnson and quickly intercepted. He ran 100 yards for a touchdown. Namath's next pass was intercepted by cornerback Butch Byrd, who returned it 52 yards for another touchdown, but that was nullified because Buffalo was offside. By the fourth quarter Namath was attempting to drive his team to the lead when Byrd intercepted him and returned it 53 yards for a touchdown. One minute, 12 seconds later, the other Buffalo corner-back, Booker Edgerson, intercepted Namath and returned the ball 45 yards for another touchdown. The Jets' last chance to get back into contention was snuffed out when Byrd intercepted Namath's bomb to George Sauer Jr. at the Bills' 5-yard line.

After the game the New York sporting press assembled in front of Namath's locker in the War Memorial Stadium dressing room. The quarterback sat on a stool, cradling his face on his lap and mumbling incoherently. The journalist closest to him was a kneeling Milton Gross, the *New York Post* columnist whose interviewing style was to place his head cheek-by-jowl to that of his subject, whispering his questions in the hope the answers would be whispered in return. Gross explained the reason for his unorthodox method as "run with the crowd; write like the crowd." The scene resembled a priest hearing the penitent's confession. Finally Gross arose and those in the back rows pleaded for a translation from Namath's mumbles, "What did he say, Milton? What did he say?" As he brusquely strode away from the scene, Gross reported, "All he kept saying was 'I stink.'"

In football, the healing process is usually a matter of a few days, sometimes a few hours. By Sunday, when the Jets returned to Shea Stadium to play San Diego, Namath's psyche was cleansed as he stepped on the field before a franchise record crowd, 63,786. The Jets won 23–10, and they would go on to win five of their next six games until they went to Oakland for one of the most bizarre endings in football history. They still call it the "Heidi Game," and it piqued interest in the AFL as nothing had before.

The date was November 17, 1968, and NBC had begun structuring its holiday telecasting with a cultural doubleheader: The late afternoon football game was a match between two of the three strongest teams in the AFL, the New York Jets versus the Oakland Raiders, defending league champions. The second half of the programming, scheduled to start at 7 p.m., EST, was the beloved children's tale of *Heidi*, the adorable little Swiss mountain girl. *Heidi* was precisely timed to air so the network engineers knew exactly when to start, when to cut to commercials, and when to end it and move on to the next program. Football games aren't nearly as predictable, and this one turned out to be a jailbreak.

It was back-and-forth explosions from the start, Lamonica versus Namath and Jim Turner, the Jets' outstanding kicker, versus Blanda. Namath fired a 50-yard touchdown pass to Don Maynard and Turner kicked his third field goal of the game to give New York a 29–22 lead halfway through the last quarter, but viewers anticipated what might happen in the remaining time and how it might effect the television schedule. Neither defense was stopping the other team's offense so the punch-counterpunch nature of the contest was likely to extend right until seven o'clock, possibly beyond. Would they see the climax of the football game or the start of *Heidi*? At about 6:45 p.m., the calls from anxious parents, wishing to have their children see *Heidi* from the beginning, began to come in to NBC. A few minutes later, a mixture of football fans, some wishing to watch the Jets win their first division championship and home-field advantage for the AFL championship, and others thirsting to see Ben Davidson, Tom Keating, and their colleagues dismember Namath, began to call the network, demanding it stay with the game.

The Raiders scored a touchdown and Turner countered with his fourth field goal to make the score 32–29, in favor of the Jets. NBC technicians were frantically trying to contact the brass for instructions, but the incoming calls from viewers were so heavy that more than two dozen fuses were blown at the network switchboard. Namath and Lamonica disappeared from the screen, replaced by a precious little girl. Finally, the technicians who would have been able to keep the game on-screen and postpone the start of *Heidi* if they had permission, received a call from Julian Goodman, the president of NBC himself, ordering them to go back to the game. Broadcast networks are multibillion-dollar operations, and when the president of the network says, "Do it," it's done. But at that time, the fortunes of a network occasionally depended on some guy who just wants to punch out and go home to have supper with his family. That's what happened on November 17, 1968. The control of televised programming across the nation took place in a switching station in the middle of a cornfield in Iowa, a one-man operation. The man who did the switching, already on overtime, had closed up the station and gone home.

So what the TV viewers didn't see were two Oakland touchdowns in nine seconds. Lamonica threw a touchdown pass to Charlie Smith, and on the resulting kickoff the Jets fumbled and the Raiders recovered the ball in the end zone for a touchdown and a 43–22 victory. The Oakland player who scored the last touchdown was Preston Ridlehuber, whose surname would have been fitting for one of the alpine yodelers in *Heidi.*

After the uproar over the missing minute and five seconds subsided, NBC finally realized that a fuse-busting reaction over the missing end of a football game had illustrated what a valuable asset they possessed in the AFL television rights.

The victory over the Jets and their late-season 38–21 drubbing of Kansas City made the Raiders the most likely team to represent the AFL in Super Bowl III, even though Kansas City tied them for the Western Division championship with the best records in the league, 12–2. Oakland demonstrated that its early November romp was no fluke when Lamonica threw five touchdown passes, three on the Raiders' first four possessions, in a 41–6 humiliation over their bitter rivals in the playoff for the AFC-West title. New York won four straight after the "Heidi Game" to earn the right to play host to the Raiders in Shea Stadium for a shot at the NFL champion.

The Jets and Raiders were AFL purebreds. The head scouts for each team, George Sauer Sr. of the Jets and Ron Wolf of the Raiders, had performed their tasks superbly. The nucleus of New York's roster included twenty-four players either drafted or signed as college free agents either by the Jets or some other AFL team. The Raiders had twenty-seven players in that category. Two of New York's best players were original Titans, wide receiver Don Maynard and linebacker Larry Grantham. Maynard was an ex-Giant, a player who came into the NFL in 1958 from Texas Western University as one of the fastest players in football, but one who needed a great deal of polishing. The NFL was then a twelve-team league with rosters of just thirty-three players, so the Giants had neither the need nor the inclination to show more than a year's patience with Maynard and Coach Allie Sherman released him. Two years later the Titans, desperate for talent, had nothing much more than unlimited patience and signed him. He developed into a Hall of Fame player.

When Weeb Ewbank was hired by the Jets as their head coach in 1963, he outlined a five-year plan for the team, the same time span it took him to produce an NFL championship team for the Baltimore Colts. The coaching staff he hired in New York consisted mostly of men who excelled as teachers, including an offensive line coach from Blanton Collier's staff at Kentucky, Chuck Knox. Ewbank had signed Winston Hill, a raw offensive tackle from Texas Southern who was an eleventh-round draft choice of the Colts, but they cut him in training camp. Hill became Knox's prize pupil and developed into one of the best offensive linemen in pro football.

December 29 is not a time to expect New York City to be at its best. At least in Manhattan you can dodge the weather between skyscrapers. Shea Stadium, the Jets' home at the time, is in Queens, where the icy winds cut across Flushing Meadow and a discarded napkin in one end zone can make it to the opposite end zone in a flash.

But this was the Jets versus the Raiders, the "Heidi Game" reprised, with Lamonica and Namath competing against the wind as well as one another. The Jets jumped in front, 10–0, with Namath throwing the first of three touchdown passes, this one to Maynard. Lamonica threw 29 yards to Fred Biletnikoff to cut New York's lead to 13–10 at halftime. George Blanda kicked a short field goal to tie it

174

early in the third quarter, but Namath found his tight end, Pete Lammons, for a 20-yard touchdown to give the Jets a 20–13 lead and it really was beginning to look more and more like the "Heidi Game," but without the TV blackout in the last two minutes.

Namath tried to break it open with a deep pass, but Raider safety George Atkinson intercepted at the New York 37, and only Namath's tackle at the 5 prevented a touchdown. "I threw the perfect pass," Namath said, "Atkinson just made a perfect play on it." As Pete Banaszak ran it into the end zone to put the Raiders ahead, 23–20, Namath was standing alongside of Ewbank. "Don't worry," he promised the coach, "I'll get it back." It took him three plays. The first was a 10-yard pass to Sauer. Then he sent Maynard on a deep route toward the goal-line flag on the right side of the field, as Atkinson matched the receiver step for step. Maynard's head snapped back—in the wrong direction—but the pencil-shaped receiver reached out and made a sensational, over-the-shoulder catch at the Raider 6.

Now Namath prepared to launch his knockout blow. All afternoon the Jets had been successful running at the right side of the Oakland line, end Ben Davidson and linebacker Gus Otto, so the Raiders expected a power sweep or an off-tackle run to that side. Instead, Namath gave a play-action fake to Matt Snell, then straightened up to throw. Running back Bill Mathis was the primary receiver, but he was covered. With that avenue blocked, Namath surveyed the end zone with one sweeping glance and picked his open receiver, Maynard, in the deep corner of the end zone. The coverage converged, but Namath fired his pass through a space the size of a porthole for the lead touchdown. "I think I was the fourth receiver on his list," said Maynard. They were the last points scored in the wild, final sixteen minutes, but it was not the last shot to be fired. Oakland stormed back. With less than two minutes, the Raiders were on the New York 24 when Lamonica tried to throw a swing pass to halfback Charlie Smith. The ball was slightly off-target, and Smith

175

neither caught it nor covered it, a critical error since the officials ruled that it was not a pass at all, but a lateral. Linebacker Ralph Baker recovered it for the Jets. "I wasn't sure it was a lateral," said Baker, "but we've been taught to cover anything that looks like that so I went after it."

The Jets were 27–23 winners and on their way to Super Bowl III and one of the landmark moments in American sports history. It would be the last game John Rauch ever coached for the Raiders. Chafing at what he considered interference by owner Al Davis in the game-planning along with personnel changes on what he considered "his" team, Rauch would leave Oakland to become coach of the Buffalo Bills in less than a month. Rauch might have resented Davis's insistence in having a large say on what the Raiders did on the field, but no owner in the history of pro football other than George Halas of the Bears ever had better coaching credentials to inject himself into the product. A day before the Bills officially announced the hiring of Rauch, Davis confided to a friend, "Ralph Wilson is hiring the wrong guy. I'm going to replace Rauch with the best young coach in pro football." The man to whom Davis referred was his linebacker coach, thirty-three-year-old John Madden.

There was no such tension in the NFL playoffs. Dallas, owner of a 12–2 record at the end of the 1968 regular season and the team most likely to inherit the Green Bay Packers' place as the premier franchise in the game, was favored in its game against the Cleveland Browns, a team the Cowboys had humiliated 52–14 in the 1967 playoffs. By the time this game was over, the prophecy about the Cowboys, "next year's champions," had morphed into a sarcastic nickname. The Cowboys turned over the ball five times, contributing to 24 Cleveland points in a 31–20 upset for the Browns.

Seldom has glory turned to gore so quickly as the seven days between Cleveland's unexpected victory over the Cowboys and their moment of truth against Baltimore. Don Shula's Colts were on a crusade of their own to replace Lombardi's Packers as the No. 1

team in the sport. The Minnesota Vikings flexed their muscles for the first time in their existence as they climbed from last-place finishes in the NFL's Western Conference to the championship of their division, but the Colts swatted them aside, 24–14, as Baltimore's huge defensive end, Bubba Smith, hounded Vikings quarterback Joe Kapp all day. Cleveland had been the only team to defeat the Colts during the regular season, but in the league championship game, Smith and middle linebacker Mike Curtis were again the ringleaders as the Colts certified their dominance, 34–0, only the second time the proud Cleveland franchise had ever suffered a shutout.

Shula had come to the Colts as a defensive specialist, and his 1968 team was a masterpiece, allowing 10 or fewer points in ten of the fourteen regular-season games, shutting out three foes and holding four others without a touchdown while allowing a paltry 144 points. It wasn't all defense; the Colts not only scored 402 points, they also outscored opponents 240–74 in the first half of their fourteen games and destroyed any thought of comebacks with a cumulative score of 62–20 in the third quarter.

Those numbers should have shaken whatever challenger emerged from the AFL as much as the Packers had shaken the Chiefs and Raiders in the first two Super Bowls. If the Colts had known the truth they would have been surprised. The Jets had been studying films of the Colts as soon as they arrived in South Florida, two weeks ahead of the game. Most coaches want their teams away from the site of a game on the road as long as possible, but Weeb Ewbank wanted his players out of frosty New York, and he didn't worry about what distractions they would find in their first week away. He knew Namath was far from the only carouser on the Jets, and he expected the playboys would find the occasions and company with which to play no matter where they were. The benefit of having the team together for a week's extra film study would reinforce their confidence. The films seemed to bear out what the Jet coaches had privately thought—that the NFL champions were slow.

177

If Vince Lombardi's persona had dominated the weeks before Super Bowl I and II, what dominated the week before Super Bowl III was Namath's mouth. The New York team's headquarters were in the Galt Ocean Mile Hotel on the beach in Fort Lauderdale. For the last three decades or more, the NFL has conducted the media arrangements with military precision, tightly restricting access and controlling information like the national security office. With hordes of media, both press and electronic as well as international and domestic, the league has little choice. But in 1968 media access was a laissez-faire matter. After Jet workouts Namath would cover his body with tanning oil, don sunglasses, and repair to a chaise lounge by the swimming pool, surrounded by reporters. They got an earful.

Some of Namath's yeastier sound bites went this way:

"We're a better team than Baltimore."

"Earl Morrall would be a third-string quarterback on the Jets. . . . There are five or six better quarterbacks than Morrall in the NFL."

A few nights before the game, Namath appeared as an after-dinner speaker before the Miami Touchdown Club. "We're going to win this game," he told the audience. "I guarantee it." The reaction from the Jets was totally different from the cringing that Fred Williamson evoked from his Kansas City teammates when he boasted about how he was "gonna lay the hammer" on the Packers before Super Bowl I. The Jets believed fervently in Namath. "When Joe talked that way," said Dave Herman, a guard who would be used at right tackle to block Bubba Smith, "he was saying what all of us wanted to believe and eventually we did." The Colts, on the other hand, were enraged. Billy Ray Smith, the veteran guard, spoke of ramming Namath's teeth down his throat. Defensive end Lou Michaels, who was also the Baltimore kicker, met Namath in a Fort Lauderdale restaurant one night, and threatened him. "You've been doing a lot of talking, haven't you?" Michaels said, menacingly. "There's a lot to talk about," Namath shrugged. Eventually Michaels, whose brother

Walt ran the Jets' underrated defense, cooled down, and Namath and the two teammates who accompanied him gave Lou a ride back to his hotel.

Shula was furious about Namath's put-down of Morrall, who had replaced the injured icon, Johnny Unitas, and was voted the most valuable player in the NFL for 1968. "How can he say those things about Morrall?" Shula demanded. "He threw 26 touchdown passes, he was outstanding all season long." Morrall and Namath represented a clash of generations. Morrall, a great athlete who had not only been an All-America quarterback at Michigan State but was an infielder on the Spartans' College World Series baseball champions, wore his hair in a crew cut and his uniform traditionally. He spoke mostly in sports clichés when he spoke at all. Namath wore his hair long, dressed in white, low-cut football cleats, and had a great deal to say about everything. The media that covered the AFL, mostly young turks, identified with Broadway Joe. The media that covered the NFL was older, more conservative, and respectful, especially of players like Morrall. They thought Namath conducted himself disgracefully, was disrespectful of the NFL and its long traditions, and, in a word of their generation, "a snot."

The reaction of Namath's coach was "I wish Joe would keep his mouth shut," but Ewbank's pregame speech to his players before they left their dressing room for the Orange Bowl field was, "When we win, I don't want you to pick me up on your shoulders and carry me off, you might ruin my other hip. I'll walk, okay?" This was greeted by a happy roar from the Jets.

The day before the game, Vince Lombardi, now exclusively the general manager of the Green Bay Packers, visited the media center at Super Bowl headquarters. He didn't stay long, but he confided to Moe Siegel, the *Washington Star* columnist, that he thought the Jets had a chance to win. "I've never seen a quicker release from a passer than this kid's," he said, referring to Namath. Lombardi was emerging from his Wisconsin cocoon and displaying, of all things, media savvy. Siegel had a lot of important readers in the nation's capitol, and Lombardi obviously saw profit in staying on his good side. Twenty-five days later he would resign from his position in Green Bay to take over the Washington Redskins. He knew that they criticized popes and presidents in Washington and that he wouldn't be able to operate as he had in Green Bay. Siegel used Lombardi's words in his column on game-day morning. Later that evening the media center had another visitor, Giants kicker Pete Gogolak, who was looking for a ticket to the game. The man who started the march to the merger between the leagues and the invention of the Super Bowl when he jumped from Buffalo to the NFL, didn't have enough pull to assure himself of a seat.

When they finally took the field the next day, the Jets were 17-point underdogs. "I'd rather be 17-point underdogs than 19-point favorites," said defensive tackle Paul Rochester. He referred to the regular-season games against Buffalo and Denver when the Jets were heavily favored. "That's when we lose," Rochester added. The Colts took the field with a definite air of confidence, and up in the Orange Bowl press box there was even more confidence. It was long before the era of luxury-box elitism, and the commissioner's box was a normal set of chair seats on the 50-yard line in press row, separated from the media only by Plexiglas windows. Commissioner Pete Rozelle sat on the left, with George Halas, who virtually invented pro football, and Art Modell, owner of the Browns and reigning president of the NFL, on Rozelle's right. They wore satisfied looks, as if they were about to donate themselves to the Smithsonian Institute.

The style of football played once the game commenced went along the lines of which Ewbank had predicted: "Probably not very pretty to watch; not much fun to play." What he meant was that the Jets were not going to put themselves into a predicament that could shatter their confidence, which is what had happened to Kansas City and Oakland in the first two Super Bowls. The rain that fell in the morning had ceased, but there was enough wind for the coaches to worry a little about their passing games. The Jets received the opening kickoff, and the second play Namath called was 19 straight, with Matt Snell carrying the ball. It would be called sixteen more times that day. Baltimore safety Rick Volk closed on the play, but he was knocked groggy in his collision with Snell and had to leave the field. It certified to the Jets that the Colts did, indeed, put on their pants one leg at a time.

On their first possession, Baltimore played as if the 17-point betting spread was an underlay. Morrall passed to his great tight end, John Mackey, for 15 yards. Tom Matte picked up another first down on a sweep. A mixture of runs and another 15-yard pass put the Colts on New York's 19-yard line. Then the unhinging began, not for the AFL upstart but for the supposedly cool hands, the proud champions of the even prouder National Football League. Morrall threw an accurate pass to Willie Richardson, who dropped it even though safety Jim Hudson, the man assigned to cover him, fell down. On the next play, tight end Tom Mitchell got open, but Morrall overthrew him. On third-and-10, Gerry Philbin, New York's best pass rusher, chased Morrall out of the pocket and tackled him for no gain. Lou Michaels then missed a 27-yard field goal.

When the Jets regained possession, Namath converted a third down and put the ball on the New York 35. What followed was one of the most famous incomplete passes in Super Bowl history. Don Maynard was sent downfield on a straight streak pattern, flying by cornerback Bob Boyd, whom the Jets' coaches had identified as the weakest link in the Baltimore secondary. Colt safety Jerry Logan came over to pick up Maynard but the swift receiver beat him, too. Namath overthrew the pass. "It was an important play," Namath said later. "Maynard got by their bomb-proof coverage. He put the fear of God in them for the rest of the game. They had to keep their double coverage, which opened things up for George Sauer."

What the Colts didn't know was that Maynard had pulled a muscle in the AFL championship against the Raiders, and he was unlikely to be capable of another all-out fly pattern like the one that shook the Colts early in the game. What the Jets didn't know was that the Colts were hiding a nasty case of tonsillitis handicapping Lenny Lyles, the cornerback who was assigned to cover Sauer. Sauer caught eight of Namath's passes for 133 yards. Had the Jets known about Lyles's illness, they might have tested him more often.

The game was scoreless until New York stepped out of character, using twelve plays to move methodically downfield with Matt Snell giving the AFL its first lead in the short annals of the Super Bowl. It was the Jets' only score until Jim Turner kicked three field goals in the second half. Baltimore had many opportunities yet took advantage of none of them, which is usually a loser's lament. In the first two Super Bowls, it was the AFL challengers who cracked, but on this day it was Baltimore's composure that crumbled early and kept crumbling. Colt running back Tom Matte broke loose on a 58-yard run, the longest in Super Bowl history at the time, and then he was tackled by several Jets at the New York 16. The last tackler on the pile was cornerback Johnny Sample, a former Colt who had played in Baltimore's famous overtime victory over the Giants in the 1958 NFL championship game. Sample arrived with his knees digging into Matte, who leaped to his feet in rage. "You're a dirty player," he screamed at Sample, whom many of his former teammates despised. A number of other Colts joined the scene, yelling at Sample. Two plays later Sample intercepted Morrall's pass to kill the scoring drive.

The next time Baltimore took possession of the ball, it was at the New York 42 with just 43 seconds remaining in the half. The pregame assumptions were that the Jets would have to resort to gadget plays in order to have any chance against the NFL champions, but with the score 7–0 in favor of the Jets and the smell of stupendous upset in the air, it was the 17-point favorite who reached into the gadget bag. Matte took a handoff and headed to his right on what seemed, ostensibly, to be a sweep, but then he stopped, turned, and threw the ball back to Morrall. Downfield in the end zone was Colt receiver Jimmy Orr, who seemed 15 yards from any Jet. Safety Bill Bair, normally the coverage man on Orr, had bitten on the running fake. A halftime tie and a game-changing atmosphere beckoned, but Morrall never threw the ball to him. Time after time for the next four decades, Morrall patiently explained to interviewers, "I never saw him." When Orr realized that, he began frantically waving his arms to attract the attention of his quarterback. He didn't see Orr, but Morrall did see fullback Jerry Hill, who was also open since Jim Hudson had slipped trying to cover him. Morrall released his pass, but Hudson had recovered and intercepted as the half ended.

No intermission would heal the Colts. They were a psychological mess. The missed opportunity with Orr was just part of their travail. Morrall was intercepted three times, Michaels missed two field goals, and in the last minute of the half the Colts roughed punter Curley Johnson but were saved by an off-setting illegal formation penalty against the Jets.

On Baltimore's first play of the second half, Matte fumbled and Baker recovered for New York, resulting in the first of Turner's field goals and a 10–0 lead. It was then that the champions of a league derided for playing "basketball on cleats" began playing ball control. In the entire third quarter, the Colts managed to run just seven plays, gaining 11 yards. As time was dwindling in the quarter, a roar from the crowd signaled that on the sidelines, warming up, was the great Johnny Unitas. By the time he replaced Morrall, the Jets had a 13–0 lead on Turner's second field goal. Once he took the field, it was obvious to all but the most fervent NFL loyalists that Johnny Unitas, now an aged athlete and a sore-armed one, was not the Johnny Unitas they remembered. His first series yielded nothing and Turner kicked his third field goal for a 16–0 lead. In Unitas's prime, hearts would beat, reasonably expecting a comeback, but now he had almost nothing to offer. Later he pushed his team toward the Jets goal line, but when a receiver broke free, Unitas badly underthrew his pass and Beverly made the Jets' fourth interception. Far too late the Colts scored a face-saving touchdown, but it required three defensive penalties against the Jets and three runs from the 1-yard line before Hill finally made it across the goal line.

By chance, I was seated at the end of the left side of press row, my right shoulder next to Rozelle's left shoulder, divided only by the Plexiglas. With about seven or eight minutes before the end and the Jets leading, 16–0, I heard a tapping on the glass. I glanced over, saw Halas and Modell in a state of biblical anguish, and then noticed that a grinning commissioner was holding a small note to the glass for me to see. The note read: "Do you think Jimmy the Greek will be allowed back in Las Vegas?" The Greek was one of the Vegas oddsmakers who established Baltimore as a 17-point favorite. Rozelle could afford to smile. He was now in charge of a united league in which parity, not disparity, reigned. Someone in the press box referred to him as czar of all the rushers!

With five minutes remaining in the game, members of the NFL's public relations staff led the media from the press box down a series of ramps to the field and then the locker-room areas. Larry Merchant, then a popular *New York Post* sports columnist and later a famous boxing analyst for HBO, was at the head of the media pack, reeling off one-liners that were the reversal of most of the put-downs suffered by the AFL, which he now turned on the established league. The best of them ended up in the lead of his column in the *Post* the next day:

> With a common draft, the NFL is sure to catch up to the AFL in two years. The thing the NFL has to work on is defense, especially at cornerback. Still, it's too bad O. J. Simpson is going to the AFL when the weaker NFL needs him.
>
> It is a time for gloating in the AFL because the Jets knocked all the smugness and pomposity out of the poor old NFL yesterday. The Jets took apart, beat up, and panicked the invincible Colts in the Super Bowl. The world belongs to the young.

184

There would be no dramatic change in the game's final minutes. The final score was 16–7. Sports history had been written.

Once Namath reached his teammates in the Jets' pandemonium of a dressing room, he assumed the role of master of ceremonies, at first rejecting questions from anyone but the New York press, quickly widening the approved group to AFL writers. A photographer asked a question, and Namath told him to get a pad and pencil if he wanted to be part of the chaotic press conference. Sample reached into his locker for his wallet and removed a yellowed newspaper clipping. Its headline read KC NOT IN CLASS WITH NFL'S BEST— LOMBARDI. "I've been carrying this in my wallet for three years," revealed the Jets' cornerback, "Nobody knew it but my wife. I guess I can put it in my scrapbook."

CHAPTER 21

The Convincer

The Baltimore dressing room in the hour after Super Bowl III was a festival of sore losers and finger pointers. Most of the fingers were pointed at quarterback Earl Morrall and coach Don Shula.

"We played the game like an AFL team, throwing the ball deep all day," wide receiver Willie Richardson said. Veteran defensive end Ordell Braase, outplayed by Winston Hill, the Jets' young left tackle, who had been driven off the Colts' roster by Braase years before, was still resentful of Namath: "Football is a team sport. If he thinks he can go out and do it alone, he's crazy. He had a lot of help."

"We beat ourselves," tight end John Mackey said. Linebacker Dennis Gaubatz said, "They still don't impress me. The breaks didn't come our way; we're a better ball club." Bill Curry, who would become a big-time college head coach years later, said, "It seems stupid to say, but we played ten or twelve teams better than the Jets." Curry was correct. It did seem stupid to say.

The Colts weren't the only ones still in denial, many NFL players, their pride scalded by the AFL victory, also refused to believe that the Jets' victory was anything but a fluke. These skeptics included the New York Giants players who wouldn't believe they had lost the battle of New York until the following August when the teams finally met in a preseason game at the Yale Bowl in Connecticut. "It was as serious as the Super Bowl," said John Dockery, a Jet defensive back who had played at the Yale Bowl when he was a Harvard undergraduate. New Haven was a Jets town, and about 60,000 people in the stadium were Jets fans. Namath cut the favorite to pieces, throwing three touchdown passes in a 37–14 Jets victory.

A large portion of the sporting press also thought the Jets' victory in Super Bowl III was a fluke. As the Jets dressing room was emptying after that game, Gerry Philbin, the fiery defensive end, was still sitting in his uniform on a bench right next to the door. A writer friend asked what he was waiting for. "I'm waiting for Tex Maule," he said of *Sports Illustrated*'s senior pro football writer and a journalist infamous for his anti-AFL bias. "When is Maule coming in here?" Maule never came. Maybe he got lost on his way out of the Baltimore dressing room.

When I arrived back at the press hotel on Miami Beach, my wife, Beverly, was waiting for me in the lobby. She had seen the miniature treasure chests the NFL caterer had picked to serve lunch to the press at halftime and she told me not to forget to bring it back since she wanted to make a purse out of it. When we got on the crowded elevator to go to our room, she asked, "Did you remember the lunch bucket?" I told her I had and that "I spilled pickle juice on my trousers cleaning out the trash in it." From the rear of the elevator came a voice: "That game made me so sick, I couldn't eat my lunch." It was Tex Maule.

As satisfying as the Jets' victory over the Colts had been, Joe Namath and the Jets had not convinced the NFL owners they should prepare any special welcome for their AFL counterparts when their shotgun marriage was to be consummated in time for the 1970 season. It's difficult to embrace your new in-laws at the wedding reception when you still consider them to be on a level with the Jukes and the Kallikaks.

That was the atmosphere when the "new" NFL convened in Palm Springs, California, in March of 1969 to start discussing realignment of the league as outlined in the original merger agreement. A number of old-line NFL owners wanted to dispense with the realignment problem by establishing a "separate but equal" football society, with the two leagues being renamed conferences but the status quo of membership retained. That would have meant the NFL would stay a sixteen-team league, and the AFL would keep Cincinnati despite Paul Brown's insistence on the Bengals rejoining his old friends from his Cleveland days. As it turned out, Brown had AFL allies in Gerald Phipps of Denver, Joe Robbie of Miami, and Gene Klein of San Diego. Phipps and Robbie wanted their teams, never before successful at the gate, to have access to some of the huge NFL stadiums. The Chargers wanted a natural Southern California rival in the Los Angeles Rams. A separate AFL identity appealed to those who found the cachet of the upstart league whose champion had just stunned the NFL very appealing.

Those who wanted a total realignment pointed to a paragraph in the original merger agreement that read: "In connection with such future realignment of the league, factors of geography, natural rivalries, stadium size, gate attendance, weather circumstances, team strength, and conflicts with baseball with the use of league stadiums shall all be taken under consideration in such fashion as not to prejudice unfairly any franchise of the realigned league."

Brown and his allies wanted a complete realignment, a new start with the twenty-six teams mixed as they hadn't been before. As soon as all the owners had entered the room for their joint session, they were handed a document titled *A Summary of Basic Information Pertinent to a Scheduling and Alignment in 1970 and Thereafter*. Its four main points were:

1. Expansion from twenty-six to twenty-eight teams in 1970 was not feasible.
2. Realignment based on the extension of the present fourteen-game schedule was not feasible.
3. Realignment in 1970 should retain as many of the smaller four and five-team divisions as possible.
4. The two leagues should maintain their identity for purposes of public image, although legally one league in 1970, with some interleague play.

Point No. 4 was the bombshell. There would be no realignment but a recommendation to maintain the sixteen teams in what had been the NFL and ten in what had been the AFL, with a few inter-league games thrown at the AFL as a financial bone. It was as if it were 1776 and King George III had told the colonial revolutionaries, "You can have your independence, but we're keeping our troops in America forever to maintain order." The AFL owners, who had already agreed to pay rich indemnities to merge, greeted the document like a skunk at a wedding reception. They saw it as a shell game conducted not on the sidewalk in Times Square but in Rozelle's Park Avenue office.

"The owners from the two leagues did not get along at that meeting, nor would we get along for years to come," said Buffalo's Ralph Wilson. "It was no surprise that some of our owners wanted to be mixed into the NFL since that's how the AFL was formed, by men who wanted to have NFL franchises but weren't allowed in.

"The AFL owners didn't trust the NFL owners either. For instance, there was still tremendous bitterness toward Max Winter and the rest of the Minnesota owners because of what they did to us at our formative league meeting in Minneapolis in 1959. They were original members of the AFL but while we were waiting for them to show up at our meeting, we got word that the NFL had offered them a franchise and they had accepted it, double-crossing us."

The NFL thought it had effectively strangled the new league in its cradle with its clandestine operation but the AFL then accepted an offer for a replacement franchise in the San Francisco Bay area, taking on the 49ers in NFL territory. That's how the Oakland Raiders were born.

"Not long afterward we received a telegram from George Halas, offering to accept the entire AFL into the NFL, but without Denver," said Wilson. "They didn't want Denver. They didn't think it was a major league city." In those days the Colorado capital still had the flavor of a frontier town. There were few tall buildings downtown, but there were a number of saddle shops that catered to cowboys from the rural parts of Colorado and Wyoming, as well as American Indians from nearby reservations. It was colorful, but the NFL considered it below its standards. "We turned down Halas's offer unanimously," said Wilson. "None of us would turn our backs on Denver."

The subject of realignment was postponed until a second owners' meeting in New York, where the fervor over the Jets' staggering upset and the Giants' string of bad seasons had created an AFL city—if only temporarily. The clock was ticking with 1970 approaching and the completion of the merger essential to avoid chaos and possibly crippling lawsuits. Again, nothing was resolved by the stubborn moguls, and Rozelle called a third, drop-dead realignment meeting in New York City for April 29. The merger, and possibly his commissionership, was at stake.

The opening day of the third realignment meeting bore no fruit, but the next day, in a separate gathering of NFL owners, a resolution was adopted authorizing Rozelle to discuss with interested NFL teams a move by three of the league's teams to what had been called the AFL but now was rechristened the American Football Conference of the National Football League. The idea was based on a suggestion floated by Al Davis, whom the AFC-AFL owners had designated their realignment chairman, to pay the three NFL teams to switch conferences. The NFL owners digested, debated, and discarded the idea for the next five days. The idea itself was found feasible by some, but getting a club to commit to moving to the new conference was the sticking point. The consensus thinking was "let some other guy do it." Especially firm about not moving his team was Art Modell of Cleveland, who had just finished his term as president of the NFL. "The Browns will never move," he said in a widely quoted vow. He also included Los Angeles, Chicago, New York, and San Francisco in that category. "It would emasculate our keynote franchises," he said. In a moment of overheated candor about his own team's feelings, he repeated his vow, "The Denver Broncos will never play in Cleveland Stadium."

On the sixth day, with progress neck-deep in disagreement, the velvet glove was slipped off Rozelle's mailed fist. The commissioner locked the door on his collection of tycoons, captains of industry, and power brokers accustomed to being the masters of their own fiefdoms. In the parlance of mobsters readying for gang warfare, they "went to the mattresses" until Rozelle could squeeze an agreement out of them. Some napped uncomfortably in chairs. Lamar Hunt of Kansas City, scion of a Texas oil fortune, and Max Winter, septuagenarian managing partner of the Minnesota Vikings, stretched out on the red plush carpet beneath a boardroom table. Finally cots were brought in.

Across town, in a large suite converted to a press room in the posh St. Regis Hotel, the media awaited word on an agreement. For days the stylish encampment lasted until early in the evening when word came that there would be an adjournment without an agreement. On Friday, Rozelle sent word to sit tight; there would be an agreement some time this day, May 17, 1969. Periodically, an emissary was sent to the press room to deliver a progress report, which, in reality, was a stalling report. The reporters couldn't even retreat to the hotel bar for a refreshment break, since the price of a drink in the St. Regis's famed Old King Cole room tested even the most generous expense accounts. As evening began to slip into nighttime, stomachs began to rumble, and someone in the media suggested that steak sandwiches be ordered for all from room service. The public relations person in charge of the room, Harold Rosenthal, was at one time a noted baseball writer for the long-defunct *New York Herald Tribune*. His paper's demise forced him to change careers and he ended up employed in the public relations department of the AFL and then the NFL after the merger. Rosenthal was unaccustomed to steak-sandwich generosity with the budget-conscious AFL, and he hadn't worked for the merged league long enough to realize Pete Rozelle always went first class with the media. When the waiter showed up with the sandwiches, Rosenthal, who had been absent when the call for food was made, banished the waiter to the kitchen to exchange the steaks for hamburgers, too accustomed to the AFL's frugal habits.

Shortly after dawn on Saturday, May 10, the commissioner announced that three NFL teams—the Pittsburgh Steelers, Baltimore Colts, and Cleveland Browns—had agreed to switch to the AFC. The realignment of the remaining thirteen teams in the NFC would be the subject of a later meeting. As it turned out, there were many meetings, and further wrangling so the last strings of the great realignment wouldn't be tied until January of 1970. There was one other item about the joining of the Steelers, Colts, and Browns to their former AFL adversaries: Each of those teams would receive a bounty of $3 million each.

The reaction of the fans in Pittsburgh, Baltimore, and Cleveland ranged from surprise to volcanic eruption. Most of the surprise came in Pittsburgh. The volcanoes erupted in Baltimore and Cleveland. Modell had been absent from the last few days of the meeting in New York, as he was lying in a bed in Doctors Hospital in Manhattan, recovering from a bleeding ulcer attack. His bedside visitors included Art Rooney, the Steelers' owner, and Rooney's son, Dan. The younger Rooney was against the move, but his father told him, "I'm with Art [Modell]. If he moves, we move."

The following Wednesday an open letter appeared in the *Cleveland Press* from Bill Schmidt, a reader in Lakewood, Ohio, a Cleveland suburb. It addressed Modell as "Dear Benedict," as in Benedict Arnold. "I greet the news of the Browns entering the AFL about like I would if someone told me my wife had been unfaithful. I wish my season ticket [which I've held since 1964] to terminate the day the Browns enter the AFL. I previously hailed you as the Bill Veeck of football. I now curse the day you came to Cleveland. I hope you made enough money on your sale of the Browns to the minor league. My family wishes you a speedy recovery by a vote of four to three."

James B. Debevec of Euclid continued in a similar vein: "I have never been so humiliated in my life. The greatest concentration of NFL fans in the world is right here in Cleveland. Never before in sports history were so many people hoodwinked and given such a kick in the pants." Baltimore fans, whose team was beaten by the Jets four months previously in Super Bowl III, were slightly less incensed, but John Root expressed the feelings for many when he said, "I'm disgusted and my wife is really burning. Three million dollars for the owner and nothing for the fans. The Rams have more stars than the whole AFL put together."

In Pittsburgh, where the Steelers had enjoyed just six winning seasons since World War II ended and never won a championship of any sort since their founding in 1933, the reaction was less fervent. Their final season in the "old" NFL was near commencement, and they would win just one of thirteen games. The civic consensus was "What do we have to lose?"

Pro football players are like Army enlisted men. They serve where they are paid to serve. The reaction of the players from Pittsburgh, Baltimore, and Cleveland to the working company they would keep henceforth was fairly uniform. "Football is football," said Johnny Unitas, the hard-nosed Colt great. "I couldn't care less where we play." His teammate, wide receiver Willie Richardson, who complained bitterly that "we played like an AFL team" when Baltimore lost Super Bowl III, claimed "I don't see where it makes that much difference."

The reaction of those closest in their organizations to the owners who took the money and switched were almost unanimous in that Rooney and Modell did what they thought was best for the league. Front office employees with the Browns said they heard Modell remark to his son David that "we have real money for the first time." But that was acknowledged to be more of an affirmation that he was not a particularly wealthy man when he bought the Browns in 1963, at least not in the same financial class as most NFL owners. It was different in the case of Baltimore's Carroll Rosenbloom. Asked why he thought Rosenbloom decided to switch conferences, then-Colt general manager Don Klosterman rubbed his fingers together and said, "The money."

Rosenbloom's decision to move the Colts out of the NFC may have played a role in his later landmark swap of the Baltimore franchise for the Los Angeles Rams. In 1953 when he led a group that purchased Dallas's NFL team and moved it back to Baltimore where it was renamed the "Colts," Rosenbloom became close friends with *Baltimore News-American*'s John Steadman, the most popular sports columnist in the city. In the mid-1950s, he hired Steadman as assistant general manager and public relations director. Steadman eventually returned to the newspaper business, but Rosenbloom assured him that if ever he wanted to return to the Colts there was a good job waiting for him. In 1959 when NFL commissioner Bert Bell died of a heart attack while watching an Eagles' game in Philadelphia's Franklin Field, Rosenbloom nominated Steadman as Bell's successor. The position eventually went to Pete Rozelle.

In the early 1960s, a rift started between Rosenbloom and Steadman when the columnist began criticizing the Colts' owner for attempting to force his season ticket holders into buying exhibition games in their ticket package, a practice already being used in the new AFL. After Rosenbloom moved the team into the AFC, the rift with Steadman deepened. The last time the two were socially amenable came at a golf outing sponsored by the Colts as they were about to open the 1970 training camp for their pioneer season in the AFC. Rosenbloom insisted on putting together a foursome that included Steadman. The owner's partner was Klosterman, his GM, who was a decent golfer even though he had been crippled in a skiing accident in the Canadian Rockies fifteen years earlier. The partner chosen for Steadman was the Colts' new public relations director Ernie Accorsi, even though Accorsi had played only once or twice that summer. What the others didn't know was that Accorsi had attended Wake Forest University on a golf scholarship.

As soon as the round started, Accorsi was on fire. After about five holes, Klosterman recognized the subtle signs of unhappiness in his employer. Quietly he sidled over to Accorsi and whispered, "If you want to keep working for C.R., I'd suggest you start making some bogeys." Immediately Accorsi began to, in effect, shave points. As the foursome approached the eighteenth hole, the match was tied. Steadman won it by sinking a dauntingly long putt. As the ball dropped into the cup, Rosenbloom literally danced across the green, hugged, and kissed Steadman. Later, after the post-tournament dinner in the clubhouse, Steadman won the grand prize in the drawing, but he never got to collect it. The rift with Rosenbloom became a chasm. The owner refused to extend to him the normal courtesies enjoyed by the press that covered the Colts by not allowing his newspaper the Colts' rate at the team hotels on the road. Nor would Rosenbloom make his hotel reservations or allow him to travel on the team plane or ride to the game on the press bus. Since he, like all journalists on an out-of-town assignment, was on expense account, Steadman accepted it as a petty annoyance. Rosenbloom tried to bar him from the press box at Memorial Stadium, but Rozelle wouldn't allow that. This was done to a man who was such a Colt loyalist that he carried a small Baltimore Colt pennant, with the team's original colors, and affixed it to the front of his space in the press box whenever he covered a road game. When he died in January 2001, the Baltimore Colts were no more, having moved to Indianapolis fifteen years earlier, but the casket bearing John Steadman's body was led out of his neighborhood Catholic church by the Baltimore Colts' marching band playing the Colts' fight song.

After the Colts' switch to the AFC, a move Steadman greeted reluctantly with his mood clear to his readers, life in Baltimore grew far less comfortable for Rosenbloom. The city is strong on tradition, wary of change, and at rest with its history, including its sports history. The change in the Colts' yearly opponents ran counter to what appealed to Baltimoreans. Rosenbloom began thinking about a change of venue for himself, if not his franchise.

It wasn't merely in the cities whose franchises had switched where there was criticism of the owners who agreed to move. In Washington, Shirley Povich, the famed and respected sports editor of the *Post*, wrote a stinging column about the surprising developments. "It will be a stunning new alignment for professional football beginning in 1970," began Povich, "with the proud Cleveland Browns and Baltimore Colts, along with the Pittsburgh Steelers, moving into the onetime unspeakable American Football League. The switch of two of the NFL's most prosperous and powerful teams into the erstwhile low-rent district is an astonishment." It was as if what Joe Namath and the New York Jets accomplished in Super Bowl III didn't matter.

Meanwhile, the 1969 season, the final one for the American Football League and the farewell to the "old" NFL for Baltimore, Cleveland, and Pittsburgh, was about to commence. For the Steelers it started with hope, as they had a bright new coach, Chuck Noll, a new stadium named Three Rivers under construction, and an unaccustomed opening victory over Detroit. After that it took on the look of the 1968 team, who had won just two games. The final NFL version of the Steelers lost its last thirteen games. The Colts did not rebound well from their monumental upset loss to the Jets. Their good-bye to their old league began with a home loss to the Rams and then a dismal 52–14 walloping from the Minnesota Vikings, definitely a team on the make. The Browns were the Browns, as usual. They didn't lose a game until November. Leroy Kelly would have his three-season streak of 1,000-yard performances snapped, but with the help of his wonderful receivers, Paul Warfield and Gary Collins, who caught twenty-one touchdown passes between them, quarterback Bill Nelson had the season of his career.

For those NFL teams who hadn't switched, it was a matter of business as usual—except for the Dallas Cowboys. On July 5 their original quarterback, Don Meredith, announced his retirement at the age of thirty, at a time when most pro quarterbacks are just warming up. Thirteen days later, when the veterans were due to report to training camp, the team's best running back, Don Perkins, retired. The Cowboys reacted to the traumatic change by winning their first six games and extending their regular-season winning streak to eleven games. Like Cleveland, they didn't lose until November.

Over in the AFL, it was a reprise of the 1968 season with the same three teams dominant—the Jets, Oakland Raiders, and Kansas City Chiefs. It never was sorted out until Christmastime. Kansas City lost just three games all season, but two of those were to the hated Raiders late in the season. Oakland won, 27–24, in Kansas City on November 23 and then again in Oakland, 13–10, on December 13. As the wild-card team, the Chiefs would have to play the Jets in blustery, frigid Shea Stadium. Two of the sport's best passers, Namath and the Chiefs' Lenny Dawson, were virtually neutered. Namath completed just fourteen of forty passes. Dawson didn't complete many, but he won the game with two clutch passes late in the fourth quarter. The first was a 61-yard shot to Otis Taylor, followed by a 19-yarder to Gloster Richardson for the game's only touchdown.

The Raiders, with their self-esteem inflated by those two late-season victories over the Chiefs, arrived for the very last AFL championship game at Oakland–Alameda County Stadium with their suitcases packed and ready for a postgame flight to New Orleans for Super Bowl IV. The bags would stay in Oakland. After a 7–7 tie at halftime, normally reliable George Blanda missed field goals of 39 and 40 yards, both wide right, which would have given the Raiders a third-quarter lead. The Chiefs then drove 98 yards for the lead touchdown on Robert Holmes's 3-yard run. The rest of the game was dominated by the Chiefs' defense, which intercepted Daryle Lamonica three times in the fourth quarter. The last interception, Emmitt Thomas's second of the game, set up Jan Stenerud's 22-yard field goal, which made the final score 17–7.

The AFL's representative in the Super Bowl was a wild-card team in its going-out-of-business final game. The NFL's representative

197

was none of its elite franchises, but instead one who was born as a device to strangle the AFL while it was still in the birth canal; a team that gradually inched its way to the top of its league in the ninth year of its existence—Minnesota. It had no 1,000-yard rushers and no flashy passing game, but it did have a magnificent defense and a commonsensical, practical-joke-playing coach, Bud Grant, who had been one of the greatest all-around athletes bred in the state of Minnesota. The Vikings also possessed a quarterback who graded just a three on the passing scale but a ten-plus on the leadership scale.

When Joe Kapp came out of the University of California, the NFL scouts weren't smitten with his passing arm, so he signed with the British Columbia Lions of the Canadian Football League. It was an era in which the CFL was at its all-time best with outstanding quarterbacks on each team: Bernie Faloney, the first-round draft choice from college champion Maryland, whom Hamilton had signed away from San Francisco; Kenny Ploen in Winnipeg, where he was coached by Grant; Sam Etcheverry in Montreal; Ron Lancaster in Saskatchewan; Tobin Rote in Toronto; Canadian homebred Russ Jackson in Ottawa; and Jackie Parker in Edmonton. In that competition, Kapp won the league's most valuable player award. In 1967, after Fran Tarkenton was traded to the Giants for four high draft choices, Kapp came back across the border to become the Vikings' quarterback the same year Grant succeeded Norm Van Brocklin as their coach.

The Vikings lost their opening game to the Giants and their last regular-season game to Atlanta but otherwise swept the board. Their great defense allowed as many as 14 points in just one game, the opening loss against the New York Giants and Fran Tarkenton. The running backs were Dave Osborne and brush-cut Bill Brown. Between them, they barely totaled 1,000 yards, but they were tough and durable, a Viking hallmark under Grant, who would not allow his players to wear gloves or have heaters to give them refuge at their bench, even though they were playing in the bone-numbing outdoors in old Metropolitan Stadium, where winter became a cruel companion.

What they had in large supply was leadership, from Grant and, more dramatically, from Kapp. The quarterback bore a strong facial resemblance to actor Anthony Quinn, and, like Quinn, a generous supply of Mexican blood coursed through his veins. The week before the Super Bowl, Grant gave an apt description of his ragged-edge star: "Most quarterbacks look for a place to run out of bounds; mine looks for someone to bump into." While some quarterbacks have finesse, Kapp was dashing, with a large mixture of charisma and testosterone that encouraged the other Vikings to follow him. His war cry was "Forty for sixty!" What he demanded was that all forty players on the roster give their all for sixty minutes. His teammates bought it.

Kapp was at his best in the Western Conference title game against the Rams, passing for 40 yards and running for 14, including the final 2 for the winning touchdown as Minnesota came from behind in the last quarter to win, 23–20. Then he set the tone in the NFL championship game against Cleveland. Kapp collided with his teammate, Brown, while trying to hand off, then tucked the ball away himself and blasted through the middle of the Cleveland defense, shedding tacklers to get into the end zone. The Vikings went on to win, 27–7. In the dressing room Kapp took a long swig out of a bottle of wine, then smashed the bottle against a locker. "I'll finish the whole bottle when we win the whole championship," he declared.

Football fans seemed to be overcome by Kapp's swashbuckling and so did the Las Vegas oddsmakers. They made Minnesota a 14-point favorite for Super Bowl IV.

New Orleans was a city made for the Super Bowl and the high-roller atmosphere that attached itself, beginning with the Jets' surprise appearance in Super Bowl III in Miami. The hospitality industry was vital to New Orleans' economy, so Bourbon Street and its randy attractions along with the most exotic menus in America—from the $35 breakfasts at Brennan's to the famous French restaurants like Galatoir's, Arnaud's, and Antoine's in the French Quarter to Pascale's Manale in the Garden District to Mosca's in suburban Gretna—were packed most of Super Bowl week. The game itself was played in the old Sugar Bowl, a name much grander than the arena itself. In actuality the "Sugar Bowl" was Tulane University Stadium and its cuffs and collar were frayed, but with seedy charm just like the rest of New Orleans in 1969.

By the time the Chiefs arrived in town, something unfamiliar accompanied them—an ice storm, which froze the fountain in front of their hotel, the Fontainebleau; something not at all unfamiliar to Louisiana and New Orleans also greeted their quarterback, Len Dawson—scandal. On Tuesday night of Super Bowl week, NBC's nightly news program, the *Huntley-Brinkley Report*, led its show with a bulletin, "In Detroit, a special Justice Department Task Force, conducting what it described as the biggest gambling investigation of its kind ever, is about to call seven professional football players and one college coach to testify on their relationship with known gamblers. Among the players scheduled to appear is Len Dawson, quarterback for the Kansas City Chiefs, who will play the Minnesota Vikings in the Super Bowl this Sunday."

The NFL made Dawson available to the media the next morning, a session at which the quarterback denied all charges. Pete Rozelle quickly came to Dawson's defense, revealing that the NFL's own security office had cleared him previously and calling NBC's report "irresponsible." Rozelle's response carried a great deal of weight, as he had a track record of being harsh on any evidence of players' involvement with gamblers. In 1963 he suspended two of the NFL's biggest stars, Green Bay running back Paul Hornung and Detroit defensive tackle Alex Karras, for a year because they bet on games. Earlier in 1969 Rozelle had demanded Joe Namath sell his stake in the Manhattan bar Bachelors Three because it was frequented by known gamblers.

Nineteen sixty-nine was a year of one amazing feat and several depressing horrors. Man walked on the moon, the Manson cult committed unspeakable murders in Hollywood, unspeakable atrocities by U.S. soldiers at Mi Lai in Vietnam were revealed, U.S. Senator Ted Kennedy swam away from the drowning of a young woman campaign worker in Chappaquiddick, Massachusetts. Now it appeared that a diversion the nation seemed to need, the climax of the pro football season, Super Bowl IV, would be stained also. It wasn't. The scandal story had no legs. There was never any evidence that Dawson had anything but a casual acquaintance with a big-time gambler. Before the game a phone call came in to the Chiefs' dressing room for Dawson. It was from Richard Nixon, president of the United States. He told Dawson not to worry about the gambling allegations.

Hank Stram, the Chiefs' coach, was confident his offense could score enough against the Minnesota "Purple People Eaters," the Vikings' aggressive defense. He would use their aggressiveness against them, with reverse plays and traps. Seven minutes into the second quarter, the Kansas City strategists had confirmed that Stram's game plan was on the money. The nation's football fans were also learning something: The Las Vegas oddsmakers, along with the NFL champions, put on their pants one leg at a time. The smart guys from the legal betting rooms had completely misjudged what a mismatch the Kansas City defense against the Minnesota offense would turn out to be. Las Vegas's 14-point spread was absurd. The Vikings' ground game was a matter of pounding the ball between the tackles, and there was very little outside speed. The focal point in their offensive line was Mick Tingelhoff, one of the finest centers in the NFL. Smart and quick, he called the blocking assignments, and his quickness allowed him to efficiently cut down opposing linebackers, helping create huge holes for Osborne and Brown. Kansas City's defense presented a much more difficult problem. The Chiefs had made seven changes from the defense that the Packers encountered in Super Bowl I. Youngsters Jim Lynch and Willie Lanier had joined Bobby Bell in a revamped linebacking trio, but Tingelhoff couldn't even get at them much less block them. The Chiefs used a 3-4 defensive front rarely seen in the NFL in those days. That meant Tingelhoff, who weighed just 237 pounds, would have to play head-on with a nose tackle, in this case 6-foot-7, 285-pound Buck Buchanan. The Chiefs also had a variety of defensive sets with Buchanan moving over to a normal tackle position and Curley Culp, a college wrestling champion who weighed 295 pounds, on Tingelhoff's nose. By the end of the first quarter, the Vikings center thought his head was caught in a snow blower.

In the pregame warm-ups, the Vikings also witnessed something that shocked them—the Kansas City kicking game. Stenerud was successful on almost every kick of 50 yards or more that he attempted. Of punter Jerrell Wilson, Minnesota offensive coordinator Jerry Burns said, "I don't think I've ever seen anyone kick a ball that well or that high." The Chiefs scored on their first possession when Stenerud kicked the longest field goal in the four Super Bowls, 48 yards. He followed with two shorter field goals for a 9–0 lead. Minnesota fumbled the next kickoff and the Chiefs recovered on the Vikings' 19 and added a touchdown to make it 16–0. Minnesota was in such shock that they desperately had Fred Cox attempt a 56-yard field goal, beyond his range, on their next possession. It got no further than the Kansas City 7-yard line. The Vikings were cooked. The final score was 23–7.

Unlike the postgame excuses and put-downs after Super Bowl III, the fallen Vikings accepted defeat with class, saluting their conquerors. "They beat us on offense, they beat us on defense, they beat us in every way," Vikings offensive tackle Grady Alderman said. "There were so many guys running around in their backfield," linebacker Roy Winston said of the Chiefs' constant shifting, "that we couldn't keep track of them." Kapp had an eye-to-collarbone view of his foes. "That defensive line was like a redwood forest," said the Northern California native. "They took our ground game away."

There were concession speeches that came from NFL players on other teams. "I still say that if we [the Colts] played the Jets ten times, we would win nine games, but I don't say that at all about the Vikings and the Chiefs. The Chiefs are a much better team than the Jets and much better than the Kansas City team which played the Packers three years ago," Baltimore center Bill Curry said.

Fran Tarkenton, who would return as the Vikings' quarterback three years later, was more outspoken than any of the NFL veterans. "That was the first time I've seen Dawson play," he said. "All I kept hearing from players, coaches and writers was that Lenny wasn't much of a quarterback. I never heard a good word about him. From what I saw today, I'd say he was one fine quarterback." Tarkenton also had a realist's view of the long argument between the leagues. "I think maybe the AFL has passed the NFL," he said, "Really. Kansas City, Oakland, the Jets, they would be great in our league. Our league doesn't have the great teams it used to. Who's got the great defenses any more in the NFL? Los Angeles, Minnesota, Detroit, Green Bay? Our league isn't as good as it used to be."

The playing field was even at last. The merger was complete. The mayhem was over.

Appendix A: Aftermath

On February 16, 1970, thirty-eight days after Super Bowl IV, Don Shula, whose Baltimore Colts team was upset by the New York Jets in Super Bowl III, a landmark victory for the American Football League, signed a contract to coach the Miami Dolphins of the NFL's American Conference, formerly the AFL.

Commissioner Pete Rozelle later awarded Baltimore a first-round draft choice in 1971 as compensation for the Dolphins' tampering with Shula. Colts' owner Carroll Rosenbloom contended that the tampering occurred around the time of Super Bowl IV, and Shula waited until the owner was out of town on a tour of Asia to get permission from Rosenbloom's son, Steve.

Shula went on to become the most victorious professional coach of all time.

With the merger completed, CBS signed a four-year contract to televise all NFC games, and NBC signed a similar contract to televise all AFC games. Earlier, the NFL had signed a contract with ABC to televise a weekly Monday night game on the network. The television contracts were the second indication that professional football was headed for a future of undreamed-of profits. The first was the gross receipts of $3.8 million for Super Bowl IV, the largest for any previous sporting event.

In the 1970 common draft, the Pittsburgh Steelers exercised the right to first pick as the team with the worst record in the combined league to select Louisiana Tech quarterback Terry Bradshaw.

In early July of 1970, on the eve of the opening of training camps, the combined Players Association announced a strike over improved pension, disability insurance, and several other demands. It was settled August 3, without much benefit to the players, leading Arthur Miller, head of the baseball union to sneer, "It wasn't a strike, it was a student demonstration. The students marched around campus and then went back to class."

Vince Lombardi died of cancer on September 3, 1970, at the age of fifty-seven. He had coached only one season in Washington, but he brought the franchise its first winning season since 1955. A week later the NFL named the Super Bowl trophy after him.

The Browns defeated the New York Jets, 31–21, in Cleveland Stadium in the first ever Monday Night Football game, September 21, 1970, before a crowd of 85,207. The losing quarterback was Joe Namath, who would play five more seasons with the Jets but never appear in another playoff game.

The Browns' victory seemed to confirm to their owner, Art Modell, the feeling he had when he agreed to switch conferences and throw in with the old American League teams. "I thought we would dominate," Modell said many years later, "but it turned out to be Pittsburgh."

In November the Browns had consecutive games scheduled against San Diego, Oakland, and Cincinnati, all former AFL teams. They lost all three games, fell out of the playoff race, and finished 7–7. The loss to the young Bengals was particularly galling, since they were the product of coach, general manager, and founder Paul Brown. Brown was Modell's former coach in Cleveland whom he had fired in a messy controversy after the 1962 season. Modell and Brown despised each other.

In the first Super Bowl after the merger, Super Bowl V on January 17, 1971, the Baltimore Colts—by then the AFC champions under Shula's coaching successor Don McCafferty—defeated the Dallas Cowboys, 16–13, in a ragged, error-filled game decided by a field goal by Baltimore's rookie kicker, Jim O'Brien, a product of the Namath generation. When veteran Baltimore tackle Dan Sullivan was asked if he was worried the rookie might flub the kick, he replied, "No, he's just like all the kids today. He doesn't give a damn about anybody or anything."

In the first forty years after the merger, the Cleveland Browns, once among the sport's proudest franchises, would not appear in any Super Bowl, but Modell did. He moved the Browns out of Cleveland in 1995, relocated in Baltimore—which had lost the Colts—and the team was renamed the Ravens. In the 2000 season the Ravens made the Super Bowl as a wild-card team and defeated the New York Giants, 34–7.

In the 1971 season, the second after the merger was complete, the Denver Broncos not only played in Cleveland Stadium but also shut out the Browns, 27–0. In the 1980s Denver had become one of the nation's greatest cities and its NFL franchise boasted a great quarterback in John Elway. In the AFC championship game on January 11, 1987, the Broncos visited Cleveland Stadium and destroyed the Browns' Super Bowl hopes, first when Elway engineered a 98-yard drive to tie the game with 38 seconds remaining and then the Broncos won in overtime. When the same teams met again in the AFC championship, this time in Denver on January 17, 1988, it marked one of the great performances in Browns' history when Earnest Byner caught seven passes for 120 yards, ran for 67 yards, and scored two touchdowns only to fumble on Denver's 3-yard line with the game about to be tied and only 65 seconds remaining. The television cameras followed Modell's excruciating torment in the owner's box on both occasions.

After his Super Bowl season of 1969, Minnesota quarterback Joe Kapp staged a lengthy holdout that extended into the next season. In October he signed with Boston as a free agent, but the Patriots discovered that charisma and team chemistry do not travel well. Kapp threw just three touchdown passes and seventeen interceptions. After the season Boston drafted Heisman Trophy–winning quarterback Jim Plunkett of Stanford, and Kapp, then thirty-three, was out of the NFL.

Without Kapp, Minnesota won Central Division championships in eight of the next nine years, 1970 through 1978, with the only miss coming in 1972. Coach Bud Grant was inducted into the Pro Football Hall of Fame in 1994.

In 1972 Carroll Rosenbloom traded his NFL franchise in Baltimore to Robert Irsay, the new NFL franchise holder in Los Angeles for the Rams. Because of the tax laws at the time it was a financially astute move for Rosenbloom and it would give his personal popularity a large boost to leave a community where he was becoming a pariah.

In 1978 Rosenbloom hired George Allen, who had been fired by the Washington Redskins, for his second term in Los Angeles, succeeding Chuck Knox, whom the owner had allowed to sign with Buffalo. Halfway through Allen's first preseason schedule, Rosenbloom also fired him and promoted assistant coach Ray Malavasi as his successor. In 1979 the Rams won the NFC championship and advanced to the Super Bowl, where they lost to Pittsburgh. Before the game Rams safety Dave Elmendorf made a private comment that seemed to speak for his teammates: "This isn't Ray Malavasi's team, nor George Allen's team. It's Chuck Knox's team."

On April 2, 1979, Carroll Rosenbloom drowned while swimming in the Atlantic Ocean in front of his winter home in Golden Beach, Florida.

Two days before Christmas, 1972, Pittsburgh was trailing the Oakland Raiders by 6 points with seconds to play in an AFC divisional playoff game in Three Rivers Stadium. The Steelers had one play left, a fourth-and-10 from their own 40-yard line. Terry Bradshaw threw a pass downfield to Frenchy Fuqua, but Raider safety Jack Tatum stepped in front of the play and the ball bounced off his chest. Before it could reach the ground, Pittsburgh's Franco Harris caught it at his shoe tops and ran for a touchdown that allowed the Steelers to win the game. The play would be forever known as the Immaculate Reception. Almost four decades later, Raiders managing partner Al Davis and his players from that team still insisted the pass completion was illegal.

Steelers owner Art Rooney was on the stadium elevator when the winning play began on his way down to offer his condolences to his team, who had never won anything in his forty years of steward-ship. He never saw the winning touchdown. Until the doors opened and he heard the bedlam, he did not know that the once-forlorn Steelers were no longer forlorn.

Two years later the Steelers would experience what arguably was the best college draft of all time. They selected four players with their first five picks who eventually would be voted into the Hall of Fame. Their first pick was wide receiver Lynn Swann of Southern California, their second linebacker Jack Lambert of Kent State, their third wide receiver John Stallworth of Alabama A&M, and their fourth center Mike Webster of Wisconsin. That draft would form the core of a four-time Super Bowl champion and cre-ate a tradition of outstanding teams that would last into the new millennium.

In January 1973, the Baltimore Colts traded forty-year-old Johnny Unitas, their franchise player for seventeen years, to the Chargers, an original AFL team.

In the summer of 1974, the Players Association went on strike, pre-senting the owners with fifty-seven demands, many of them calling for the freedom to move from team to team. The first game affected was the annual exhibition played in Canton, Ohio, just before the Hall of Fame induction. The entire day was a three-ring circus.

The competing teams were Buffalo and St. Louis, and both teams flew in clandestinely the morning of the game to avoid picket lines. The striking players were supported by young members of the United Auto Workers from the Chevrolet plant in nearby Lordstown,

Ohio. The strikers themselves were picketed at the gates by older players, "pre-59ers," who had been shut out of the NFL pension by the union because their careers had ended before 1959.

Against that chaotic background, the speaker of the day was Gerald Ford, the old Michigan center who had been invited by the Hall of Fame board when he was still Republican minority leader in the U.S. House of Representatives. By the time induction day arrived, however, it was in the midst of the Watergate scandal and Ford was vice president of the United States, appointed by President Richard Nixon to replace the disgraced Spiro Agnew.

Among the inductees was Dick "Night Train" Lane, the great defensive back. His acceptance speech wandered from topic to topic, but at its end he turned to Ford and said, "It is a special honor to share this stage with the next president of the United States." The audience went bonkers, screaming and cheering. Ford blushed and shifted uneasily in his chair, but two weeks later he was, indeed, the president of the United States.

The strike ended before the regular season began, with the players not much nearer to free agency. Eight years later, in 1982, the players struck again, this time two games into the season. The union, led by its firebrand executive director, Ed Garvey, meant business. The strike lasted thirty-seven days, and when it ended, some satisfactory form of free agency was on the way along with a much larger share of the immense profits that flowed from the merger.

At the end of the 1974 season, the two coaches who directed their teams to landmark AFL victories in Super Bowls III and IV, Weeb Ewbank of the Jets and Hank Stram of Kansas City, were out of football. Ewbank retired, and Stram was fired by the Chiefs.

211

In the middle of the night on March 28, 1984, moving vans from the Mayflower Company pulled out of Baltimore with blocking dummies, desks, coaching film, uniforms, helmets, and everything else that belonged to the Colts, taking them to Indianapolis where owner Robert Irsay was moving the franchise without advance notice.

In 1996 the Cleveland Browns franchise was moved to Baltimore and renamed the Ravens, the second of the three teams that sealed the merger by switching from the "old" NFL to the AFL in 1969 to relocate. Cleveland received an expansion team, also named the Browns, who began play in 1999.

In 1989, after twenty-nine years on the job, Pete Rozelle resigned as commissioner of the NFL. He was widely regarded as the most successful commissioner in the history of professional sports in America. He died December 6, 1996.

In 2002 the NFL expanded to Houston, making it a thirty-two-team league, more than 2½ times the size when it was first challenged by the AFL. Many of the teams are now playing in recently built luxurious stadiums.

In 2005 the San Francisco 49ers and Arizona Cardinals competed in the first regular season NFL games played outside the United States. In 2007 the New York Giants and Miami Dolphins played the first NFL regular-season game contested outside of North America.

In 2006 the NFL began its own cable network, a hint that widespread pay-per-view of league games was in the future. Many cable systems, however, balked at carrying the NFL Network because of its high costs.

By 2008, the average salary of an NFL player had reached $1.5 million. Ironically, the merger of the AFL and the NFL was finalized to staunch the financial bleeding from the high cost of players.

In April of 2008, the sale of one-half interest in the Miami Dolphins' franchise was finalized for $550 million. In 1966 entertainer Danny Thomas, the original investor in the Miami expansion franchise, was shocked when the asking price had escalated to $6.5 million.

The lowest and highest tickets for Super Bowl I in Los Angeles on January 15, 1967, were $10 and $13. The lowest and highest prices for NFL-issued tickets to Super Bowl XLII in Glendale, Arizona, on February 3, 2008, were $700 and $900. Somewhere Manny Celler, the late chairman of the House Judiciary Committee, was frowning.

Appendix B: Team Relocation and League Expansion

Since the merger, eight franchises have changed their cities. The Cardinals and Raiders each changed twice. The list:

- In 1982 the Oakland Raiders moved to Los Angeles.
- In 1984 the Baltimore Colts moved to Indianapolis.
- In 1988 the St. Louis Cardinals moved to Arizona.
- In 1995 the Los Angeles Raiders moved back to Oakland and resumed their former name of the Oakland Raiders. The Los Angeles Rams moved to St. Louis.
- In 1996 the Houston Oilers moved to Nashville, Tennessee, where they became the Tennessee Titans. The Oilers name was permanently retired, the first such name retirement in NFL history. After fifty years in Cleveland, the Browns moved to Baltimore where they took the name Ravens.

The NFL has expanded six times since the merger:

- In 1974 Tampa Bay and Seattle were added. The Tampa Bay Buccaneers went to the National Conference and the Seattle Seahawks to the American Conference, where they stayed until the NFL realigned in 2002 and Seattle joined the NFC.
- In 1993 Charlotte and Jacksonville were awarded expansion franchises. The Charlotte Panthers went to the NFC and the Jacksonville Jaguars to the AFC.
- In 1998 Cleveland and Houston, which lost their franchises to other cities, received expansion franchises. The city of Cleveland had never given up the name "Browns," so a new team with a familiar name, the Cleveland Browns, began play in 1999. The new Houston team was named the Texans.

Appendix C: Evolution of the National Football League (1959–2008)

NFL 1959

EASTERN CONFERENCE
- Chicago Cardinals
- Cleveland
- New York
- Philadelphia
- Pittsburgh
- Washington

WESTERN CONFERENCE
- Baltimore
- Chicago Bears
- Detroit
- Green Bay
- Los Angeles
- San Francisco

NFL 1960

EASTERN CONFERENCE
Cleveland
New York
Philadelphia
Pittsburgh
St. Louis[1]
Washington

WESTERN CONFERENCE
Baltimore
Chicago Bears
Dallas Cowboys[2]
Detroit
Green Bay
Los Angeles Rams
San Francisco

AFL 1960

EASTERN CONFERENCE
Boston
Buffalo
Houston
New York Titans

WESTERN CONFERENCE
Dallas Texans
Denver
Oakland
Los Angeles Chargers

[1]Transferred from Chicago
[2]Expansion franchise

NFL 1961

EASTERN CONFERENCE

Cleveland
Dallas[3]
New York Giants
Philadelphia
Pittsburgh
St. Louis
Washington

WESTERN CONFERENCE

Baltimore
Chicago
Detroit
Green Bay
Los Angeles
Minnesota[4]
San Francisco

[3]Switched conferences
[4]Expansion franchise

AFL 1963

EASTERN DIVISION
- Boston
- Buffalo
- Houston
- New York Jets[5]

WESTERN DIVISION
- Denver
- Kansas City[6]
- Oakland
- San Diego

[5]The Titans were renamed the Jets.
[6]The Dallas Texans moved to Kansas City, becoming the Chiefs.

NFL 1966

EASTERN CONFERENCE
Atlanta[7]
Cleveland
Dallas
New York Giants
Philadelphia
Pittsburgh
St. Louis
Washington

WESTERN CONFERENCE
Baltimore
Chicago
Detroit
Green Bay
Los Angeles
Minnesota
San Francisco

AFL 1966

EASTERN DIVISION
Boston
Buffalo
Houston
Miami[8]
New York Jets

WESTERN DIVISION
Denver
Kansas City
Oakland
San Diego

[7]Expansion franchise
[8]Expansion franchise

NFL 1967

EASTERN CONFERENCE

Capitol Division
Dallas
New Orleans[9]
Philadelphia
Washington

Century Division
Cleveland
New York Giants
Pittsburgh
St. Louis

WESTERN CONFERENCE

Coastal Division
Atlanta
Baltimore
Los Angeles
San Francisco

Central Division
Chicago
Detroit
Green Bay
Minnnesota

[9]Expansion franchise

AFL 1968

EASTERN DIVISION	WESTERN DIVISION
Boston	Cincinnati[10]
Buffalo	Denver
Houston	Kansas City
Miami	Oakland
New York Jets	San Diego

[10]Expansion franchise

Merged NFL 1970

AMERICAN CONFERENCE

Eastern Division

Baltimore[11]

Boston

Buffalo

Miami

New York Jets

Central Division

Cincinnati

Cleveland[12]

Houston

Pittsburgh[13]

Western Division

Denver

Kansas City

Oakland

San Diego

NATIONAL CONFERENCE

Eastern Division

Dallas

New York Giants

Philadelphia

Washington

St. Louis

Central Division

Chicago

Detroit

Green Bay

Minnesota

Western Division

Atlanta

Los Angeles

New Orleans

San Francisco

[11]Agreed to switch from National Conference, the former NFL, to the American Conference, the former AFL
[12]Agreed to switch from National Conference to the American Conference
[13]Agreed to switch from National Conference to the American Conference

NFL 2008

AMERICAN CONFERENCE (AFC)

East Division	North Division	South Division	West Division
Buffalo	Baltimore	Houston	Denver
Miami	Cincinnati	Indianapolis	Kansas City
New England	Cleveland	Jacksonville	Oakland
New York Jets	Pittsburgh	Tennessee	San Diego

NATIONAL CONFERENCE (NFC)

East Division	North Division	South Division	West Division
Dallas	Chicago	Atlanta	Arizona
New York Giants	Detroit	Carolina	St. Louis
Philadelphia	Green Bay	New Orleans	San Francisco
Washington	Minnesota	Tampa Bay	Seattle

Acknowledgments

I would like to thank the following people for their assistance and support, without whom this book would not be possible:

Commissioner Roger Goodell, Joe Browne, Pete Abitante, and Greg Aiello of the NFL;

Joe Horrigan, Pete Fierle, and Saleem Choudhry of the Pro Football Hall of Fame;

Kevin Byrne of the Baltimore Ravens; Scott Berchtold, Chris Jenkins, and Matt Heidt of the Buffalo Bills; Jack Brennan of the Cincinnati Bengals; Rich Dalrymple of the Dallas Cowboys; Jim Saccomano of the Denver Broncos; Jeff Blumb of the Green Bay Packers; Craig Kelley of the Indianapolis Colts; Dan Edwards of the Jacksonville Jaguars; Bob Moore and Patrick Herb of the Kansas City Chiefs; Harvey Greene and Michael Pehanich of the Miami Dolphins; Pat Hanlon of the New York Giants; Mike Taylor of the Oakland Raiders;

Two of the foremost characters in a town famous for its characters: Jim O'Brien and Beano Cook of the city of Pittsburgh;

The players: I've seen the best football could offer on the field over fifty decades—the great passers, receivers, runners, blockers, and tacklers—but for a writer the great players who are also great storytellers are frosting on the cake. Thanks for the entertainment and the conversations to Floyd Little of the Denver Broncos; Ted Hendricks of the Raiders and Packers; Joe Schmidt of the Detroit Lions; Bobby Mitchell of the Browns and Redskins; Chris Spielman of the Lions and Bills; Jack Ham, Mel Blount, Terry Bradshaw, and Andy Russell of the Steelers; Bobby Bell, Jan Stenerud, Willie Lanier, Len Dawson, E.J. Holub and the late Jerry Mays of the Kansas City Chiefs; Nick Buoniconti and Gino Cappelletti of the Patriots; Bart Starr, Forrest Gregg, Paul Hornung, Bill Curry, and Willie Wood of the Packers; Tom Keating and Daryle Lamonica of the Raiders; Joe

Namath and Jim Turner of the Jets; Ron Mix and Dave Kocourek of the Chargers; Archie Manning of the Saints; Dan Dierdorf of the Cardinals; and Jack Kemp, O.J. Simpson, Billy Shaw, Stew Barber, Booker Edgerson, Butch Byrd, Mike Stratton, George Saimes, Ernie Warlick, Cookie Gilchrist, Charlie Ferguson, Mailon Kent, and Joe DeLamielleure of the Bills;

The coaches: Sid Gillman once described coaches by admitting, "We're all a little nuts." Maybe so, but mostly it's an enjoyable brand of nuts. Whether discussing quarterbacks with small hands ("The only good one I recall," Gillman said, "was Norm Van Brocklin.") or the best receivers with Weeb Ewbank, the "46" defense with Buddy Ryan or just about anything with Chuck Knox, they all fall into the category of unforgettable characters. Thanks to Chuck Knox, Sid Gillman, Jack Faulkner, Don Shula, Weeb Ewbank, George Allen, Hank Stram, Mike Holovak, John Madden, Tom Landry, Chuck Noll, Marty Schottenheimer, Marv Levy, Lou Holtz, Lou Saban, Sam Rutigliano, Wade Phillips, Vince Lombardi, Jeff Fisher, Buster Ramsey, Buddy Ryan, and Bill Walsh;

The GMs: I can't imagine any of these general managers doing anything else but brainstorming football to make a living, and they talked so fervently about it. Thanks to Ernie Accorsi, Ron Wolf, Bill Polian, Carl Peterson, George Young, Jim Finks, Dick Gallagher, Ozzie Newsome, Joe Thomas, and Lou Spadia;

The owners: Yes, Virginia, there are genuine sportsmen and these gentlemen fit that category. Thanks to Ralph Wilson, Lamar Hunt, Bud Adams, Billy Sullivan, Art Modell, Wellington Mara, Wayne Valley, Sonny Werblin, Barron Hilton, Art Rooney, Dan Rooney, and Edward Bennett Williams;

In a class by themselves, the all-around wizards of football: Al Davis, George Halas, and Paul Brown. They had enormous respect for the sport of football and the people around the game.

The young turk sports writers who covered the AFL with me: Paul Zimmerman of the *New York Post* and *Sports Illustrated;* Dave

Anderson of the *New York News-American* and the *New York Times;* Will McDonough of the *Boston Globe;* Larry Fox of the *New York Daily News;* Dick Connor of the *Denver Post;* Edwin Pope of the *Miami Herald;* Jack Gallagher of the *Houston Post;* Jerry Magee of the *San Diego Union;* Scotty Stirling of the *Oakland Tribune,* Bill Richardson of the *Kansas City Star,* and Jack Horrigan of the *Buffalo Evening News;*

Finally, friends who listened to my stories through the years and suggested I shut up and write a book (so I did!): Eddie Abramoski, John DeMerle, Murph Procknal, Budd Thalman, Don Aniskiewicz, Milt Northrop, John Murphy, Leo Roth, Howard Simon, Chuck Burr, Steve Cichon, and Van Miller, the all-time voice of the Bills.

Index

About the Author

Larry Felser is a former president of the Pro Football Writers of America. In 1983 he became the youngest winner of the McCann Award for distinguished writing about professional football and was elected to the writers' wing of the Pro Football Hall of Fame. He covered his first pro football game in 1957 and reported on the Buffalo Bills from their inception through 1960 for the *Buffalo Courier-Express* and from 1963 through 1976 for the *Buffalo News*. He was a sports columnist for the *Buffalo News* from 1977 through 2001, adding the title of sports editor in 1982. He wrote a football column for *The Sporting News* for twenty-five years and for *Street & Smith*'s pro and college annuals for twenty-five years and has written articles for many other magazines, including *Pro Football Weekly*. Felser resides in Buffalo, New York.